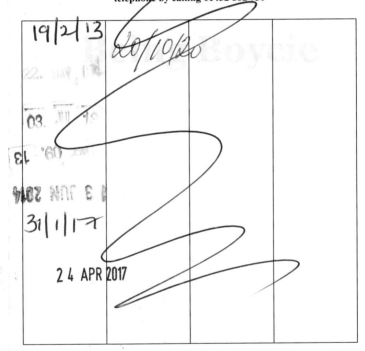

Being Boycie

An autobiography

by

John Challis

First published in Great Britain in 2011

By Wigmore Books Ltd

Copyright © 2011 John Challis

The right of John Challis to be identified as the author
of the work has been asserted by him in accordance
with the Copyright, Designs and Patents Act 1988

ISBN 978-0-9569061-0-6

Wigmore Books Ltd
Wigmore Abbey
Leintwardine
SY7 0NB

Printed in Great Britain by the MPG Books Group, Bodmin and King's Lynn

To Carol, my wonderful,
long-suffering wife

Acknowledgements

I'd like to thank Peter Burden, Nina Hely-Hutchinson, Damian Russell, Martin Ellis and my wife, Carol, for their invaluable help in getting this, my first book, off the ground.

FOREWORD
Sir David Jason OBE

I first met John Challis on the set of "Only Fools and Horses" but knew him as an established actor with a long, prestigious career behind him. What was to be a big part of his life to come was his portrayal of one of Britain's finest characters, Boycie, the wheeler dealer car salesman from such a popular show televised for three decades and still going strong. John is much more than Boycie - not only is he a kind and generous actor and friend, but he is a sensitive actor capable of many genres. We all had such a laugh making "Only Fools" which was down to the capabilities and charisma of such a lovely cast. John deserved every success with his strong role in such an iconic show and that is why the public want to hang on to such a colourful character. I too loved seeing him down at the "Nags Head" and amongst many other things, for being Boycie.

Sir David Jason

Prologue

'*Only Fools and Horses*?' I asked. 'What kind of title's that?'

Absurd as it sounds, at the time the four words didn't mean much at all; but then, it isn't always easy to spot the turning points in life until you can stand back and view them from a distance.

I certainly didn't see this one coming. It was April 1981, and I was sitting in the living room of my house in Alexandra Road, Twickenham. I'd just had a phone call from my agent. BBC producer Ray Butt and writer John Sullivan wanted me for a part in the second episode of John's new comedy series, which wasn't due to air until the following September. This was the call that led to the birth of *Aubrey Boyce*.

Ray sent me a script which I sat and read to myself, laughing out loud. I'd had fun with a similar part in an episode of Sullivan's last series, *Citizen Smith*, which Ray had also produced, and I guessed that was what had prompted the call.

I felt pretty relaxed when I turned up six weeks later at the familiar surroundings of BBC Television Centre in London's White City. It was good to see John Sullivan again. He was a man who saw the comical side of everything and knew how to communicate it; I was desperately upset when he died, quite young, earlier this year.

Ray, too, had been fun to work with on my one outing in *Citizen Smith* and I was sure I would enjoy working with them again, albeit for a single day's filming.

I'd met the show's star, David Jason, several years before, when he'd been playing Ronnie Barker's dogsbody nephew, *Granville,* in *Open All Hours* and I'd made an appearance as a baker's van driver. *Derek 'Del Boy' Trotter* was David's first leading role in a sitcom, but he seemed absolutely right for the part. He wasn't too nervous about it and, though a fairly private individual, he's not too difficult to get along with. The part of his younger, much taller brother, *Rodney*, was being played by the experienced former child actor, Nicholas Lyndhurst, who'd made his name in *Butterflies* with Wendy Craig.

The episode I'd come to do – '*Go West, Young Man*' – was only the second of the first series. Although the first show hadn't been aired, I'd heard that the studio audience reaction had been terrific. The characters were still bedding in, so John Sullivan and Ray Butt seemed happy to let me play my character the way I thought best.

Aubrey Boyce was a successful second-hand car dealer – at least, successful compared to the *Trotters*. He was an old-fashioned spiv with flashy apparel, a penchant for bling and a taste for cigars. Without any specific instructions from John or Ray on how to play him, I brought on a version of the character I'd created for *Citizen Smith* and, using my own quite intimate knowledge of second-hand car dealers, I made the appropriate adjustments, and *Boycie* was born.

Boycie's costume posed a bit of a problem, because although he was bound to wear a bit of flash, *Del Boy* already sported a strong line in big rings, medallions and watches (usually counterfeit, naturally) – so *Boycie's* predilection for flamboyant embellishment had to be expressed with more subtlety: the bogus Oyster, the loud, not quite 'designer' tie, the double-breasted shiny suits, dark shirts, and white blazers with a hint of the golf club about them.

For this first and (so far as I knew then) only outing as Peckham's leading pre-used motor trader, I wasn't given any specific instructions about costume, but when I went shopping with Robin Stubbs, the wardrobe master, I already had a good handle on the character and his milieu. I had a pretty clear image in my own head of how he should look, and, luckily, this seemed in line with the designer's ideas. I chose a cream coloured suit with a dark shirt – a dash of gangland deemed appropriate to a south London car dealer – and a multicoloured tie of spectacular garishness.

Also for *Boycie's* first appearance, I'd deliberately grown and trimmed one of those thin pencil moustaches that are so closely identified in the public imagination with men of less than honest trading habits. I've always been rather fascinated that this particular style of upper lip hair should indicate such specific characteristics – perhaps the most eloquent of the many available variations of face-fungus.

Again in contrast to *Del*, who favoured big fat Churchillian cigars which he smoked with flamboyance and an expansive flourish, *Boycie* preferred the more discreet style of long, slender panatella, airily waved around between two fingers and sucked through thin, pursed lips.

Although he put in only one appearance in the first series (which was no more than I'd been led to expect) it was clear that *Boycie* represented an important touchstone in the mind of *'Del Boy' Trotter*. *Boycie* was every bit as dodgy a merchant as *Del*, but he carried it off with more aplomb and an appearance of financial solidity. He also generally made a decent profit, and hung on to it. Coming from the same background (even the same school, the *Martin Luther King Comprehensive* in Peckham) as *Del* and his mates at the *Nag's Head*, he was definitely one of them. However, Boycie was also very conscious of having elevated himself, which he liked to show by putting *Del* and the others in their place at every opportunity, at the same time, thriving on *Del's* obvious envy of his success.

'Go West, Young Man' is a classic *OFAH* story, with the key characters anxious to pull one over each other, to squeeze the most points from each transaction. It's also full of the absurd posing and fantasizing that *Del* thinks will (and sometimes does) impress his peers. *Del* and *Rodney* don't see why they shouldn't sell second-hand cars at least as well as *Boycie,* and they buy one from him – a rusty old Cortina ragtop with dodgy brakes. *Boycie* wants £50 for it; Del offers him £25 and a week's storage for an E-type Jag which *Boycie* has bought for his 'bit on the side' and wants to keep hidden from her.

The *Trotters* triumphantly drive away their knackered old Cortina, swiftly turn back the mileage and stick on a price tag of £199. *Del* uses his own special brand of sales pitch to flog it to a visiting Aussie. The punter coughs up and *Del* assumes he's seen the last of the car. But he and *Rodney* decide to go out to a couple of clubs to celebrate their first car deal. *Del* announces that they'd be more impressive in *Boycie's* E-type than the battered yellow three-wheeled van they normally use, so they borrow the Jag for the evening – of course, without telling *Boycie*.

After a few mishaps (like chatting up some transvestites) they meet a couple of Chelsea girls, who agree to a date the following week, and give them a phone number, which *Del* scribbles on an empty cigar pack. On the way home, *Rodney* carelessly chucks the packet out of the car window. *Del* jams on the brakes, to jump out and go back for it, but *Boycie's* E-type is rammed in the rear by the car following them – which turns out to be the Cortina with the dodgy brakes they'd sold that morning. The Trotters grimace but take it on the chin, while the Aussie punter is less philosophical.

It was terrific to work on this first appearance of *Boycie*. I liked the team, felt that the chemistry was there between the characters, including my own, and went home with the hope that, if the thing was a success once the public saw it, there might be more in it for me. By then, though, I'd been in television long enough to know there's no such thing as a certainty – especially in sitcom. It had been a nice little earner to set me up for another month or two. And I was chuffed that the part I'd nearly turned down in *Citizen Smith* had gone on to open up this new possibility – in a way that is one of the pleasing serendipities of my profession.

I'd been in the States when my agent, Marina Martin, had called me for the earlier *Citizen Smith* job with John and Ray. It wasn't a big part – a few days' work – and, frankly, if I'd been having only a tad more luck with a play I was trying to put on in New York, I would probably have turned it down. At the time, I was romantically optimistic about forging a career in the US, fraught with obstacles though that could be.

Three and a half years before, in 1977, I'd been as surprised as anyone when I'd been offered a role in Tom Stoppard's *Dirty Linen*, which I played in South Africa and London's West End, before joining an American tour of Stoppard's next play, with a reprise of *Dirty Linen*. That's why I was still in the States in 1980, after some great reviews and encouragement to find a venue for a play of my own, still trying to secure a green card and, partly with that in mind, juggling a love life that would have challenged an amorous jackrabbit.

My first introduction to the United States was a haphazard business, and like a lot of the more regrettable incidents of my earlier life, it started with a woman – on this occasion, Sarah Venable, a warm, lovely American actress with whom I imagined I was deeply in love, at the time.

It was 1979; we'd been working together in London and fell on each other while we were both preparing for a short tour in the US. The British American Repertory Company had been cast from either side of the Atlantic with the idea of producing plays from both sides, although, as yet, no one had come up with a suitable American product.

The blow to my pride – and to what I saw at the time as my enduring love life – came when Sarah announced, without any preamble to soften the blow, that when we got to the States she'd be going back to her husband.

Like everyone does, I'd been getting very keyed up about the idea of going to America for the first time and working there, but on the day I left London, I boarded the plane in a state of deep depression and non-existent self-esteem, and I made the not uncommon mistake of deciding to confide in a bottle of Scotch.

As any fool knows, whisky and six-hour flights don't mix. My arrival at Dulles International Airport, Washington for my first ever visit to the States was an ignominious event. I could speak – loudly and passionately, I was told afterwards – and I could walk, sort of. My first encounter with American officialdom inspired me to deliver a vociferous plea for peace and harmony in a world where passports would be an irrelevance.

'Who needs a passport, anyway? We're all citizens of the world!' I declaimed woozily at a pair of surly immigration men who wanted to see my passport, which, owing to the whisky, I couldn't find. Meanwhile the company manager, a worried American who'd come from London with us, flapped frantically, foreseeing a key member of the troupe being turned around and sent home before he'd even entered the country.

He summoned up a lot of tact to avert this disaster, or perhaps he just found the missing passport in my pocket, for I was only vaguely conscious of being bundled through a swirling terminal building and into a capacious but battered taxi. My confusion increased as we set off through the hot summer night and the wholly unfamiliar townscape of Washington's western suburbs, past signs to mythical-sounding places – West Virginia, Blue Ridge Mountains and the Shenandoah River (where Jimmy Stewart hung out).

We arrived in the south side of Washington in the suburb of Alexandria, where somehow – though I remember no details of it – someone shunted me into the lobby of a large building and I was transported up towards the apartment I'd been allocated. When the lift reached the right floor, I headed for the nearest open door and stumbled in, waving my key, more or less aware that at last I'd reached my destination.

Being Boycie

I remember being confused and a little taken aback to find that I was, apparently, sharing the apartment with an hysterical and completely unknown female – fortunately clothed – who seemed convinced I was there either to rob her or to rape her, neither of which I could have done even if I'd wanted to. As she screamed and waved her arms at me in rather an aggressive way, I gathered groggily that I was in the wrong place, tried to apologise and tottered off to fumble around with my key in other doors until one opened for me, and I fell in.

I found a bedroom and flopped onto the bed.

The next thing I knew, it was three in the morning and I was still lying on the bed in my clothes, wondering where the hell I was. Like Dudley Moore bursting out onto the balcony in *Ten*, I lurched to the window and thrust it open.

The scent of acacia, the sultry air and the buzzing of cicadas reminded me I was in subtropical America, and suddenly I was hungry for the excitement of being there, as well as for anything that would fill up my hung-over stomach.

Some instinct got me stumbling downstairs, out of the building, into the muggy night and the bright lights of a wide boulevard, where gleaming vehicles of absurd proportions still cruised. And there, a hundred yards down the road, like a mirage in a desert, was Nirvana – a shiny zinc diner whose blue and red neon signs beckoned enticingly.

I wanted nothing in the world right then as much as I wanted a plate of bacon and eggs, and I staggered gratefully towards the place. I pushed through the glass door and was met by a blast of chilled air as I blinked in the lights, bemused by this cinematic vision come to life, while, with a stab of déjà vu, the universal aroma of frying hamburger and onions transported me back to the Wimpy Bar in Epsom where I'd spent a few high points of my youth.

The punters – quite a few of them, even at that hour – slowly turned their heads, regarding me with deep suspicion from beneath the peaks of battered baseball caps. I had the impression they didn't see too many strangers in them there parts – at least, not in that there diner.

Rising to the challenge of charming these hostile natives, I pulled up a stool at the counter and leered at the short-order cook, who menacingly brandished a steel skillet.

He plonked a large glass of iced water in front of me before I'd had a chance to speak.

'Thanks,' I muttered.

He looked puzzled. 'What? OK, buddy, what'll it be?'

'Bacon?'

'Bacon? What else?'

'Eggs?' I mumbled.

'Eggs? What kinda eggs? Over hard? Over easy? Sunny side up?' he demanded brusquely, while I could sense the sniggers of the truckers and rosy-necked insomniacs behind me.

'Well, you know – as they come?'

'Where the hell are you from?'

'England.'

'England? London? You a cockney? Do you do cockney?'

'Yeah – bit Brahms & Liszt, atcherly,' I obliged.

'You what?' he bellowed, shaking his head in disbelief and turning to cook my order.

I sat back happily, feeling this was it. This was America and – drunk or not – how great it was to be there.

After I'd filled myself with the most delicious fried food I'd ever tasted, with no more challenges over my identity, I stumbled back to my apartment a happy man, dimly aware that some time next day I had to turn up at the Kennedy Center in downtown Washington to get ready for the launch of my career in the US in the first performance there of *Dogg's Hamlet; Cahoot's Macbeth*, the latest product from one of the world's hottest playwrights, Tom Stoppard.

Perhaps, before I go rambling on, I should fill you in a little with what screenwriters like to call the 'back story' – in other words, the bizarre string of happenstance, accidents, lucky (and unlucky) breaks that had brought me in my 35th year from an ordinary, single childhood in a West London suburb to these unusual circumstances.

The 1940s and 1950s

During the Christmas holidays of 1949, my parents, Joan and Alec, took me to London's West End on my first visit to a theatre. We were going to see *Peter Pan* at the Coliseum in St Martin's Lane; I was seven, and quivering with excitement. As soon as we arrived I was gripped by the magic of the place – the vast, rococo proscenium arch, the red plush seats and gilt-edged boxes. I was thrilled by the show, the colours and the excitement – Brenda Bruce flying across the stage as *Peter Pan* and, above all, Douglas Wilmer as *Captain Hook*. I can still picture vividly his voluminous shoulder-length black wig, the glittering red brocade coat, vast feathered tricorne and, of course, the terrifying hook which protruded from an ample gold-trimmed sleeve.

My parents told me I couldn't stop talking about it for months, and it's no coincidence that nearly sixty years later every Christmastide sees me wigged and hooked, enjoying myself in that same role in pantos all over the country.

I think, probably, that I enjoyed mimicking and entertaining from a very early age. It was certainly the dominant characteristic of my schoolboy life, but the first time I was truly conscious of the acting 'bug', the thrill of pleasing an audience – or at least extracting a little applause from them – occurred not long after I'd seen *Peter Pan*, when I appeared as *Michael Darling* in a youth club production of the play, put on by my mother at the village hall in Tadworth where we lived.

I didn't need much encouraging and I loved the experience. From then on, although a grown-up career on the stage had to compete with the possibility of playing cricket for England, tennis at Wimbledon or lead guitar in a rock'n'roll band, it continued to lurk in my consciousness as a desirable option. However, while my mother, Joan, was happy to go along with the idea, my father always made it clear that it wouldn't please him.

As a young man Alec Challis had committed himself to carving a decent career for himself. The son of a Sheffield steel worker, he had made the most of a good state education and managed to get himself a job in the Civil Service. This led, when he was twenty-two and war had broken out, to his being posted to the Admiralty in Bath, where he soon mastered the mysteries of the Royal Naval stores. He'd been desperate to sign up for the army, but his rotten eyesight precluded that option, and he regretted enormously that he hadn't taken part in the Dunkirk evacuation. Nevertheless, he was in demand for his special organisational skills and had an important role to play. It was here in Bath that he met a pretty young female ambulance driver from the city, whom he courted and married in the autumn of 1941. On August 16th the following year, they welcomed baby John Spurley Challis into the world ('Spurley' after a Sheffield football grandee my father admired).

We were living in Bristol, in a rented house in the salubrious hilltop surroundings of Clifton, where my father soon became leader of a Home Guard platoon. He used to love telling stories with great gusto and laughter about his duties with his intrepid troop. The highlight of his military career occurred one night in the semi-rural surroundings of Lansdown outside Bath. The patrol heard sounds of serious activity in the woodlands which, in their excitement, suggested to them the presence of a detachment of invading German paratroopers. Unarmed, but alert and braced for confrontation, they stood their ground on the edge of the copse..... until a bemused, and very lost cow emerged.

When Dad was eventually given a pistol – the only weapon in the platoon – he was very pleased with himself, although his pride was somewhat diminished by having no ammunition for it. After a while, he told me, he'd been issued with half a dozen bullets – not enough, one might have thought, to stop the Wehrmacht marauding up the Avon Gorge.

About a year after I was born, my father's job was transferred to London, so I had to go too, the only child moving *into* the metropolis while tens of thousands of kids poured out of London in the opposite direction, evacuees from the Luftwaffe's target area. As a result, of course, I have no memories of those early days in Bristol, but because my mother was from Bath, I've always retained a connection with that fair city and the West Country.

In London we seemed constantly to be on the move from one rented house to another. For a while we stayed in Sidcup and Bexleyheath, where I dimly recall German bombing raids, wailing sirens, searchlights piercing the night sky and the raucous blast of the ack-ack guns on Blackheath. I have a distinct memory of being grabbed from my bed one night and carted downstairs to be shoved under the kitchen table until a raid was over. I can't imagine that the tabletop would have protected me much from a direct hit, but I suppose it reassured my mother.

Later she told me how once she'd come back home after popping out for a short while to find I wasn't there. She panicked, launched a hue and cry, and eventually found me with a small girl, a year or two older than me, sitting at a broken table amidst the rubble of a bombed out house. We were acting out a tea-party scenario, in which she was pretending to pour me cups of tea and hold polite conversation – my first liaison with an 'older woman'.

By the end of the war, my father had progressed up the Civil Service ladder. It seemed that he was one of the few who knew where all the Royal Navy's stores were located and what was in them. He was promoted to the Ministry of Energy, going on eventually to become secretary to the Minister. Now he was in a position to buy a house and settle permanently at Cherry Cottage, Epsom Lane South, in Tadworth. Here, on the south west fringes of London, I lived with my parents for the next fifteen years.

Cherry Cottage was a comfortable 1930s semi, at the top of a hill with views across the lane to the other side. In the snow-filled winters that seemed the norm in the late '40s and early '50s, I loved tobogganing down the hill with Rosemary, our neighbours' daughter, and my friend Christopher from over the road. The gardens behind the house were covered in a rash of sheds and outhouses, among thick shrubs and what in my younger years seemed like a forest of cherry trees. These provided loads of scope for a kid like me who enjoyed fantasy, and my memories of early childhood there are mainly of carefree, contented days.

As far as one can judge these things from a child's perspective, my parents' marriage was happy enough during those immediately post-war years, when they were still enough in love to obscure the rifts sometimes created by their differing personalities. Photographs of them strolling arm in arm along seaside promenades show two young people clearly enjoying each other's company. However, my father – jovial, certainly, and well meaning – could also be pedantic and cautious, whereas my mother had a distinctly cavalier, artistic side to her.

It was only in my teens that the strains became visible, while my father was becoming more bitter, and less forgiving of his flighty wife. He was commuting every day to London, to the Ministry office on Millbank, while my mother pursued her love of amateur theatricals, and a moustache-twirling visitor, known to me only as 'Uncle Charlie', who often came round in his sports car to play tennis with her. He would bring small presents for me, and linger in the house while I played on my own in the garden.

The growing discontent between my parents became more evident to me as I grew up, through my father's increasingly cantankerous manner, to the point where the only emotions he ever showed me were disapproval and anger; his only communication through pursed lips or gritted teeth. I couldn't understand what had happened or what I was supposed to have done. I yearned for his approval and felt guilty that nothing I did seemed to please him. There was no longer any apparent affection in him and no warmth, and I became a little fearful of him and the sporadic physical chastisement he dished out. When I was younger, as I lay in bed, I would hear my parents arguing about whether or not I should be beaten. My mother was clearly against it; he disagreed. 'You're too soft! It's about time that boy had a bit of discipline,' he said. 'When I was growing up, if I put a foot wrong, my father let me know with the back of a brush. And I didn't forget.'

It was only after he'd died and I was reading his diaries that I realised just how hard he had striven to move himself on from his Sheffield working-class background, with entries like 'Learn to speak English'. This referred to a conscious suppression of his South Yorkshire accent, which did indeed diminish a lot, although never completely, especially in anger. It was clear that he knew he had gained a big advantage by having been to the Grammar School, and he was determined to make use of it.

A tall, trim, handsome young man, he kept himself fit with his love of hiking, and broadened his mind by taking an interest in everything around him. He'd learned to dance, and played hockey and badminton for the Civil Service. But, already by nature an introvert, when he first met my mother he'd been acutely conscious that she was a few rungs up the more clearly defined social ladder that existed then. Presumably with this in mind, he worked hard at learning how to play tennis, at a time when membership of the local tennis club would have been a sure sign of upward mobility for him.

I was always comfortable with my mother – an extrovert, brave and, I suspect, passionate woman. She was an admired teacher of drama and elocution in several local schools and to private individuals; she was even called on to help the Surrey Cricket skipper, John Edrich, to overcome his reserve and master the art of public speaking. Like my father, she enjoyed physical activity too, especially tennis, riding and dancing. She was much more outgoing than my father. She even intimated to me how he lacked confidence and how she'd often had to reassure him in his efforts to 'better' himself. But, strangely, my mother wasn't particularly touchy-feely – not very physically demonstrative, perhaps thinking it 'not quite the thing' to show too much affection. It was her mother, my grandmother, whom I remember as the most tactile and inclined to give one a cuddle. As a result I always felt very close to her and missed her enormously when she died.

For a brief while at the end of the war, we'd lived in Harrow, where I went to my first school. I had a nasty experience there when another boy picked up a brick from a partially demolished air raid shelter outside the school and threw it at my head. He ran off, and as soon as he got home he blurted to his mother, 'I never threw a brick at John,' which was thought to have confirmed his guilt. It could be that blow to the tiny Challis bonce which led to charges of lack of concentration at my next primary school in Tadworth.
    Even at that early stage, my fondness for observing the world and the people around me and doing my best to imitate them were already getting me branded as 'childish' in school reports. However, I was developing a good ear for taking off any interesting sounds or voices, and my mother would have to tell me off for staring at people, when I was just studying their behaviour and mannerisms. I was fascinated, for instance, by the dozens of different ways in which people smoke cigarettes – the short sharp puffs, the long luxuriant drags, the clasping between the tips of index and ring finger, or keeping the fag hidden between thumb and forefinger – all distinctive and clear expressions of the inner self. I remember

clearly a chap who always placed his ashtray in a precise spot where he could knock off the ash without having to alter his posture, while at the end of each inhalation, he waggled the tip of his tongue as he sucked in the remaining smoke.

I would also study the way people walked and afterwards try to imitate them as closely as I could. This instinct to observe and replicate behaviour has never left me. All the time, I still take note of how people sit or arrange their legs, pick up a wine glass, eat peanuts or speak on the phone, and these are all stored away, often for later use.

However, at school my antics were perceived as low concentration and were not appreciated by my teachers. My propensity for reproducing what I'd seen and heard in front of other children didn't excuse me at all in the teachers' eyes, but it kept me in with the kids. Playing games – cowboys and Indians, maybe – I was much in demand because I could do the best 'deaths'. I could, and did, fall from the branches of trees and land on the ground, writhing around in agony and moaning in a way that thrilled and convinced my playmates. That mattered, because even at primary school, I was always eager for the approval of the girls. There was a tiny, special girl with Bambi eyes and a naughty smile called Christine Shaw, whom I especially liked to see and show off to. I would wait to make sure we were on the same bus to and from school, and would get very upset if I missed her. I was rewarded for my persistence with my first ever kiss, a tentative effort behind a shrub on Burgh Heath.

My next school was a distinct step up, although I don't suppose I appreciated it at the time. My father had evidently decided to incur the costs of private education to reflect his higher status within the Civil Service. So, at the age of ten, I was kitted out in smart grey flannel shorts, long grey socks, blue blazer and cap, and sent off to board at Belmont Preparatory School, set in the Surrey hills at Westcott, near Dorking.

It was, in 1952, a traditional sort of place, housed in a comfortable Edwardian mansion, where doves cooed from a dovecote on the wall outside our dormitory windows. Most of the masters were authoritarians who sported moustaches and spurious heroic war records. The headmaster, Mr Sharples (who ten years later would undoubtedly have been known as 'Ena') could have walked off the pages of a *Jennings* book, and had no late twentieth-century qualms about physical chastisement; while the French master, a gimlet-eyed despot with a withered arm, whom we knew as 'Foxy', was known to use a long oval clothes brush to impose his will.

On the whole I was well behaved for this brief period of my life, but got led astray on one occasion with my friend Bracebridge. We were walking, as we often did, up an ancient track to the woods on Ranmore Common where the hedges were thickly clad in wild clematis, or 'old man's beard', as we knew it.

A young know-all with us announced with the supreme confidence of boyhood ignorance that 'people' used the white fluffy weed as an alternative to tobacco. This seemed to present an opportunity for a very cheap thrill, and Bracebridge and I set about making a limp, loose roll-up using a page from a weekly comic and some old man's beard. Someone produced some matches. I lit the thing, tentatively sucked in half a lungful of the disgusting smoke it produced, and immediately erupted in a convulsion of coughing, just as a junior master caught up with us.

'Smoking, Challis?'

'No sir, not properly,' I gasped between coughs. 'It's jus' the weed off the hedge.'

'Smoking is smoking. I'll have to report you.'

We knew we were in for a 'whacking'. We just hoped it wouldn't be from Foxy (who seemed to relish the job). As we'd been caught by a junior master, he reported us to Mr Sharples. That was a relief; Sharples, though a beater, was generally more relaxed about the process, diffidently announcing that, much as he'd rather not, he would have to beat me – for my own good. He proceeded to pound my backside for half a dozen strokes with a fairly flaccid gym shoe, certainly preferable to the clothes brush favoured by Foxy. In any case, I'd grown up with corporal punishment as part of my life, so it was no great shock to me.

We still had to suffer a lecture on the evils of smoking, and how, if it happened again, our parents would be told – which, in fact, was a bigger deterrent for me than the whacking, painful as it was.

Generally, though, I prospered at the school, and for a brief period in my life was happy to become engaged with what I was being taught. I experienced a slightly embarrassing moment, tinged with pride, when Dad played in the fathers' cricket match. I was in the 1st XI and fielding when he came in to bat – too far down the order – and leathered our little bowlers all over the place. I tried hard at cricket, athletics and football, and was in all the top teams. One end of term report even describes me as 'a credit to the school'. At the same time, I loved the open air time we spent learning fieldcraft, making camps and racing round across the Pilgrims' Way on the wooded slopes of Ranmore Common. It was a happy, untroubled time of pre-pubescent innocence which I look back on with fondness, for it was all soon to change.

My education continued in 1954 at Ottershaw School, a strange hybrid establishment – a boarding school run by Surrey County Council along the lines of an old-fashioned public school (but with no fagging or flogging). It had been set up just after the war as a kind of experiment to provide boarding education for boys in tricky family circumstances, or anyone else who wanted the benefits of a boarding education for their sons, but couldn't afford the fees of a regular public school. I guess this reflected in some way my father's social aspiration to rise above his own background, although I never really felt that I'd been at a 'public school'.

The school occupied an eighteenth century mansion called Ottershaw Park, surrounded by a park of 150 acres in which four boys' 'houses' had been built. The founding headmaster, still in control when I was there, was Arthur Foot, an impressive chap (known to the boys as 'Six Inches'), who had previously taught at the Doon School (the Eton of India, and as pukkah as any school in the world). He had introduced a lot of strange educational ideas, some of which strike me now as thoroughly flawed. A chap like me, for instance, who was strong on English and History but as much use as a haddock at the long jump when it came to Chemistry and Physics, was ordered to do less Eng. and Hist. and more Phys. and Chem. Talk about being made to play to your weaknesses! It certainly did nothing for my academic attainment, which ended up being no more than a short handful of O levels.

My father, evidently concerned about my academic shortcomings, decided that I would stand a better chance of speaking French if I went and learned it on the spot. He liked to display his own grasp of the language by declaring, apropos nothing in particular, *'Voici l'Anglais avec son sang froid habituel!'* This he translated as, 'Here comes the Englishman with his usual bloody cold.' As it turned out, when I set off for France, at the age of fifteen, I found no occasion to use this sentence.

The plan to send me to a kind of foreign lingo boot camp had been suggested to my father by one of his work colleagues, and my mother, always pleased to see me improve my communications skills, was right behind him. It was described to me as a holiday camp in the west of France to which kids from several countries would gather and share the experience of being abroad. It was also, without doubt, a chance for parents to offload their kids onto some other poor mug for a few weeks of the long summer holidays.

In order, presumably, to maximise the experience I was to make the journey unaccompanied. My parents put me on a train at Victoria, but after that I was on my own. I found the ferry in Portsmouth easily enough, and didn't even have to think about the sea-sickness pills my mother had slipped into the small canvas rucksack which was all the luggage I carried (toothbrush, toothpaste, one spare pair of trousers, gym shoes, two shirts and a change of underwear) plus my tennis racquet – as if I was going to play tennis in France! I thought.

It all went fairly smoothly until the ferry reached St Malo. Once ashore, I looked around for a Frenchman to aim me in the right direction.

'Ou est la gare?' I asked, proud of sounding really quite French, and embellishing the few words with suitable Gallic gestures that I'd observed watching Jacques Tati films with my father – a lop-sided shrug of the shoulder and a quizzical pout.

'I dunno, mate,' the man answered in distinctly London English. 'I'm a stranger round here. I'd have thought you'd have known, being French.'

Flattering of course, but not helpful. As I was casting around for a Frenchman to ask – someone wearing a striped matelot shirt and a beret with a string of onions round his neck, smoking a yellow Gauloise and reeking of garlic – I spotted a sign in the form of an arrow with the words, *'La Gare.'*

The train journey from St Malo to Nantes introduced me to a lot more raw Frenchness – a man pulling a cigarette from a blue packet of *Gitanes* and sucking in the pungent smoke with extravagant vigour; a tall, shingle-haired woman who could have walked off a 1940s film poster, and a dumpier, more matronly sort with her two ridiculously obedient children.

I sat there drinking in these exotic creatures and longed to try out some French, ready even to resort to discussing my aunt's pen on the bridge at Avignon. I was quite keen, too, to have a go at *'Ouvrez la fenetre,'* or *'Fermez la porte,'* but after my difficulties in St Malo, I chose instead to grin foolishly and watch the French landscape fly by.

At Nantes, I had to seek further directions. *'Ou est l'autobus gare, s'il vous plait?*

The man I'd asked looked at me as if I were simple. *'Ici!'* he said.

I was standing in it – bang outside the train *'gare'*.

I was about to ask for the bus to St Brevin, when there it was, with my destination clearly signed on the front, being entered by hordes of French peasantry, slinging luggage and chickens on the roof, and dragging kids onto the bus behind them. I did the same (minus chickens and kids), found myself a seat and happily settled in.

A jovial, rotund little chap looked at my ticket and was transformed instantly into an arm-waving maniac, from whose torrent of French and gesticulations at another crowded charabanc I quickly gathered that this bus was not going to my destination, St Brevin-*les-Pins* (no relation, I discovered later in life, to the more exotic *Juan*-les-Pins – where Peter Sarstedt's *Lovely* was to spend her summer vacations.)

Having retrieved my bag from the roof, I migrated to the other bus and, now sure that I was on the right route, settled down again to enjoy the journey.

It was, for me, a wonderful, almost fantastical voyage as I revelled in everything that was so different to what I was used to – the sounds, the smells, the people, the fields and crops, the houses and farm buildings that all made me feel I was in an alien world, and not quite in control.

After an hour or so we arrived at St Brevin-les-Pins, where I clambered down with the rest of the passengers and joined in the scramble to retrieve my bag from the roof. After quite a bit of shouting and remonstration, when everything was out, the bus rattled off in a cloud of dust to go back the way it had come. In the eerie silence of the warm late afternoon sun, I stood there like Cary Grant, waiting for the unknown in the middle of nowhere in *North by Northwest*.

Consulting my father's old *Bravington Wetrista* military watch, which he'd lent me for the trip, I found I had arrived just four minutes before the scheduled time in the detailed itinerary my father had drawn up for me. The rest of the passengers seemed already to have been absorbed into the fabric of the small, sleepy town, while a mad-eyed mongrel dog appeared, running in circles around the leaf-shaded square. The silence was shattered when it started barking hysterically at nothing, stopping only to pee on the base of a tree or scratch its neck with manic vigour; I thought about rabies and took a step back.

On the far side of the square, untroubled by this potential danger, an old man was sweeping leaves away from the front of his house, which the breeze instantly deposited back into his small garden. Beyond him, two women fluted at one another in French that was incomprehensible to me, the mad dog loped off, silence fell once more and I wouldn't have been a bit surprised if *M. Hulot* himself had cycled lazily into view from around the corner.

I heard a car approaching and picked up my bag in anticipation; it appeared and drove slowly past without stopping. The silence resettled until another car, a grey-blue Citroen with great sweeping mudguards and old-fashioned chrome carriage lamps had crept up behind me. The door swung open – the wrong way, I thought – and a large chap with a jolly visage and colossal moustache stepped out.

'*Bonjour... Monsieur John Challis?*'

'*Oui,*' I replied succinctly. '*Bonjour.*'

'*Ca va?*' he enquired, which left me floundering a moment.

'*Oui, merci beaucoup,*' I managed.

He opened his boot, took my bag and dropped it in before ushering me into the passenger seat. Back then in 1957, it didn't seem at all odd for a boy of my age to get into a car with a total stranger, even a foreign one.

He drove me without incident to the place where I was to spend the next three weeks. It looked more *Concentration* Camp than

Holiday Camp, surrounded by high, chain link fences topped with barbed wire. I wondered, as I was greeted by a pugnacious little sergeant major type, if the wire was to keep intruders out, or us in. I was quite surprised not to see guard towers with search lamps protruding from each corner. The camp reminded me of the sort of place I'd seen on innumerable war films where gung-ho, moustachioed Johnnies with implausibly plummy accents would tunnel their way to freedom (usually to be caught a few hours later by saying, "I say, I'm *so* sorry," in their best English, when they bumped into a member of the Gestapo at the nearest railway station).

The only buildings were a series of low, two-storey blocks of sandy-grey concrete panels, with incongruous floral curtains in the window, perhaps to make the grim barracks more homely for us boys. It occurred to me that not much over a dozen years before, the place must have been some kind of military installation. From the second floor, I discovered, looking north across the broad mouth of the Loire, one could easily see the opposite shore and the site of the wartime German U-boat base at St Nazaire.

There, in 1942, HMS *Campbeltown* had brazenly steamed up the Loire estuary under intense German fire and struck the floating dry dock in the middle of the night. A raiding force of commandos leaped from the bows and set about destroying the dock in a daring and brilliantly successful operation that produced five Victoria Crosses, four DSOs, seventeen DSCs and eleven MCs. It made me tingle just to think of it.

The sense of a former military presence at our camp was reinforced by the sleeping arrangements – four large dormitories to house an assorted gang of spotty youths from a variety of countries, all of whom, more or less, spoke English. There were a few other English boys, whom I rather resented; I wanted to be the sole representative of my country to have been incarcerated in this floral-curtained barracks. I gravitated from the start towards a gang of French Canadians with their almost American accents.

I went to bed that first night a little uncertain of what to expect but excited at the thought of getting down to the beaches we could see from our window.

This hope was quickly dashed next morning at 6.30, when we were bellowed out of bed and marched down to the St Brevin Lido.

Being Boycie

The sergeant major type, whom I came to think of as Camp Kommandant, put us through a punishing series of physical jerks and made us plunge into the unheated pool.

If this was supposed to turn us into strapping, healthy young fellows bursting with well-disciplined energy and spiritual fortitude, it wasn't going to work – not with me anyway. If there was one thing that made me want to rebel and do the opposite, it was discipline. Besides, we all agreed, the whole process smacked of Hitler Youth activity, and we knew what had happened to them.

On the march back, I looked across at the rebuilt industrial landscape of St Nazaire, and at the not much more attractive view offered by St Brevin, and wondered what on earth had possessed my parents to send me to a hellhole run by angry little tyrants.

Back at the camp, I studied the view inland, towards tempting signs announcing *Boulangerie, Patisserie, Charcuterie*, and most excitingly, *Bar*.

Within a few a days, with a group of French Canadian boys about my own age, I'd found a way to scramble under the fence and into the open, which led to the new and exciting experience of ordering drinks in the nearest bar.

Apart from a glass of my Uncle Lew's scrumpy, which I hadn't enjoyed, I'd never had alcohol before, and a beer at St Brevin-les-Pins was my first ever proper drink, though, it must be said, by no means my last. We managed to escape several more times, until we were caught red-handed wriggling under the wire, which provoked an hysterical tirade from the sergeant major.

This wasn't the only thing that excited his wrath. One of the FCs, as I called them, had brought a guitar and one evening performed his version of the Muddy Waters classic, *Hoochie-Coochie Man*. Of course, we had no idea what a Hoochie-Coochie man was supposed to do, but it sounded fun. I borrowed the guitar and responded with a Vipers version of *Cumberland Gap* – vastly superior, in my view, to the more successful Lonnie Donegan recording – but halfway through, the Camp Kommandant came storming in and yelled at me to stop. It seemed that he did know what a Hoochie-Coochie man was supposed to do, and he wasn't having it sung about on his camp. Determined to impose cultural as well as physical discipline, he announced that only 'folk songs' were now permissible.

Luckily, he wasn't privy to our interminable, and frankly ill-informed discussions about girls – mainly focussing on the local French girls whom we ogled from a distance on our trips into town or to the lido. Graphic as our talk became, it was never translated into action. But the heat generated by this forbidden, or at least, unreachable fruit was none the less intense.

In the course of other, official jaunts around *la Bouche du Loire*, my Canadian friends and I slipped the main group for our own slightly more dangerous excursions, on one occasion nearly drowning as we teetered along a sea wall with the tide rushing in at St Nazaire, across the estuary from Stalag St Brevin. I was loving my first taste of being abroad, and despite the discipline issues, would happily have stayed on for the rest of the summer.

Although I had questioned my father's insistence that I take my tennis racquet, it did get a surprising amount of use in France. I had played with some of the other 'inmates' a few times and was spotted by a local worthy who had come to visit. It seemed that he rated his own son – about my age – quite highly as a tennis player.

While I don't want to sound immodest, I was a pretty good player myself at the time. I'd played in the English Southern Area Junior Championships, where I lost in the quarter finals to one Mark Cox, and just missed out on the All England tournament.

I accepted a challenge to play the French boy, and in what was clearly a well-advertised encounter, he turned out looking pretty confident. When it came to it, he played a bit too deep and was therefore vulnerable to the drop shot, which, at the time, was one of my best. I won in two sets, 6-4, 6-3, to much cheering from my fellow inmates and the whole local community who'd come out in a spirit of entente cordiale. I was walking away from the scene of my triumph when the French boy's tubby little father blustered over and challenged me to play him, too. Although this match was a little tougher, I won again, in three sets, 6-4, 4-6, 6-2.

I didn't really gather what this challenge was about – whether it was a matter of family honour, national pride, or sheer pique at seeing his son beaten by an Englishman; but I had the impression he wasn't too happy with the result.

Shortly after that, my French sojourn was over, and I was seriously disappointed. I don't remember anything of the journey back, but the wanderlust it instilled in me remained – a first manifestation of a gypsy feeling that I didn't really belong anywhere – a feeling that stayed with me for a long time to come.

Luckily, at Ottershaw I played a lot of sport besides tennis – mainly rugby, cricket and football, which I still love, despite the frustrations of supporting Arsenal for the last fifty odd years. I was in most of the school teams and tolerably handy on the footer pitch. Unfortunately the coach was also the physics master and therefore treated me as a dozy thicko. I was particularly mortified when I played in an Ottershaw junior team against Eton, and he kept yelling 'Get stuck in, Challis!' But I was more of a creative, play maker, which didn't involve 'getting stuck in'. As it happened we won the match and went back in the coach happily singing, 'We've beaten Eton.'

I generally fared better at tennis and cricket (although seeing me perform against Andrew Flintoff's XI in Shropshire last summer, you could have been forgiven for doubting that).

Now I look back on my four years at Ottershaw with affection, and, surprisingly, I still feel that by boarding, I learned a lot about how to live with my fellow men – and I mean 'men', because one of the obvious downsides of a single-sex boarding school, especially for an only child like me, was the lack of regular contact with girls. I'm sure it took me longer than those who went through mixed day schools to learn how to act naturally and easily with young women, which possibly affected my relationships and caused my inability to commit properly for the next thirty years.

I did have contact with one girl while I was at Ottershaw, who lived thousands of miles away in Vancouver. She was my penfriend, Leni Hindmarch, acquired for me through a sympathetic friend of my mother's. Leni was an attractive and well-developed teen, judging from the small black and white photo she sent and we did seem to have some kind of empathy, as the communications between us became, albeit very subtly, more and more saucy. These missives, evidently doused in scent by their sender, described all sorts of arousing activities, as yet unknown to me, like pyjama parties and, with imaginative extrapolation, heavy petting. The school's censorship process (Six-Inches) began to interfere when Leni took to putting *SWALK* on the back of the envelope – a pretty harmless sentiment, you might think, and a lot less worrying, than, say, *NORWICH (translation: Nickers Off Ready When I Come Home)*, but too steamy for our moral guardians to ignore. Inevitably, I was called up to explain why a fourteen-year-old boy should be communicating like this with a young member of the opposite sex. It seems a very long time ago, when you consider how teenagers these days swap snapshots of their genitals on their mobile phones the whole time – if the *Sun* newspaper is to be believed.

But I was a slow developer in these things, even when opportunities were handed to me on a plate. During the school holidays, when I was fifteen, my mother suggested I should join the *Junior Drama League*, an organisation which used to gather for tuition and workshops in Fitzroy Square, London. I went along willingly, only to be a little alarmed to find that there were more girls than boys there, and I was almost overwhelmed by this rich source of sexual arousal. One keen girl, with the perfect prettiness of teenage innocence, had me sweating up with a galloping pulse every time I saw her. Penny Ede was the daughter of well-known stage director, Christopher Ede. They lived in Barnes, where I visited Penny a few times. We'd wander together around the quieter fringes of Barnes Common, when it became clear that she was a lot more advanced than me; I really didn't know how to respond to her adult suggestions and would depart from each encounter throbbing with excitement, confusion and frustration.

Following my trip to France and my adventures with the FCs, I certainly learned at Ottershaw how the 'pack instinct' can manifest itself among a group of male adolescents. It wasn't always admirable and often went against my own instincts. I felt deeply sorry for one boy, whose name I won't divulge, who excelled at all the academic subjects but was useless at games. He wasn't in my house, and I didn't know him well, but I knew he was despised by some of the other boys for being a 'swot' and 'sucking up' to the masters by being conscientious in his work. He was also horribly teased for being Jewish. It hadn't occurred to me that he differed in any way from the rest of us; he certainly didn't *look* different, but some of the boys had made the connection, and old-fashioned anti-Semitism was still common then.

In inter-house rugby matches in which he was forced to play – without regard for his complete lack of aptitude or his own wishes

– he was put in the scrum, where he would deliberately be given the ball, then kicked and trodden on by the opposing scrum *and* most of his own side. I saw it, and didn't take part... nor did I say anything about it to anyone.

I'm sorry to say that the torment went on until one day it became too much for him and he came running out of his house, up towards the main building, clutching a knife and screaming that he was going to throw himself off the roof.

A group of us walking down to the games fields tried to stop him, but he had completely flipped. The alarm was raised, he was prevented from getting up to the roof, and restrained until an ambulance came to take him away, and we never saw him again. Although I'd not played any part in what happened, I still feel remorseful about not intervening to help him.

I came alarmingly close to suffering some harsh ridicule myself when one of my contemporaries found out I'd been into hospital during the holidays to have my testicles nudged on their downward journey into their natural adult resting place. I had to use all my wit and ingenuity in explaining that the same operation had to be done sometimes to horses and bulls who went on to become champion sires, which seemed to nip any potential taunting in the bud.

One of my stranger school contemporaries was John Romer, who later became well known as a television presenter of ancient archaeology. A powerful man with a great interest in the infamous Satanist, Aleister Crowley, he was also an outstanding draughtsman and had gone on from Ottershaw to the Royal College of Art, where he developed his interest in drawing the ancient monuments of Egypt, which led him into archaeology.

Also as a result of the school's policy of making boys do more of what they were manifestly not good at, I suffered for my swimming. I was a rotten swimmer then, and always have been; I've never even learned the crawl, and can only manage a few metres in the 'Drowning Cow' style of breaststroke. Seeing my inadequacy in aquatic sports, the sports master appointed me swimming pool life-saving attendant, which meant patrolling on a pontoon that jutted several yards out over the water. I had to stroll back and forth, looking out for boys who had got into difficulties, ready to extend to them the long bamboo pole with which I'd been issued. The idea was that they would grab the end of the pole and I would pull them into the side where they could rescue themselves.

Inevitably, almost the first time I was on duty, I had to proffer the pole to a flailing, distressed eleven year old, who grabbed it, panicked, fell back into the water and pulled me in with him. It became a case of the blind leading the blind as we thrashed about both trying to reach the edge, and dry land...

On the whole, I kept out of trouble, but there was a quick reprise of the smoking episode that had led to the whacking at Belmont. We were smoking real cigarettes this time, albeit tiny spindly little things called Woodbines, unfiltered and loosely packed – five good draws could get the flame to your fingertips.

We had carefully selected a secluded cluster of rhododendrons to hide ourselves while we 'experimented'. We stood beneath the canopy of dark brittle leaves, certain that no one could see in. But we'd overlooked all the escaping smoke which five illicit young smokers could produce finding its way up through gaps in the leaves into a kind of funnel and streaming out of the top like smoke from a tepee.

The smoke was spotted, we were flushed out, and subjected to punishment. But instead of a short sharp burst of pain (physical chastisement being banned at Ottershaw), we were allotted endless dreary duties doing things around the grounds – weeding, repairing fences, or cleaning the stairs in the main buildings. I would rather have had the thrashing (I say now).

Despite my ineptness at swimming, the testicle trouble and my lack of progress with some of the academic stuff, I didn't suffer from too much teasing; I had a fairly broad range of friends, both in my house (North House) and elsewhere in the school. With one in particular, a jovial little fellow named Michael Bywaters, I shared my enthusiasm for the *Goon Show*, broadcast on the BBC Home Service.

In fact, I'd first listened to the wonderfully surreal *Goons* with my father, who, despite the moroseness that clouded much of his life, had started out with a great sense of humour. When I was young, he made me laugh lot, and he enjoyed extracting the humour from any situation. If two people were hammering away in some passionate debate, he would interject, 'That's all very fine and large... if true,' or, from Evelyn Waugh's *Scoop*, 'Up to a point, Lord Copper' –

meaning 'No'.

He introduced me to the Marx Brothers, and Jaques Tati's *Monsieur Hulot*. He also loved the pioneering humorous radio shows of the '50s, like *Take it from Here* (with the *Glums*) and *Beyond Our Ken*. He and I would sit at home in Cherry Cottage, both of us listening to the *Goons*, falling about and crying with laughter while my mother didn't get it at all and looked on with faint disdain. I very quickly cracked the whacky voices created by Spike Milligan, Harry Secombe, Peter Sellers and Michael Bentine for *Eccles, Neddy Seagoon, Moriarty* and *Bloodnok* – a pleasure which I shared with Bywaters at school.

Strangely, when I was older and making noises about my ambition to go on the stage and use my skills in mimicry and timing – both of which had to a large extent been triggered, or at least encouraged by the funny films my father took me to and the radio shows we loved – he gave me absolutely no encouragement, and even when it was a something we regularly shared, he never suggested I might follow suit.

His default demeanour was critical, and grew more so as I grew older, and perhaps as he became more embittered about the life he led and the work he did. Most of our communication seemed to centre around criticism and instruction, so that I became very accustomed to his sharp censures.

'What are you doing?' or 'Don't do that!'

One evening, when I was about twelve, I thought he and my mother had gone out. Fancying a piece of fruit, as I often did, I wandered into the dining room where there was always a bowl of fresh oranges and bananas, and helped myself to a big juicy Jaffa. I'd just stuck my fingernails in to start peeling it, when he appeared from behind the door, ashen faced and furious.

'I knew you'd been stealing fruit!' he declared triumphantly. 'And now I've caught you red-handed. You do *not* steal – not from us, not from anyone. When you want fruit, you ask for it – understand!'

I could scarcely believe that he'd actually been lying in wait to catch me, and put up no fight when he announced that I was to be chastised and he laid into me with a slipper.

I was easily led into trouble at school, too. Once, finding myself with two friends on the fringes of the school grounds while we performed some tedious chore, one of my companions suggested that we slip through the perimeter fence and catch a bus into Woking to see the new Hammer House of Horror production of *Dracula*, with the inimitable Christopher Lee and Peter Cushing.

At the cinema, I bought our tickets to overcome the 'X' rating (I was just fifteen, nudging six feet tall), I insisted that as I wouldn't be scared like the others, I wanted to sit on my own. Within ten minutes, I'd found my friends, and stuck by them for the rest of the film. When we were caught getting back late and owning up to what we'd done, we were punished not with a caning but by having a few privileges withdrawn, while our parents were sent letters containing the damning information that we'd been to see a film, and an X film at that.

The next time I saw Christopher Lee, fifteen years later, he was leaning over my shoulder in a West End club, breathily demanding a Bloody Mary. Was it my imagination, or were those canine teeth just a little too long?

Above all, though, the great benefit of Ottershaw School for me was the number of opportunities to act that it provided.

I enjoyed French classes, and 'Tubby' White who taught me also produced the school plays, and cast me in all of them. Before my voice broke, it was inevitable that I should be cast in female roles and, though I say it myself, I made a dashed fine-looking woman. My first experience of this was as *Alizon Eliot*, the daughter of the house in *The Lady's Not for Burning*. I did notice that after that I seemed to have quite a few more friends among the older boys, although, thank God, there were no physical approaches. I also noted that the interest waned as soon as my voice broke. Before that happened, though, I had played *Anna, Tobit's* wife in *Tobias and the Angel* which, in hindsight, must have been a tricky part for a boy to play, while my first part as a man was *Sir Benjamin Backbite* in Sheridan's *School for Scandal*.

Acting when I was a child and teenager seemed the most natural thing in the world to me, and the stage was where I felt most at home. When I wasn't acting, I was always pulling voices out of my repertoire – real people, surreal fantasy folk like the *Goons*, children's voices, animals, birds, ghosts, railway trains, car crashes – anything that a human voice could reproduce.

Being Boycie

I'd always been encouraged to act by my mother, too, who had appeared in several am-dram productions for the Tadworth Players, where soon after I left school I joined her as *Feste*, the clown in *Twelfth Night*.

While I was developing a taste for theatre, I was also getting into rock'n'roll, which was emerging then as a distinct new form of popular music and replacing the boring older crooners and balladeers like Guy Mitchell and Johnny Ray (although, incredibly, teenage girls in the mid-1950s had screamed and wept at the sight of their tone-deaf, Brylcreemed idol).

One or two of the boys had Dansette gramophones, and these machines were in constant demand for playing the new records that we'd go off to buy in Chertsey and Woking. The transition from the clumsy 78rpm records to the altogether sexier 45s happened while I was at Ottershaw. I was thrilled by my first 45, with the words printed on the label: '1957 Super Rhythm Style Series'. Who wouldn't want some of that?

Regrettably, the playing of rock'n'roll records at school was strictly banned on the grounds that at the time anyone over thirty thought the music was utterly subversive and sexually arousing in a dangerous way. We were caught listening to the latest records by our housemaster, Mr Oettinger, who – like the Camp Kommandant in St Brevin-les-Pins – seriously chastised me for listening to 'dangerous' music.

Before doling out whatever punishment he deemed appropriate, he couldn't resist peering over his glasses at me with an eyebrow raised and asking, 'Well, Challis; are you *getting the message?*' – a musical buzz phrase of the moment.

My passion had been sparked originally by local and home-grown skiffle bands that started to appear in Britain in the mid-'50s, like Wally Whyton's *Vipers*, whose rhythm section used a washboard and a tea-chest bass – purer skiffle, I thought, than Lonnie Donegan (who had a drummer). After that, through the growing reach of Radio Luxemburg, I discovered the truly thrilling sounds of the new black American rock'n'rollers – Little Richard, Fats Domino, Chuck Berry, Bo Diddley – as well as white bands like the Champs (remember *Tequila?)* and Johnny and the Hurricanes, whose great

Red River Rock was a hit on both sides of the Atlantic.

When I told my mother I wanted to play rock'n'roll, she didn't tell my father, but she bought me my first cheap, orange-box guitar. As soon as I'd learned my E, A and B7 chords, I traded in the instrument for a better one, and recruited three more enthusiasts from school into my own new group, *Johnny and the Bandits.* With a bass made from a tea-chest, piano wire and a broomstick, plus washboard percussion, my friend David Coxall could play a few recognisable riffs as lead guitar while I played rhythm. We used to practise in the games changing rooms – a kind of underground tunnel with great echoing acoustics that could only make the cacophony sound better.

The school music master, excited by the chance to get boys playing instruments without having to bully them into it, taught us more chords and suggested new things to play. What made him think the old Delta blues song, *The House of the Rising Sun*, was suitable, I can't imagine, especially when he arranged for us to perform it at a concert in front of the parents, and 'Six Inches', the headmaster. Of course, we had no idea that the song was about a New Orleans whorehouse, but Six Inches did, and he leaped up on to the stage to stop me singing before I'd even got to '*that ball and chain*'.

What to do? The end of the '50s

To my father's obvious disgust, I left school without going on to do A levels, having pursued what could only be called an undistinguished academic career. I'd had promise, some of my teachers averred, but I'd never applied myself – not to the subjects I professed to like, nor to the sports I'd enjoyed. The only thing I'd really thrown myself into with a naturalness that didn't feel like effort was acting.

Arthur Foot was candid. 'We all want to be actors,' he said with a flick of his hand to emphasise the flippancy of such an aspiration, 'but what you need is a safe steady job, gaining practical experience while passing exams to get the qualifications you'll need for a long-term career.' This was a view with which my father entirely concurred, and was the basis of several heated debates about my future.

By that time we had moved from Tadworth to a bigger, detached house at 8, Sunnybank, Epsom. I was living there, still dependent on my parents for survival, and I let myself be pushed into a compromise. My mother's father, Wallace Wyndham Harden, was an auctioneer's clerk in Bath, and very good at his job. He had a reputation for being a whizz with money, and was a tireless dabbler in company shares and local property.

My parents sought his advice and he came up with the name of a contact who was a partner in Osenton & Lamden, Chartered Auctioneers and Estate Agents in Leatherhead. Only vaguely aware of how an estate agent went about the business of selling houses, I ambled along to an interview, in which I felt afterwards I had not excelled. Evidently, however, I did well enough for them to offer me the most junior post available in their Ashtead office.

Although I soon passed my driving test, I only occasionally had access to my parents' car, and each morning after donning my grey flannel suit, I took the short bus journey from Epsom to Ashtead. My duties at the office consisted of making tea, running off Roneoed copies of property details, and occasionally going out to look at houses and preparing their descriptions – good modern bathrooms always had '*H&C Running Water and Low-level Flush Pedestal Toilet*'; a pocket handkerchief sized garden with a flower bed and an apple tree were described as 'Extensive Gardens laid to Lawn, Herbaceous Border and Fruit Trees'. A house described as 'imposing' was usually an ugly great beast of a place whose only hope for.the future was as a Borstal or a mental institution. I quite enjoyed this creative side of the business, heavily prescribed though it was, but I was just getting bored with the job when it was announced that staff cuts were to be made. I had, as it happened, recently met a man who worked for Douglas's, another firm of estate agents in Leatherhead, who'd told me about a job vacancy there. Although Douglas's were more Red Brick Semi than Gent's Res compared with where I was, the pay was double, and I jumped ship at Ashtead before I was pushed.

The job at Leatherhead wasn't much better, and I still found it hard to focus. I knew that at heart I was just not driven enough to make much of it. However, life at home was at least tolerable as long as I stuck it out, and I was beginning to make a little headway with some of the girls I'd met at the Epsom tennis club, just down the road.

Like most suburban tennis clubs in the '50s, it was the social centre for young things of vaguely middle-class or mercantile backgrounds. I was good at tennis – indeed a master at Ottershaw had told me I might have become a professional, if only I'd learned to focus – and I could see no harm in watching fit, slender teenage girls running around the court in tantalisingly short white skirts. It was inevitable that I started a bit of a relationship with one of them, a girl called Christine Boyt, the daughter of a local butcher. Her father gave me a few driving lessons, and once took me to see his abattoir.

When my Sheffield Grandad Challis came to stay, I told him about it. He was impressed.

'By goom!' he said. 'You're a looky young booger, and no mistake! A loovely lass, and free meat! Who could ask for more?'

Shortly after that, I'd left home and I thought I'd never see Christine again. But those teenage tennis romances stay with you forever. I was delighted when, fifty years later, she turned up to see me in a play.

As well as Grandad Challis, my mother's parents came to Epsom from time to time, and we often stayed with them in Bath. I loved my mother's mother very much; she was a sprightly little silver-haired woman, who never said an unpleasant thing about anyone, and probably never had an unpleasant thought, either. She was one of the most life-affirming people I've ever met. For reasons lost in the mist of early childhood, I used to call her 'Khaki', which was my own special name for her.

I spent many happy hours playing games and cards with her, when, through some kind of telepathy, she often seemed to know what I had in my hand, and there was always a great empathy between us.

One day, coming home from work in Leatherhead, I walked back from the bus stop, up Sunnybank and was a few houses from home when I spotted her – small, sparrow-like and silver haired – in the front garden of our house. I called a greeting, which she returned with a big smile and a wave before disappearing through the side door to the back garden. I hadn't known she was coming, and guessed my mother had simply forgotten to tell me.

In the house, my mother greeted me tearfully. 'I'm afraid I've got some sad news about Grandma.'

'Grandma?' I asked. 'She looked fine to me.'

My mother looked puzzled. 'What are you talking about?'

'I've just seen her, in the front garden. She saw me and gave me a wave, then went through to the back.'

'Don't talk nonsense, Johnny; you can't have done. She died at home in Bath, at eleven o'clock this morning.'

I was utterly astounded. I'd seen her, a few minutes before, without any question.

Bizarre as it may seem, I still believe that she appeared to me then so that she could say a final goodbye. It was exactly the kind of thing she would have wanted to do.

Despite the intensity of emotion I experienced with Christine Boyt, I was still pretty innocent in my late teens, and none of my first relationships ever got beyond the kissing to medium-petting stage, so I had a terrible shock when I first came across an incidence of illicit leg-over in the Ashtead office of Osenton & Lamden. I'd left to go home one evening, but before I reached the bus stop, I remembered I'd left something back at the office. Having my own key, I went back and let myself in. As soon as I was inside, I heard a terrific scuffling going on in the senior partner's room just above the front door. When some embarrassed female squeaking was added to the scuffling, I guessed what must have been happening. Sure enough, a dishevelled senior partner soon emerged from the front room, still adjusting his dress and harrumphing awkwardly. Up until then I hadn't been absolutely sure that people really 'did' it. And frankly, the sight of this 'old' man (probably about twenty years younger than I am now) looking so uncomfortable about it didn't encourage me to try 'it' out myself too soon.

Working in Leatherhead did have a few advantages over Ashtead, including the presence of the original Leatherhead Theatre, where I saw several shows. By far the most notable was a production of Ian Rodger's *Cromwell at Drogheda*, starring one of the great thespian knights of the time, Sir Donald Wolfit, as *Cromwell*. Before I saw the play, I had seen the great man a few times strolling up and down the broad streets of Leatherhead, wearing a spotless Homburg and astrakhan collared coat, with a silver-topped cane. He pushed his obvious personal presence before him like a bow wave as he progressed along the street, stopping every so often to admire his reflection in a shop window. But this didn't prepare me for his extraordinary stage presence. When he made his entrance, it was as if every other player on the stage was blown away, evaporated or shrunk in stature. It was the power of this performance as much as anything that implanted in me a real sense of purpose about becoming an actor, and increased my frustration with the job I was doing.

My boss, who lived for estate agency and with whom I got on pretty well, was observant enough to be aware of this.

'Let's face it, John,' he said to me after I'd been there about three months, 'your heart's not really in the job it, is it?'

I couldn't deny it, and although I knew what ructions it would cause at home, we agreed that it was probably time for me to move on... to what, I had no clue.

There were ructions at home. My father was furious and dished out some bitter assessments of my character and my unsatisfactory ambitions.

'Well, what do *you* want me to do?' I asked him, more or less aware that I needed direction, like a lot of young men of eighteen.

'I don't care if you're a bus driver,' he fumed, '*as long as you're a good one.'*

In order to keep his anger at bay, I went straight out to find work for myself – anything to show him I was trying – and talked my way into a job delivering orders for Hudsons of Epsom, the local grocer. This brought a little respite from my father's harassing and at least gave me the chance to drive around the villages in the grocer's van, stopping off to drink tea and talk cricket with a succession of middle-aged housewives.

In the meantime, I was getting to play some music. I'd made friends with another local rock'n'roll enthusiast, Tony Instone. We played together a little and managed to get a few gigs at village halls and a church fete in a vicarage garden.

This hadn't developed any further when I met three other guys and formed a more folksy band with them – three guitars, a banjo and drums – called the *Dustbowl Refugees.* In this guise we managed to get a few better gigs than I was used to, on a circuit of South London pubs, and the high point of the band's career was reached at a gargantuan boozer in Stanmore, where we played the interval between sets by *Terry Lightfoot's Jazzmen.*

Tony Instone and I carried on hanging about together, and we used to go up to London to sit around in Soho coffee bars, like the ghoulish *Macabre* in Meard Street, where the tables were coffins, and skeletons dangled in corners, the *Cat's Whiskers* or the *2i's*, which had set the scene for an early Cliff Richard movie, *Expresso Bongo*, and where the *Vipers* were then the house band. These places got so packed (not to say sweaty and malodorous) that there wasn't always room to dance, and the punters would practise instead what became known as the hand jive – just moving the hands and forearms in time to the music, which must, at least, have kept the sweat level down a bit.

Tony got to know a lot of the musicians we came across in those early expeditions to the West End, and even at that stage it was obvious that he was determined somehow to make his way into the music business. He soon got himself a job in the industry as a song plugger for Essex Music and moved full-time to London. I rather lost touch with him after that, when my own life also took a critical turn.

What to do?

It was towards the end of 1961, I was nineteen and I knew I wasn't cut out for a career in grocery, any more than estate agency. Like a lot of feckless youths, I was still trying to identify a job that would accommodate my idea of fun and my innate idleness, when I came home one evening to Sunnybank and my mother excitedly announced that she was going to introduce me to a friend who knew the assistant to Michael Macowan. Macowan was a former actor and well-known theatre director who, since 1954, had been head of the *London Academy of Music and Drama*, or LAMDA, one of the country's leading stage schools. As a keen thesp herself, my mother had loved my appearances in the school plays and in *Twelfth Night*, and she was by no means opposed to my taking up acting as a career, as long as I had a strategy of some sort. I think she felt that a formal training at one of the great drama schools would give me this, as well as a clearer idea of what I wanted to do.

While my father listened in stony silence, it was arranged that I would go for a preliminary audition with Michael Macowan's assistant, and we set off for a nondescript office in Coulsdon. Here I had an informal, as it were preliminary, audition with two people I'd only just met. Inevitably the meeting kicked off with a lecture on the incredible insecurities of the profession, and how absolute dedication to the theatre was essential. 'Absolute dedication' didn't sound much fun to me, nevertheless I happily performed a speech from *The School for Scandal* which I'd learned at school. They evidently liked what they saw, and I was told that if I applied in the normal way for entry to LAMDA, I would very likely get in.

That was exciting in a way – flattering, at least, if only I'd realised it when my mother was busy taking credit for her son's talents – but I couldn't see how learning about the theory of acting was going to help me. From what I'd seen among the boys in school plays and the members of the Tadworth Players, either you could do it, or you couldn't; and in any case, the idea of at least three more years effectively 'at school', with people telling me what to do all the time, appalled me. I was already gathering my things to leave the room while my mother was promising she would get me along to an audition.

The next day, I was back in the real world and the grocer's van, but the reaction of the people who'd auditioned me – people involved in the real theatre – had fired up my determination to look further afield for opportunities to get a proper acting job. So as soon as the next issue of *The Stage*, the theatre trade paper, appeared in the Epsom newsagents, I made sure I got one. Leafing through this publication the following weekend, I spotted an advertisement on the back page for an actor with a schools touring theatre company. The number to ring was quite nearby, in Purley. This seemed like a good omen, and an opportunity not to pass up, despite everyone telling me how impossible it was to find work as an actor, especially without training. (My father also used to warn me how much time I would have to spend doing nothing between jobs, which seemed to me a positively attractive aspect of the job). I sometimes wonder if the address had been in Hampstead or somewhere equally inaccessible, if I would have bothered.

As it was I rang the number and a friendly woman asked me a few questions before inviting me to come over to Purley for an audition the next day. My parents were away on holiday and hadn't taken their car, so I borrowed it and drove myself to the appointment.

The interview was held on a winter's day in a fairly plain semi in an undistinguished street of the Surrey suburb. Another hopeful was leaving just as I set off up the path to the front door. My immediate reaction, as it was for some years to come, was that he was taller, more handsome, more composed and altogether more suitable for the job than me. The door was opened with a friendly greeting by a middle-aged, housewifely sort. She led me into a small front room brimming with aspidistras, stagy pictures of actors, stacks of old playbills and dog-eared copies of *Spotlight* and *The Stage*. This woman didn't strike me as being remotely theatrical, but she put me at my ease and asked me what I'd done.

With hindsight, I realise it was my theatrical experience she was asking about, but I was quite naive and didn't have a clue.

'Oh, this and that,' I said, trying to sound amusingly sophisticated and blasé. 'You know, a spot of estate agenting, but I got rather bored with that... then I did a bit of grocery delivery. A few shows with my skiffle group, tennis in the summer....' I faded, conscious that I wasn't perhaps stressing the right experience.

'Acting?' my interviewer prompted.

'Oh yes, I played *Feste* in *Twelfth Night*.'

Her ears pricked up. 'Oh good. Where?'

What to do?

'With the Tadworth Players.'

I'm sure I saw her ears unprick, nevertheless she decided to press on and asked me to read a few pages of the part of *Geppetto*, the old carpenter in *Pinocchio*, which I did my best to deliver in an old man's voice.

Then I had to be a fire-eater – a theatrical circus performer with lots of arm flourish and raised eyebrows.

She was beginning to look more interested, and asked me to show her how I thought an owl might speak.

Interspersing long, lugubrious words with a few *Tu-whoos* and *Tu-whits*, I felt I acquitted myself all right. More encouraged now, she laughed and asked me if I could drive. I didn't realise then, but this was an important qualification for the job. So, too, was my lack of an actor's Equity card – although she made nothing of it at the time.

'When can you start?' she asked.

I yammered incoherently for a moment or two, not certain that I'd heard right.

'Could you start next week?' she pressed.

'Yes, of course!' I gasped at last.

I set off on the return drive to Epsom in a state of majestic euphoria, feeling that my first unlikely attempt to find a future for myself, which I'd considered a very long shot, had paid off spectacularly. A short way into the journey home a heavy snowstorm got up, but I carried on, singing my head off, thrilled to have succeeded at something I'd done on my own initiative, and astonished at how easy it had been to get the job when everyone had told me it was impossible.

I had to wait impatiently before my parents arrived back from their holiday a few days later. I had terminated the grocery job and was all ready to go. I told them the good news – to my father's gritted teeth disgust – and announced that I was taking the train to Birkenhead in the morning.

I felt like Dick Whittington, with a sandwich, a toothbrush and a spare pair of pants wrapped in a red spotted hanky as I set off next morning, to arrive shortly after lunch, as requested, at Birkenhead's Argyle Theatre.

My new place of work was still more or less a bombed-out wreck, except for one end which was occupied by the Argyle Theatre for Youth. This company sent out tours of basic stage productions to put on in schools all over the country. I knew I was going to love the job, and was very happy at the idea of being paid for doing what I most enjoyed – fooling around with mimicry and voices, recreating and caricaturing the characters I'd observed and retained over the years.

From the very first run-through, I was in no doubt that this was what I'd always wanted to do, and I would be happy to go on doing for as long as I could move.

And fifty years on, I haven't changed my mind.

The Young Actor - The 1960s

The Argyle Theatre for Youth had been set up to tour the country, putting on simple productions of plays in schools. Whether this was done with a view to educating the kids or simply shutting them up so the teachers could get a bit of a rest for an hour or two, I never really gathered. I suppose it was a commercial enterprise, but being of a naive and unworldly frame of mind at the time, I never enquired. The schedule of performances was frantic, but for a nineteen year old with itchy feet and a fanciful nature, it was a great way to live.

After just a week's preparation and rehearsal for a production of *Pinocchio*, we set off in the company's Commer van. There were five of us, three girls, and another man – a gloomy middle-aged Scot – packed into the aging vehicle, along with a collapsible 'fit-up' Dexion stage, complete with proscenium arch, curtains and drawstrings, a few lighting boxes and a couple of costume hampers. When I found that I was expected to do most of the driving, it dawned on me that if I hadn't been able to drive, I wouldn't have got the job; and a few weeks in, once I'd begun to appreciate that I was doing up to twenty-four shows a week for a wage of £11, I understood that my lack of an Equity card had also been strongly in my favour. I must have been getting less than half the minimum for that number of performances. Nevertheless, I enjoyed the travelling, and got to see a whole lot of Britain – albeit in a perfunctory way – in a short space of time. As a child, I hadn't travelled much beyond a few holidays with my parents in touristic destinations – the Peak District, the Isle of Wight and the River Wye at Symonds Yat; now I was staying in a different town every night for three months on the trot.

We would drive from school to school, book into digs, and sometimes do two or three shows a day at different schools in the town. We became very adept at leaping out of the van as soon as we'd arrived, putting up the stage in a matter of minutes, and adapting it, too, for a separate glove puppet show – in which I found a good use for my owl impressions.

I was loving it, and the only thing that spoilt my first tour was our Scottish colleague, a man of such angry pessimism and dark humour that it was almost impossible to coexist with him.

Being Boycie

Glasgow was an eye-opener. Although now it's more or less commonplace to see inebriated young women in scanty frocks stumbling around our provincial capitals with their knickers around their ankles, in 1962 I'd never seen so much overt drunkenness as I saw in Glasgow. I noticed, too, that a lot of the boarding houses had signs outside saying, 'Sorry, no Theatricals please'. I guessed that previous visiting 'theatricals' must have behaved very badly indeed to provoke a ban like that. And the plain-speaking landladies, in the digs that *would* have us, came as a shock.

'D'ye like kippers?' one asked me.

'No,' I answered emphatically, remembering the hideous foul-smelling slabs of salty orange shoe leather that had been served up under that name at school breakfasts.

'Weell, you'd better start likin' 'em, 'cos that's all ye're getting for breakfast' – which taught me, at least, how delicious a good kipper could be.

When I'd started the tour, I was a nineteen-year-old virgin, not out of choice, but because in 1962 the so-called sexual revolution hadn't happened. As Philip Larkin succinctly put it...

> Sexual intercourse began
> In nineteen sixty-three
> (which was rather late for me) -
> Between the end of the *Chatterley* ban
> And the Beatles' first LP...

Without going into any moral analysis of this, I was damned sure I didn't want to be a twenty-year-old virgin. But it seemed the women in our troupe – two of my age, and an 'older' woman (perhaps in her early thirties) – could somehow *smell* my lack of carnal knowledge, and to begin with I made very little headway in advancing it.

I wasn't helped by my male colleague, who seemed to get an evil buzz from constantly ragging me. He was a man of sociopathic tendencies whose idea of fun was to see his fellow men looking as uncomfortable as possible, and he would regularly set up practical jokes and ambushes to catch people off their guard, especially me. One night, early in the tour, he insisted that he should play my part of *Geppetto*, while I took on his, the main part of the *Wicked Fox*. During the performance, he kept coming in from the wrong side, to unnerve me, and throw me off my lines, and he would stand there, deliberately not giving me my cues. This was typical behaviour, designed to make his fellow players as uncomfortable and on edge as possible. I never did understand why he was particularly nasty to me, although I've since thought maybe he was trying to compensate for his homosexuality, which was still illegal to practise in those days, and often uncomfortably concealed.

In general, though, I was enjoying the experience, relishing my independence, and pleased, frankly, to be away from my father's increasingly black moods and harsh criticism. I was especially conscious that this colossal change in my life had happened through my initiative, and no one else's, and I felt very much that now I was ploughing my own furrow. When the *Pinocchio* tour was over I had little hesitation in signing up for another one, on the strict condition, which was granted, that I wouldn't be touring with my Scottish antagonist again. This time we were to do a play called *The Emperor's Nightingale* – a children's play based on a Hans Christian Andersen story, packed with songs and humour. It was a tale of dragons and tigers, of sacred mountains and stolen treasure, and a little bird who manages to win the heart of the young Chinese Emperor.

The children made great audiences, although they would often chatter and heckle the whole way through, like a Shakespearean audience. Sometimes participation could be so enthusiastic as to be inconvenient, like the time I thought I'd collided with a piece of furniture, only to find a child hiding in the Emperor's robes I was wearing.

During the course of this happy tour, we found ourselves in the south of England, indeed, in the southern suburbs of London, not far from the place where I'd auditioned for the job. I could have gone and stayed at home, but I didn't choose to, which allowed another unexpected and long-awaited event to occur. Frances, the 'older' woman in the company, suggested I come with her to the hotel where she was staying. There, with my full cooperation, she proceeded to seduce me and give me, at last, my first sexual experience: the Full, as it were, Monty.

Being Boycie

Like most young men achieving this critical rite of passage, I found it had released a flood of pent-up sexuality and a colossal sense that now, finally, I was a man. The most noticeable effect of this was the change it produced in the reactions of the other girls in the troupe. And the one I'd been fancying for months without requite started suddenly to notice me. This provoked swift retribution from Frances, who told me at the first plausible opportunity that she was pregnant by me. As a ploy for retaining the interest of a callow nineteen year old, it couldn't have been less effective. I was shocked, smitten with guilt and appalled that my very first encounter should result in such a potential disaster, and I fell instead on the tender mercies of the eccentric – and frankly voracious – sexual appetite of a girl in the troupe called Carmen.

By the end of 1962 after two very full tours where I'd learned more in six months about acting by working on the hoof than I'd have learned in three years at drama school, I felt the set-up closing in on me, and knew that it was time to move on. I didn't have much of a clue what I was going to do next, but somewhere along the way someone had told me I should get in touch with Vincent Shaw. I went to London and found my way to his chaotic office on the corner of Greek Street and Old Compton Street.

Vincent was a would-be actor who had gone on to become a well-known agent. He continued to harbour his own thespian ambitions, however, and would sometimes put himself up for auditions under a bogus name. On one occasion a producer who'd auditioned him rang him later in the day – in his agent persona – and asked, 'Who was that useless twit you sent me? He couldn't act to save his life!' Vincent didn't own up; nor did he send himself to many more auditions.

His speciality had become finding work for young actors; as a result, whenever any provincial rep or small company had an urgent space to fill, he was the first agent they called. He could always place an actor prepared to play any part that came along, and ready to act as assistant stage manager (euphemism for furniture mover), provided they could work for a wage that hovered somewhere just around or below the poverty line.

After giving me a minimal interview, Vincent made up his mind I'd be ideal for the fairly demanding and quite high-class company currently at the Cambridge Arts Theatre, and the incumbent tough actor/manager, Charles Vance.

In early 1963 I took myself off to Cambridge, settled into a set of gloomy digs and got stuck in. Charles was a hard taskmaster who did little to bolster one's confidence. This trait was probably made worse by the fact that, for no obvious reason, he was putting on a play, *Two Stars for Comfort*, which had already toured, had done a West End run, and flopped – despite starring Trevor Howard. I played one of four troublesome 'youths' or sat in the prompt box.

We took the production up to the Empire in Sunderland, a massive and grand Edwardian theatre. In the week we were there, we seldom filled more than 100 of the 1,500+ seats. It was in a very subdued mood that we returned to Cambridge.

I liked the old university city, though, and had made a few friends in the pubs, but I hadn't got involved with any particular girl, I wasn't too well, I wasn't looking after myself or eating enough. While in this weakened condition, my life was thrown into mayhem when, out of the blue, Carmen, the sexual acrobat from the Argyle Theatre Company, turned up. I hadn't heard from her since I'd left the company a few months before, and I was pretty glad to see her again, despite knowing how disruptive and heavy maintenance she could be.

It was only after she'd stayed with me for a couple of hot, steamy nights, furtively dodging my landlady, that she told me she was pregnant... by me.

'That was a bit quick!' I said, startled by this second paternity claim within six months of my first Full Monty.

'No, no. I mean from last time, when we were at Bedford.'

I was puzzled. 'But wouldn't you be a bit, you know... plumper by now?'

'No, not necessarily.'

I wasn't surprised when she said she didn't want to have the baby, and could I help out with some cash. Obviously, on wages of £12 a week, I didn't have any cash, but, appalled and feeling hideously guilty, I managed somehow to rustle up the enormous sum of £100 from friends, so that she could take whatever course of action she deemed best; my own instinctive preference was that I should not become a father – at least, not yet – and it was already clear that I was not going to become Carmen's husband. I guess she agreed; she took the money and disappeared as suddenly as she'd come.

By now, I was at a pretty low ebb. Our director, Rolf Kruger, castigated me for not being more engaged with all aspects of theatre. Besides acting, he said, I should take a passionate interest in the sets, lights, costumes and props – everything to do with a production. But then, at just twenty, I simply couldn't; I only cared about the acting, and I didn't have it in me to fake an interest in the rest of it.

The last straw was laid on my cargo of woes when Charles Vance flew at me in a rage after he'd performed the lead in *Edward My Son*, a play heavy with opportunities for him to strut and pose. I'd been in the prompt box – 'on the book' – and he'd been on stage when he obviously and completely dried. I sang out his line, loud and clear, as I'd always been told to do. (Mumbling from the prompt box could lead to even greater confusion and embarrassment.) Charles gave me a hell of look, very grumpy about being shown up for forgetting his lines, and no doubt had carried on fuming for the rest of the performance. He came off stage looking murderous. He charged round and took out all his pent-up fury on me for making him look an arse.

Two days later, I was stuffing my paltry possessions and a lot of unwashed laundry into my case before taking the train to Liverpool Street, on to Epsom and home.

I was in no doubt that this was the end of my theatrical career. I'd been summarily sacked with no other prospects of work in sight. I wasn't expecting a sympathetic reception from my father, and I didn't get one. With lips pursed, he made it clear that all his worst fears had been realised. He was more bitter than ever, it seemed, and ready to tear into me for my lack of perseverance and discipline. He was appalled that his useless son couldn't even keep a job that paid £12 a week, and made it clear that he considered me a colossal failure.

I went straight to London the next day, with my tail between my knees, to tell Vincent Shaw the terrible news.

To my amazement, he wasn't remotely fazed.

'Oh, so you've left that one, have you? They haven't been doing well; I expect they're running out of money. Well, we'd better see what else we can find for you.'

He flipped through his Rotadex, picked up the phone and, after a brief conversation, put it down. 'How do you fancy going to the seaside?'

I nodded dumbly, and was told I had a job as *ASM* and *actor, as cast* with the Penguin Players, a company based at the De La Warr Pavilion, a 1930s modernist extravaganza on the seafront at Bexhill. And so I spent the summer and autumn of 1963, and my 21st birthday, in the balmy, ozone-laden air of one of England's most placid seaside resorts.

But before heading for the coast, I spent a short time at home, where my mother tried to feed me up after my self-neglect in Cambridge. While I was there, I escaped my father's brooding disapproval one evening to have my first experience of something that became an integral part of my life, and more or less laid down the soundtrack to it. My friend, David Smith who lived by the RAC Country Club, had a car – a mildly flashy convertible, maybe a Hillman – and I persuaded him to drive me and a couple of other mates to a club I'd heard a lot about.

The *Crawdaddy Club* had groovy little lino-cut posters up all round the area, advertising the appearance of rhythm & blues bands and a few American blues singers who knew they were more appreciated here in England than in their own country. This groundbreaking venue was in the middle of the cosy, wealthy, West London suburb of Richmond, housed in the unlikely Station Hotel, opposite the Southern Railway Station.

We had to park some way off, but we could feel the tension and excitement of the place when we were still a hundred yards from it. There was a cluster of terrific looking girls and outlandish guys around the entrance and a great sense of expectation. We squeezed our way in and had the back of our hands stamped with some luminous stuff. Inside, the sticky, tobacco-stained function room was packed to bursting point, hot, smoky, sweaty, and very exciting even before the band came on.

When a voice over the PA system announced the Rolling Stones, the place erupted, and six young, skinny men, dressed variously in cord jackets or leather jerkins, with tab collar shirts, narrow ties and hi-heeled Chelsea boots, walked onto a makeshift stage cluttered with battered black speakers, a piano and a drum kit. Three held guitars, one – Ian Stewart, the sixth Stone – sat at the piano, one sat himself behind the drums, and in the middle, Mick Jagger, still only nineteen, stood and stared moodily at the audience before bursting into a driving, irresistible version of *Route 66*.

I was completely seduced by the urgent pulse of the R&B, and Mick's strange skippy, clappy, snaky movements as he delivered the songs, shaking his maracas over his shoulder, pouting and prancing in a way I'd never seen or heard. As the set went on – *I'm a King Bee, Down the road, down the road, down the road apiece* – I wondered why I felt so cold until I realised... it was the music that was chilling me. I'd only ever heard this kind of rock'n'roll played by American singers on records. Now everyone else was feeling it in a tribal sort of way, all transported, taking off bits of clothing and waving them over their heads.

At the end of the set, Mick just stood there with one hand on a cocked hip, the other clutching a tambourine, while we all went mad.

'I s'pose we'll have to do another little number,' he said in a nasal drawl, 'seein' as you all seem to be enjoyin' yerselves.' And Keith Richards broke into the opening riff of Chuck Berry's *Memphis, Tennessee* ...

It was the most exciting gig I've ever been too, before or since, and we drove away mesmerized and high as larks – just on the music. We'd hardly drunk a thing, and we knew nothing about dope or Purple Hearts.

But on the way home in the convertible, with the roof down, me playing the guitar and all of us singing our heads off, David lost it on a corner, and the car took off down a bank, tipping us all out like peas from a pod, before rolling on down to the bottom of the slope, flattening itself on the way. I landed on top of my guitar, and it shattered – Down the road down the road in several pieces.

A few weeks later, the Stones released their first single, 1 minute and 45 seconds of *Come On*. Forever after, I was a committed Stones fan.

The De La Warr Pavilion arts centre in Bexhill was a bold piece of public architecture – a white monolith with glass inserts and embellishments. It was pretty advanced for the 1930s, and a great project undertaken by the 9th Earl De La Warr, former Mayor and grandee of the town.

The Young Actor

In the Pavilion Theatre which it incorporated, Dickie Burnett's Penguin Players ran a busy and well-supported summer season of safe, undemanding Agatha Christie plays, with the odd racier item by William Douglas-Home or even Peter Shaffer. The company was composed of good quality if not highly celebrated actors, including Dickie's wife, Peggy Paige, then generally reckoned to be the oldest Principal Boy in the business.

I was allocated digs in a handsome Victorian villa a few streets back from the sea. It was run by Mrs Crossman, who often put up one or two of the players. There was no Mr Crossman in evidence, but by lucky chance her lovely daughter, Janet, was also ASM/actor with the company, and I soon found myself spending a lot of time with her, at the theatre and at home. I stayed for six happy months in her house, where they held a party for me on my 21st birthday. It was here, a few months later, on November 22nd, that we heard the shattering news of John Kennedy's assassination. Janet, Mrs Crossman and I looked helplessly at each other, shocked and unable to comprehend the sudden elimination of this huge world figure. It seemed to me that the world was coming to an end.

The Penguin Players were, I suppose, a step down from the Cambridge Arts, but it was a much jollier company. I was given a few good parts and soon began to believe that I could be an actor after all.

I was encouraged in this by one of my colleagues, Oliver Fisher, a lovely old chap who was neither tall nor especially handsome, but had a good strong voice. He was also a consummate actor who knew a great deal about the nuts and bolts of theatrical performance. Generally cast as a bumbling old colonel or eccentric detective, week after week, with the subtlest of changes, he produced an absolutely different character. I would watch with awe, whether from the wings or on stage playing opposite him. He would use little props – a fob watch, a cigar holder, a monocle – or small tricks with make-up or his physical stance to present a new character each week to the regular punters who made up the bulk of the audience.

I cherished all the tips I gleaned from him, and stored away in my head all the little tricks and techniques he pulled out of the bag. He was a kind and thoughtful man who was happy to take me under his wing. He would sometimes invite me for a drink in a little club in the town, where he would share his experiences.

When I told him my ambitions to play the West End, he shook his head. 'I wouldn't, my dear boy. With your talent, you'll always find work in the provinces. And I can tell you from my own experience that it is better to be *some*one in Bexhill, than *no* one in London. And repertory will suit you best; you're a good actor, but you're too tall to tour.' He also added, less enigmatically and with some prescience, that as a character actor, I would probably have to wait until I was forty before I got my just rewards. Among the several parts I played in Bexhill was my first and last all-black appearance, when I was covered on every visible part of my body with the blackest make-up on the trolley in order to play the *Nubian Steward* in *Death on the Nile* – not quite as absurd as Peter Sellers playing an Indian doctor, but it wouldn't happen now.

The audiences at Bexhill did not always demand the most rigorous of intellectual standards in what they came to see, and indeed for some matinees I got the impression we were simply providing a kind of background noise, as alternate rows of seats would be taken from the auditorium and replaced with tables. Here the old things who made up much of the audience could sit and have tea, and make quite a racket asking for sugar, clattering their cups and saucers, while whispering about their granddaughters' misdemeanours.

In one of these matinées, the leading lady, Vilma Hollingbery, had come over from the senior company in Eastbourne and was quite a formidable presence. Sitting down, stage left in a lengthy drawing room scene, Vilma felt a tug on her dress. She glanced down and saw a little old lady looking up anxiously; she haughtily ignored the woman, until the third tug. 'What is it?' she whispered brusquely.

'I just wanted to say.... you were very good last week,' said the fan.

Besides my acting, my value to the company was that, like Janet, I was a multitasking dogsbody. In a single production I could be 'on the book', producing a glass crash or some other offstage sound effect, shifting scenery and furniture, and coming on stage in costume to say, 'Your carriage awaits, m'lord.' The company, I realised, was getting two or three people for the price of one.

Another of my jobs was to rush around the dressing rooms, knocking on the doors to deliver the ten- and five-minute calls. One of the actors – a regular Penguin Player – would sometimes call out, 'Come in!' When I did, he would engage in a bit of camp banter and, as I went out, flip up the back of my jacket and with a loud intake of breath, gasp, 'Oooh... ten out of ten, my dear,' which always got me out a bit quicker.

The Penguin Players also appeared in two other theatres, the Devonshire Park in Eastbourne and the Assembly Hall Theatre in Tunbridge Wells. I was excited to get the chance play in the two man/one woman cast of Peter Shaffer's new and very successful *Private Ear* when it transferred to Eastbourne. My mother came to see me (without my father) and told me that it was the first time she had watched me in a play and completely forgotten she was looking at her own son – a compliment which pleased me very much.

I had great time with the PPs and was sorry to go, but Vincent Shaw had managed to get me my first role in a film, *Where Has Poor Mickey Gone?* – written and directed by Gerry Levy. My boss at the Penguin Players, Dickie Burnett, seemed genuinely disappointed when I told him I was going to do the movie.

'You don't want to go to London and do that,' he insisted. 'Stay here – I'll always have something for you!'

After Charles Vance's bollocking at the Cambridge Arts, it was great to feel wanted again, but I couldn't resist the chance to be in a film.

I was cast as Tim, one of four unruly youths in the movie. It was a slightly macabre fantasy, in which the youths are chucked out of a nightclub before going off and breaking into a magic shop, where they try to bully the owner, an Italian magician played by Warren Mitchell (before *Till Death Us Do Part* had raised his profile). The magician starts to use his magic, and the boys get their creepy comeuppance.

I loved the excitement of filming on location around the streets of Soho, and in studios in Maida Vale as much as I expected to. My agent, Vincent Shaw had also put himself up for a bit part as a club bouncer, and thus received his only film credit. Ottilie Patterson recorded an original song for it, and I thought it was going to be pretty good.

Unfortunately I've never found out, because I've never seen it. *Where Has Poor Mickey Gone?* didn't get a release or distribution, although I was very excited when a friend rushed round to tell me when it popped up as a support for a bigger feature in Kingston. Since then it has sunk without trace and hasn't even been released on video.

At the start of 1964, although Dickie Burnett might have had me back at Bexhill, if I'd asked, Vincent had got me a spring season at the Playhouse Theatre in Kidderminster.

Kidderminster, where the West Midlands meet the Marcher counties, was a strange town of middling size, dedicated to the manufacture of carpets, where a lot of the most famous carpet makers in the world had their factories and headquarters. There had also been a long tradition of support for the performing arts in the town, and they were proud of the fact that since the war, a voluntary organisation called the *Nonentities* had kept the Playhouse going, bucking the growing trend of provincial theatre closure.

I appeared in four plays there and was beginning to think I really was a proper actor now. Perhaps the best of them was *The Private Ear and the Public Eye*, which I'd done in Eastbourne, although on this occasion, as the more playable and rambunctious of the two males. *Trap for a Lonely Man* was a terrible play, but good fun. I was a tramp, *Merluche*, playing opposite David Griffin, a good-looking young chap who later became known in *Hi di Hi* and *Keeping Up Appearances*. David's character was a detective disguised as a Catholic priest, who is supposed to shoot me. In one performance, he pulled out his revolver, pointed at me and pulled the trigger.

The dialogue could have been written: "Click... click....Fuck!' Someone hadn't done their preparation, and there was no dramatic blast of gunfire, while I stood there, poised to collapse in a heap, suffering from terminal bullet wounds, and David gazed with apparent disgust at the dysfunctional six-shooter (although it was the starting pistol held by someone in the wings that had let him down).

I carried on standing there, dithering, while David thought on his feet, picked up a convenient knife from the table beside him, as if in slow motion, and lunged at me, stabbing furiously. Inevitably I had to rethink my death. As a child (you may remember, if you've been paying attention) I was famed among my peers for the quality of my dramatic death scenes, and it was the work of a split second to transport myself back into an appropriate one. I responded to David's plunging knife by clutching the place where the blood should have been, and sinking with agonised slowness to my knees before hitting the stage floor.

There were some awkward moments later in the play when references to the 'shooting' had to be hastily replaced with the 'stabbing'.

The effect of this cock-up was that every other time we came to play the scene, David and I, with absolutely no control over our actions, dissolved into hopeless giggling.

The spring season was rounded off by a production of *Distinguished Gathering,* an itinerant production brought to the theatre by the tremendously famous and popular Vic Oliver. He cast most of the play from our company, giving me initially a fairly insignificant role, although, encouragingly, before the run had started he came down and said, 'No, no this casting is wrong. He – ' he stabbed a finger in my direction ' – should play the policeman.'

Unfortunately I didn't possess an appropriate suit to wear. Vic didn't waste any time; he went off and came back with one of his own suits which, though a little baggy on me (for I was a slender waif then), did the trick. Once again, playing opposite David Griffin, I was questioning him – '*Where were you on the night of the fifteenth?*' – and we found ourselves giggling uncontrollably. It kept happening – a comprehensive 'corpse', night after night, with the management getting very pissed off, although we explained we could do nothing about it – the strangest of physiological reactions, as testified by Brian Johnston's famous prolonged giggle after inadvertently talking about 'leg-over' in the midst of a radio commentary on a cricket test match. The process, once triggered by the 'stabbing' in *Trap for a Lonely Man,* seemed irreversible, and I think if I played opposite David again now, it would still happen.

In the middle of my run at Kidderminster, as if by some miracle designed to keep me happy, on March 26th the Rolling Stones came and did two gigs at the Town Hall. I could only get to one of them, and in this larger venue, a year on since the first time I'd seen them,

Being Boycie

I just knew they were the most exciting band I was ever likely to see. They'd released three singles by then, and an EP (with four tracks). *Not Fade Away* had got to No. 3 in the UK charts and just snuck into the US Top 50 – it seemed they were already getting known around the world. I was very glad I'd seen them in their early days at the Richmond *Crawdaddy*.

A couple of weeks into my stint at The Playhouse, the company's designer, Jean Burkenshaw, told me she knew Colin MacIntyre, who ran the Civic Theatre in Chesterfield and was then putting together his autumn/winter season. Evidently she thought I was up to the job, because she suggested I ring and ask if I could go over to audition.

I took a punt and hired a Mini to drive up to Derbyshire, and returned to Kidderminster in triumph, having scored my first job as 'actor only' to start in October. That left only the summer months to sort out.

I enjoyed the Kidderminster Playhouse, and admired the almost alarming dedication of the *Nonentities* who had kept the place going. I understood that they felt very strongly that this theatre was their baby, and they guarded it jealously. They came around a lot while we were there, checking that we were looking after their precious theatre properly, and to make sure that these callous professionals would maintain the same standards as their amateur groups.

Sadly they were somewhat betrayed by their local council, and within four years the place was flattened and serving as hard core beneath the Kidderminster ring road – in the name of Progress.

By the time the Kidderminster season closed, Vincent Shaw had arranged an audition for me with David Kirk's company. They were doing a summer season of two North Country plays at The Palladium in Llandudno, North Wales's premier resort.

I got the job and was asked to turn up at rehearsal rooms in Kilburn. Here I met the rest of the company, including Carol Robertson, one of the most attractive stage managers I'd yet come across. Although she'd never aspired to be an actress, Carol was lovely looking, and almost a caricature of a theatrical, with a soft drawling voice (with an edge of steel when required), vast, expansive gestures and a long, gold-tipped cigarette always clasped between two long fingers and waved in the air like a conductor's baton.

The star for the Llandudno summer season was a battle-hardened, fortyish North Country comedian, Ken Platt, remembered for his grim catchphrases – 'I won't tek me coat off; I'm not stoppin', which he produced at the drop of a hat for years, with variation – 'I won't tek me coat off; I've got me pyjamas on oonderneath.'

Ken was also credited with coining the term, 'Daft as a Brush', which I suppose deserves a mention. A former wartime Combined Services Entertainer, he was also guilty of that crime against humanity, playing the ukulele while singing George Formby songs – only marginally less heinous than his 1958 recording of *Snowy the Christmas Kitten*, which included the deathless couplet, '*He's my pretty, Christmas Kitty.*' He'd appeared in a lot of big radio variety shows, and had an early TV show of his own. In 1958 he'd had some success in a straight play which David Kirk had written, *Love Locked Out*, at The Alhambra in Morecambe, which was to be revived as the keystone production of the season at Llandudno.

While we were there, we went to see Ken in a recording of a BBC Light Programme variety show, at the Grand Theatre (now the *Broadway Nightclub & Disco*). He was second on the bill to a rather irritating little Arthur Askey ('Ello, playmates!'), and further up the ladder from Eddie Reindeer, who came on wearing a full reindeer outfit, including head, to massive applause. I was sitting just below Mr Reindeer as he was bowing very low to acknowledge the applause at the end of his turn, with antlers nearly scraping the floor, using the opportunity to yell, 'More! More!' at the top of his voice, in the hope, I suppose that the BBC microphones would pick it up without identifying him – evidently a popular ploy among the 'turns' when they were on the radio.

The Palladium itself was a grand old theatre (now a Wetherspoon's), then still doing good business with the holidaymakers and weekenders who streamed down from Merseyside and Manchester for their seaside breaks, although there was a fair bit of competition for the punters' money from the four other theatres in the town: The Happy Valley, The Pier Pavilion, The Arcadia and The Grand.

So venerable was the theatre that it had retained some very old connections. The dressing rooms were located off a musty corridor, high up the back staircase behind the Victorian fly tower. One night while I was busy being ASM, I came up to do something after the show while the rest went off to the pub. I was just tidying things away up when suddenly from the gloomy, cobwebbed corridor outside a door slammed, followed by urgent, angry footsteps clumping past the dressing room. I felt suddenly very cold as I heard them carry on, down the stone steps. I couldn't understand; as far as I knew there was no one else left up there. I went out into the passage, and glanced where the door had been slammed. At the end of the corridor through which the interloper must have come was a door to an old abandoned lavatory, which was padlocked shut, evidently unopened in years. Yet it was the only door that could have been slammed. I shivered, nervous as hell, and couldn't wait to get out.

I rushed down to the pub, where I was greeted by a couple of the local stage hands.

'My God,' they said, 'you look like you've seen the ghost!'

I was obviously looking pale and drained. I told them what I'd heard.

'Oh, yes – that's him. He's back, is he? He hasn't been out for five or six months.'

I was quickly surrounded by other interested people offering their reassurances. 'Don't you worry; he won't harm you. He was disappointed in love, see – unrequited, so he killed himself.'

I was deputy stage manager for the two shows we were putting on, *Glamour & Chips*, along with *Love Locked Out*. Apart from Ken Platt, ours was a typical little provincial company with all the oddballs and eccentrics I'd learned to expect. *Love Locked Out* was fun – a North Country version of the *Lysistrata*, when all the women go on strike and withhold their sexual favours, until their men finish the strike which they are staging. In *Glamour & Chips*, the daughter of a chip shop owner has gone off to become a famous actress, only to get bored with it all, and decides to come home to work in the fish'n'chip café – as if that ever happened! I had a small part in it as a photographer, though nothing in *Love Locked Out*, and I was mainly occupied with stage management for the summer season, with the bonus of working every day with Carol Robertson.

She and I went out when we could to taste the giddy nightlife of Llandudno in August. The choice venue was the Happy Valley, a gift from Lord Mostyn to the town to celebrate Queen Victoria's Golden Jubilee in 1887. The area was landscaped as gardens, acres of lawns, two miniature golf courses, and the *Happy Valley Entertainers* open air theatre, where Carol and I went a few times

The theatre was owned then by Scottish comedy actor, Alex Munro. One night, before the show, he came out with a great flourish to make a big announcement.

'Ladies and gentlemen! I've got some wonderful news about my daughter. My lovely daughter Janet – I'm sure you'll have seen her in *Swiss Family Robinson* and *The Day the Earth Caught Fire* – has just got married to the world-famous actor, Ian Hendry.'

The audience gave a great sigh of appreciation and applauded, while Alex Munro beamed with pride.

Another time we went to see a comic called Kenny Cantor where he was appearing at the *Pier Pavilion Theatre*. It emerged that he had been pursuing Carol fairly vigorously, although I didn't get the impression he'd made much progress.

I was surprised by how much this affected me, although Carol and I had certainly been getting on well. We always seemed to have a lot to talk about and, although there was no great *Hallelujah!* moment between us, before the six-week season was over, we found that our relationship had developed organically into something serious, and we'd become an item.

When the season came to an end, Carol was offered a job as stage manager at the Theatre Royal, Windsor. The first thing we did when we arrived in the South was to go and see her parents at home in Surrey, and things looked set for a long lasting if not permanent relationship. I helped her settle down into a house in Windsor, and at the end of September headed off for a longish season in Chesterfield.

At the Civic Theatre I'd been engaged for the first time as 'actor only', and in the ten productions we got through up until Christmas, not all performances sank entirely without trace. One cub critic on the local paper, aspiring to be the next Kenneth Tynan, even declared that 'Challis's performance was so strong that every time he left the stage he left his aura behind him'. In the absence of more subtle interpretations, I took this as a compliment, although the stage manager when he'd read it muttered something about having to clear it up afterwards.

Colin Macintyre was a terrific director to work for. He'd acted in the past but now restricted himself to directing, and ran the show with the help of a very able theatre manager, Derek Coleman. It was a good company with several notable actors, one of whom, Jon Finch, went on to work in Hollywood with Polanski and Hitchcock. Jon was our matinée idol and had all the girls waiting for him at the stage door. One of the girls in the company was Hazel Williams, a beautiful but vulnerable creature who'd been crowned *Miss Wales, 1963*. Hazel was hopelessly in love with Jon.

When Elizabeth Counsell, the actress daughter of John Counsell who ran the Theatre Royal in Windsor, came to Chesterfield to take a part opposite Jon Finch for two weeks, it was a safe bet that a relationship between them would develop. During that fortnight, some mysterious and not very flattering descriptions of Elizabeth were scrawled in lipstick on the playbills outside the theatre. The lipstick was the same colour as Hazel's, but it was never entirely established that she was responsible.

I didn't envy Jon too much, though; there were other actresses in the company – one especially, Penny Dixon, a pretty girl with whom I fell briefly in love, until I realised how much Carol meant to me.

After that I became quite used to thundering up and down the noisy concrete thoroughfare of the M1 to snatch the odd Sunday night with Carol. She was doing well at the theatre in Windsor and happily settled in a pretty early eighteenth-century terrace, close to the Long Walk in Windsor Great Park – an oasis of calm in my frenetic life.

I gained a lot of experience in Chesterfield with the variety of material, and found myself genuinely dedicated to making each show a success. In Wilde's *The Importance of being Ernest*, I played *Dr Chasuble* (showing, at the age of twenty two, my capacity for character roles without having to wait until I was forty as Oliver Fisher had predicted in Bexhill). I played *Trinculo* in *The Tempest*, after just a week's rehearsal, *Sergeant Rough* (with ill-fitting wig) in *Gaslight*, and *Jack the Ripper* in *The Lodger*.

I was enjoying the season, and as often happens, even over a short sojourn in a provincial theatre, the company soon became known around the town. We were treated to a lot of conviviality, usually in a great barracks of a watering-hole in the middle of Chesterfield called the Queen's Park Hotel, where the whole life of the town seemed to be played out in its never-closing bars and function rooms.

After ten productions, finishing off with a great Christmas Revue, although Colin wanted me to come back and do another season, I was ready to move – ready, I thought, to take London's West End by storm. I left Chesterfield and, in the new year of 1965, moved more or less permanently into Carol's house in Windsor, from where access to London was easy.

After Christmas, my next 'job', in the absence of any immediate prospects via Vincent Shaw, was as a 'dresser' at the Theatre Royal, Windsor, where Carol was working, and I found myself helping out with quick changes for such luminaries as Hugh Paddick (Huge Padlock) in the *Farjeon Review* with Dilys Laye and Joan Sterndale Bennett, as well as Jenny and Elizabeth Counsell, twin daughters of John Counsell.

One of the regular directors at the theatre then was Joan Riley, a woman of some presence and a salty tongue. I was surprised once to hear her during rehearsals speaking very loudly to the cast. They were fooling around, cursing and giggling, which prompted her to bellow, 'If you're going to bugger about, you can all fuck off for lunch!'

I had never heard a woman swear before, and I was rather shocked; I'm used to it now, of course. Joan was married to a fine character actor, Frederick Piper. Their son, Mark, a stripling of fifteen, was also working with me at the theatre. He and I became friends, though after I moved on, as happens too easily in my job, we lost contact.

In a nice touch of serendipity, some twenty years later when I met and worked with actress Sue Holderness, I discovered that she was married to Mark and we've known each other for twenty-five years since.

The arrival of spring in 1965 provided a critical watershed in my life when Vincent Shaw got me two important auditions. One was with the Royal Shakespeare Company, where I was seen by Peter Hall's sidekick, Maurice Daniels (known affectionately as Doris Manuals).

The other was for a part in *Portrait of a Queen*, in which Dorothy Tutin played *Queen Victoria* in a big and powerful performance.

The very day after I'd been offered – and had accepted – a part in *Portrait*, I was offered a job at the RSC. I almost cried with frustration, I would have so loved to have gone to Stratford-upon-Avon. Nevertheless, after my various excursions around the country and five seasons in provincial rep, miles from the centre of things, I was more than happy to be working in the heart of Theatreland My part was in a very classy production which was coming to the Vaudeville Theatre after a short, successful run at the Bristol Old Vic. Dorothy Tutin's husband, Derek Waring, was playing *Prince Albert*, Paul Eddington, a much praised *Disraeli*, and Peter Vaughan, *Gladstone*. The minor parts were being recast, and it was in the role of *A Gentleman of the Press* that I made my West End debut on the 6th May. I could hardly have been said to have taken London by storm, though I like to think that my original part was quickly excised from the text to shorten the show (no doubt to fit in with popular train timetables), not because I was so useless in it!

I'd also been booked as understudy to Nicholas Smith, in his linking role of *Ballad Singer*, a narrator who sang to his own guitar accompaniment. This was quite complicated and daunting for me, and several times, Nicholas, who liked a little real-life drama, would come in looking deathly and tragic, and announce that I should prepare myself to go on. Sadly, he always survived and I never played the part in public. For most of the play's year-long run, I was a kind of visible stagehand, dressed as a Victorian footman, shuffling around pieces of furniture between scenes with the curtain up. Nevertheless I was very happy to be involved. The play, based on material culled from Queen Vic's own diaries, was a great success, commercially and critically.

It was a buzz to be involved in a critical hit, and like the rest of the cast I was inclined to be sniffy about the inescapably lowbrow offering in the Adelphi Theatre next door, a very popular musical called *Charlie Girl* starring Anna Neale and Joe Brown (now without his *Bruvvers*). In the Opera, the pub between us, we would mingle with their company, with a distinct hint of condescension on our part; needless to say their show, well seasoned with common touch, went on to outrun our own by many months.

Now that I was in the West End, I began to see more of my old friends, and soon ran into Tony Instone at the 2i's in Old Compton Street. I was still sort of in touch with him, as my mother had been doing some vocal work with his sister, Vanessa. Tony was doing well in the music business, working in A&R and writing a few songs himself. He was impressively up to date with what was going on in the industry.

As we gulped our big mugs of fawn froth, he nodded at a bunch of grubby-looking fellows in the opposite corner.

'See that mess over there,' he scathed. 'That's the Sorrows. They've had half a hit and they think they rule the world!'

I looked at Tony's disparaging visage, and felt a little sorrow for the Sorrows.

Shakespeare and Marriage

Dutifully, from time to time I used to go down to Sunnybank in Epsom to visit my parents. I found I was getting on with my father no better than before, although now I could be more circumspect about it. I told him how much I'd enjoyed the pressure and workload of a crowded repertoire at Chesterfield, but he made it clear that he still didn't consider this real work. Work, he suggested, could not be regarded as 'work' if you were enjoying yourself. This brought home to me the bald reality that he was getting absolutely no enjoyment or satisfaction from his own work, which was why he was beginning to drink to compensate for it. Sadly, I still couldn't communicate with him, and he had a curious way of standing back from me. But, as far as I could tell, he liked Carol, and my mother certainly did.

I was twenty-three, and I think I still saw the world as if through a gauze mask, where the present was blurred and the future lay no more than a week ahead, and was so indistinct as to be irrelevant. I loved Carol and being with her, but up until then when long term plans had arisen, marriage seemed to me like an alien condition. Nevertheless I found myself drifting, by default, into a life of domestic contentment, and discussions about marriage became more frequent. Then, before I knew it, it was a fait accompli.

As if by osmosis, I compounded this idea one chilly moonlit night in a ploughed field somewhere between Windsor and Ascot. We had gone out for a drive and pulled into the field for a little romance. Before I knew what I was doing, I had issued a stuttered proposal. 'Do you want to get married, then? What do you think?'

Not the most unequivocal of proposals, but she said 'Yes.'

Almost as soon as the wedding date was fixed, I found myself becoming increasingly worried that I wasn't quite ready for it; but Carol had been so loyal and supportive that I didn't doubt that it would work in the long run, once I got used to the idea.

Although a little apprehensive, I was happy to go along with wedding plans, and not long after I'd got back from Chesterfield, our marriage banns were announced at St Edward's Roman Catholic Church in Windsor.

For the wedding arrangements, I didn't have to do much more than agree with Carol and her mother. Both of them were enthusiastic initiative takers and very comfortable deciding everything between them. It seemed my only responsibility was to recruit a best man, a task I went about with characteristic woolliness. I asked Richard Fentiman, an old friend from Epsom, if he would do it. We weren't particularly close but he'd been a pupil of my mother's and I'd discovered that he shared my taste in music. He was a good pianist too, and used to put on gigs and charity shows.

My mother, however, had doubts about the whole idea. 'Are you sure you want to get married, John?' she said, scaring me a little. 'You are a bit young, and used to doing what you want.'

But Carol was an impressive, achieving sort, and my parents were generally relieved and happy with her as a daughter-in-law, while her bossy mother and, frankly, hen-pecked father decently tried to disguise their obvious misgivings.

On the appointed day, 26th February, 1966, Carol looked amazing. I wondered why on earth she'd chosen me, although I felt grateful that she had. We said 'I do' with enthusiasm and without any major gaffes, beyond the non-appearance of the carnations for the men's buttonholes. After a modest knees-up in the back of the Theatre Royal and a Sunday off, I went back to work in *Portrait of a Queen* at the Vaudeville – promising like a good thesp, that we'd go on honeymoon as soon as I was next 'resting'.

We moved into a bigger flat on the ground floor of a large early Victorian house near the big roundabout on the edge of Windsor Castle's Home Park. Carol filled the large rooms with tasteful junk and found a surprising number of chores for me to do, however much I protested that pursuits like carpentry and DIY were as alien to me as Greek dancing and petit-point. We were, though, just a short walk to the wonderful open spaces that lay between the castle itself, and the enormous copper statue of George III on a horse that stood on Snow Hill at the end of the Long Walk, two and a half miles away. It was a wonderful walk which we both enjoyed, and when we reached the great metal beast, we would always remark on the size of its colossal copper testicles.

Almost from the start, however, I'm ashamed to say I was feeling ambivalent about being married. While I relished the sense of closeness that it brought, it was inevitable that I would also find the business of being accountable rather tricky; I didn't want to be unfaithful to Carol, but I suppose some unruly, wicked hormone within me wanted me to feel that, if the opportunity arose, I could – without feeling guilty about it. This began to rankle (for which I make no excuses), and at the same time Carol began to behave as if, now she had me, she no longer needed to disguise her natural bossiness.

When *Portrait of a Queen* closed in May 1966, I'd been out of work for barely a week, when, by lucky happenstance, the RSC found themselves let down over some smaller roles in their current production of *Hamlet* – the David Warner version which had been running to breathless reviews since just before Christmas. Somehow my audition the year before had lingered in someone's consciousness, and my agent Vincent Shaw was asked if I might now be available.

I was ecstatic; I could hardly believe my luck. I was engaged to 'play as cast' at £14 a week, possibly, I think, because I was agreeable to doing a bit of furniture shifting, again.

I finally came in front of the mighty Peter Hall when they were seeking to cast the *Poisoner* in the *Play* scene, and was given the role partly because I was good at the powerful histrionics the role called for, and partly because I was tall enough to fit into the quite elaborate (and no doubt expensive) costume assigned to the part.

When I joined the production, David Warner was still playing to unanimous acclaim, although Janet Suzman had been replaced as *Ophelia* by Estelle Kohler. Michael Pennington was *Fortinbras* and James Laurenson, *Guildenstern*.

It was a wonderful experience to be involved even at such a modest level with one of Peter Hall's greatest shows, and I was thrilled when we moved to Stratford-upon-Avon for the summer season. Although in some ways playing there with the RSC might have seemed like peaking too early, I was a lowly member of the company, and I loved being there.

The theatre in Windsor gave Carol leave to come with me to Stratford, and she managed to get a job in 'Wardrobe' among all the other RSC camp followers. It was a wonderful summer, and although I didn't play anything of great importance, it was inspiring to work among some of the country's best actors at the time.

We stayed in a house across the bridge, off the Banbury Road overlooking the Avon, from where, if we were feeling energetic or romantic enough, we could hire a rowing boat to reach the great red brick Royal Shakespeare Theatre by the water's edge. When I wasn't rehearsing, I played a lot of tennis – often with Ian Holm, who was a star of the company that summer – and I helped the other actors in propping up the bar of the *Dirty Duck* public house. Malcolm McDowell, already emerging as a talent, with a few speaking parts in the *Henrys*, was a regular in the *Duck*. He was likeable, but very focused. Even in one of our cod-cricket matches, when I ran him out, he got very cross.

However, between the drinking, tennis and cricket, we had a very full repertoire, including *Henry IV, Parts I & II*, *Henry V* (with Ian as *Hal V*), *Hamlet* and *Twelfth Night*. On one occasion we gave complete, consecutive performances of all three *Henrys* – morning, afternoon and evening. This was a marathon, confusing and knackering. We small players had so many parts to play that in the darkness and confusion during scene changes, it was quite easy to grab the wrong tabard from the racks in the wardrobe and end up on stage as a triumphant English bowman when one was meant to be a bloodied fleeing Frenchmen, while Ian Holm leapt onto the great siege engine in Harfleur and delivered an unforgettable summons to Close the Wall up with Our English – or possibly French – dead...

There was no doubt that the stars like Holm and Warner were a different species from us humble spear carriers. But that season, for some reason, the company was short of stagehands, so that often the whole company would be shifting furniture and props between scenes, and would sometimes find myself heaving a brazier into *Mistress Quickly's* tavern with Ian Holm in a very democratic way.

One of my tasks in *Hamlet*, besides being *Poisoner*, was to 'drive' the machine on which the *Ghost of Hamlet's Father* appears. This was a contraption shaped a little like a Dalek. It ran on large wheels and was draped in ethereal drapery to suggest the ghostly plasma through which Brewster Mason, who was playing the part, appears, standing on a platform at the back. My job was to get inside the thing and wheel it around into position, giving the *Ghost* the appearance of floating. The thing had been made for a far smaller man than me, and I was finding it impossibly uncomfortable to steer properly.

During the first day's rehearsal, Brewster, unhappy about being transported to the wrong spot on the stage opened a little panel at the back and peered in.

'Are you all right, dear boy?' he asked.

I told him the problem I was having.

'I will have it dealt with forthwith,' he boomed encouragingly.

After several more days nothing had been done to make the machine more manageable for me.

When Brewster asked me about it, and I told him, he summoned me out of the thing, and addressed the stage managers. 'How on earth can you expect this tall, strapping young man to operate a contraption designed for a midget?'

It was, apparently, a rhetorical question; he didn't wait for an answer. He was a big man, and he picked the whole thing up, carried it to the edge of the stage and hurled it into the empty auditorium, where it collapsed in a buckled heap.

'*Now* sort it out!' he bellowed.

I was mightily impressed by the sheer bigness of the man's presence, and the next day, the machine had been replaced with one into which I could comfortably fit.

In our production of *Twelfth Night* that summer I had my only non-speaking part, as *Courtier*, wearing a splendid Elizabethan slashed doublet and hose. It was in this attire that I and the rest of the cast were going to have to watch the great England v Germany World Cup Final, which took place, rather inconveniently, during a performance of the play in the Royal Shakespeare Theatre. We were all very excited but worried about how we were going to watch the game as it unfolded.

A resourceful and obliging electrician called Basher rigged up a TV aerial of chicken wire on the outside wall, which he connected through to a small black and white television set up in the band room in the bowels of the theatre. The game started and sporadically, between appearances on stage, we all clustered into the tiny space, in full Elizabethan costume, with the tannoy interrupting every so often to announce our cues, while we jostled and craned our necks to watch the game without disrupting our courtly magnificence – Diana Rigg as *Viola*, Ian Holm (a big football fan) as *Malvolio*, Brewster Mason as *Sir Toby Belch*, Alan Howard as *Orsino* and David Warner as *Sir Andrew Aguecheek*. We were all jumping up and down, yelling at the telly like a bunch of punters in any pub, anywhere in the country that afternoon. This was, after all, an event which the whole nation (except, presumably the full matinee house in the auditorium upstairs) had been anticipating for months with huge excitement, especially now England were in the final.

Loud, well-articulated and actorly cries of, 'Are you blind, ref?'... 'That was a bloody penalty!'... 'Give it to Hurst, you pillock!' echoed off the bare walls, without a thought for what was going on upstairs on stage. We seemed to have been dragged away for our cue at each crucial moment, and most of us had to get back onstage towards the end when England were leading 2-1.

When David Warner as *Aguecheek* entered a few minutes later, he mouthed to the rest of us, *'They've equalised!'*

There was a discernible droop and lack of concentration in all the cast after that, and the final scene was played like a record player cranked up to double speed, producing some mad, gabbled Goon Show sequence in what must have been the fastest last scene of *Twelfth Night* in the history of Shakespearean drama. We lined up at the end, bowed hurriedly and rushed offstage, down to the band room to catch the final minutes, just in time to see Hurst's controversial goal eleven minutes into extra time, and as the game was about to end, Bobby Moore passing to the unmarked Hurst who banged the ball into the net as hard as he could in the very last minute, while the home crowd burst onto the pitch, provoking Kenneth Wostenholme's most famous of commentaries: "... people are on the pitch. They think it's all over! It is now!"

There were a few complaints from the audience that day, though, as far as we knew, nobody asked for their money back.

I stayed with the company until the end of the summer season of '66, when I was called in by Peter Hall, rather like being called in to see the headmaster to receive my 'end of term report'.

'Well, we've had a very good season, haven't we?'

'Oh yes,' I answered keenly, trying to show how much I wanted to stay. 'I really enjoyed playing the three Henries on the same day. And...'

'Yes, yes, we're very pleased with you; you played all your little parts with terrific energy; we thought you showed a genuine streak of unique talent.'

I could barely control the trembling or the excitement that was welling up.

'We'd like you to stay,' Hall went on. 'You've been so useful and such a good walk-on.'

'Oh...' My crest, rampant a moment before, was on the floor. 'Is that it?

'Well, it's up to you. We can't guarantee you any parts.'

The room dissolved in a blur for me. I had so badly wanted to be taken on as a full player and, with encouragement from others, had thought I'd be offered that.

I didn't need long to make up my mind; I mumbled my intention not to stay. After all the joy and vicarious glory over the *Hamlet*, I left the room feeling pretty low.

Ian Holm, one of the company's stars, knew I was having this interview and had been a loyal supporter of mine, I think putting my name forward to Hall as someone to keep in the company. He was waiting for me, to see how I'd got on. He was disappointed that his suggestion had been ignored.

But despite this final let-down, it had been a happy season which Carol and I had both enjoyed. I was still only twenty-four, and although a little discouraged at rejection by the RSC, I had done enough by then to feel that I would certainly find more work.

Back at home in Windsor, I didn't have a lot to do until I was given a part in the Theatre Royal pantomime, always a big hit among the locals and folk from the smoke looking for a bit of old-fashioned entertainment.

The Counsell family, who owned and operated the theatre, were well represented in *Cinderella* by John Counsell's daughters, Jenny (*Cinders*) and Libby (*Dandini* – one of two Principal Boys.) I was *Major-Domo*, a feed part for the *Ugly Sisters* (Andrew Sachs and Stephen Moore).

Tony Hilton was *Buttons*, and panic-stricken when one of his old chums was due to come and watch. The chum knew this, and, after the show, popped his head around the dressing room door, looking for Tony. 'What happened?' he asked cruelly.

I enjoyed the traditionally relaxed approach to panto, when anything could happen. The *Ugly Sisters* kept larking about and corpsing – once dashing off in fits of mirth, leaving me standing in the middle of the stage clutching an umbrella. I had to improvise, and burst into an impromptu version of the Gene Kelly song and dance routine for *Singing in the Rain*. A little corny, you may think, but the punters liked it, and that is the joy of panto; if you have to go off piste, as it were, it often adds to the show.

Carol and I spent our first Christmas as a couple at her parents' house in Surrey. It was a salutary experience. I had never until then (though often since) witnessed such a display of female ascendency as I did in the Robertson household, where Mrs R's rule over her husband was absolute. The poor man couldn't express a thought, a hope or a view about anything without being comprehensively sat on. His wife was his self-appointed censor and spokesman in almost all matters of fact or opinion. I began to realise that Carol was very like her mother and already making decisions for me. 'OK,' she said, 'this year we're at my parents, so next year we'll be at yours.'

I found the prospect of such forward planning quite daunting and was worried that my whole life would be mapped out by my wife. She was telling me where we would be spending next Christmas... and the Christmas after that. I couldn't come to terms with the inevitability of it all, stretching away into the future. Most of the time, when we were alone, the easy comfort of being together was still there. We laughed, though not as much as we had, and talked about the theatre, which dominated both our lives. But there were distinct signs of impatience in her if I didn't quite come up to the mark in getting things done, and there appeared to be an astonishing number of things I didn't get quite right. I would even sometimes feel a little as if I'd had a summons to attend Mr Sharples' room for a whacking. I was just too easy-going to put my foot down over trivial things but I knew I didn't want to turn out a hapless cipher in our marriage, like my poor father-in-law in his. Carol's tendency to tell people what to do – a great asset in a Stage Manager – was pretty exhausting, and it was with a sense of relief that I went back to work in *Cinderella* the day after Boxing Day.

Metropolitan Man

After Christmas and the end of *Cinderella's* run in February, I had the impression that my agent Vincent Shaw had lost all interest in me, or perhaps he was just focusing elsewhere. Whichever, despite the earlier efforts he'd made for me, he wasn't sending much work my way now. Although not ungrateful for what he'd done for me up until then, I was more than ready for a change.

Besides, I'd been travelling around for half a dozen years, played hundreds of roles, appeared in the West End and with the RSC and I felt that I knew what I was doing; it was perhaps time to move to lusher pastures with a new agency.

I'd recently come across a theatrical photographer called John Vere-Brown. John lived in Primrose Hill and was well known for the moody lighting of his work, and his unabashed campness. When he suggested it, I easily succumbed to having a new set of mug shots taken for my entry in *Spotlight*, a kind of trade catalogue of the nation's actors. After they were done, he showed them to a friend of his who was a top actors' agent, particularly for films and television. Afterwards, he suggested I should talk to her.

Caroline Dawson came from a theatrical background and was now a fizzy, up-and-at-'em young agent working for International Artistes. I was invited to come and see her in their offices which were housed within the Noel Gay Organisation in Denmark Street – the music industry's *Tin Pan Alley*. I was impressed; she was a bombshell, a blur of well-placed curves and big chestnut hair who deployed these assets and a matching personality to network her way deep into the business. She can't have been more than twenty-six or twenty-seven, but she seemed to know everyone and, more to the point, they appeared to know her. She already looked after a number of successful movie actors, and she had her finger right on the pulse of the burgeoning world of television drama and soap opera.

She chattered away to me as she shuffled through my shots with a non-committal smile.

'Who's your agent now?' she asked.

'Vincent Shaw,' I admitted.

'Oh God! You could do better than that.'

I felt quite hurt on Vincent's behalf, but didn't disagree.

She went on, 'I would be happy to represent you, and I suggest you consider my offer very seriously. '

She told me she thought I should try working in television, where demand was exploding. She had a penchant then, and more so when she started up her own agency, for representing quirky actors – and apparently that included me, for I signed up almost at once.

Caroline started putting me up for TV jobs right away, and I soon got my first television part ever in *The Newcomers*, the BBC soap which had already been running for over two years with the aim of challenging the already mighty *Coronation Street* on ITV. The *Newcomers* were a group of families who had moved into a new suburb, somewhere in East Anglia. Like *Coronation* Street, it was about the interaction of neighbours imposed on one another through accidents of geography and town-planning, but aimed at a more middle-class audience than *Corrie*. In it I played a flashy London rag-trader, *Harry Kapper*, who turns up in a big shiny car (a Vauxhall Cresta with twin headlights and a few extra shiny chrome bits) to seduce the young daughter of the central family over three or four episodes.

When Caroline had sent me up for the part, she had failed to tell the producer, a woman called Paddy Russell, that I'd never done TV before, and I didn't tell her either. At the end of the first day's shoot, she came up to me with a sardonic look on her face. 'You're a naughty boy, John. You've never done telly before, have you?'

'How could you tell?' I admitted.

'You're acting too large – your gestures are all stage gestures. You're not at the RSC now, you know! You need to rein everything in – reactions, facial movements, waving your arms about – all that stage stuff. Let me show you...'

She didn't chuck me off the set – it was too late for that – but she gave me an instant and valuable tutorial on the difference between acting in the theatre and in the TV studio. I was more than happy to learn whatever new techniques I had to, without unlearning the stagecraft, the bravura style of acting by projecting which I had absorbed on the hoof over the past five or six years. Where I was in the habit of clearly stated expressions of mood and reaction, she encouraged me to play it right down, and internalise it, in a way that suits the smaller screen.

In between episodes of *The Newcomers*, Caroline sent me up for a part I could only have dreamed of while I was with Vincent. It was for the Beatles' next venture into the movies. They'd already produced *Help!* and *A Hard Day's Night*; now they were working on the more psychedelic *Magical Mystery Tour*. Caroline had heard through her spider's web of contacts that they couldn't find anyone for the part of the *Courier* on the magical coach trip; she got straight onto the case and sent me round for it.

This meant trotting round from Caroline's office in Tin Pan Alley to NEMS House, off the top of Bond Street, on a Sunday, where I met three-quarters of the Fab Four.

John was lying on the floor delivering a sardonic commentary; Paul sat behind a desk, acting the producer, and Ringo ended up on the arm of my chair. All very relaxed, their look then was facial hair and kaftans.

'We don't really know what we're doing; we haven't got a script yet. Are you any good at making up words?'

For a twenty-four-year-old in 1967, this was an ultimate fantasy, to be sitting around with John, Paul, and Ringo, exchanging gags! They were terrific – self-effacing, charming and funny – and I felt completely at ease, which says an awful lot about the way they handled themselves.

I was even bold enough, when they asked if I liked their music, to say, 'I prefer the Stones.'

John gave a Scouse chuckle. 'So do I,' he said.

As I left I could still hear him. 'He's great! Get him.'

My heart gave a mighty leap. I was going to work with the Beatles! They'd been incredibly friendly and they seemed to like me. I left NEMS House feeling about ten feet tall.

But – cruel fate! – they couldn't have me. On the dates they wanted me I was already booked by the BBC to play *Harry* flaming *Kapper*; the BBC wouldn't release me, and I had to turn the Beatles down. Strange as it seems, the part of the courier, *Buster Bloodvessel,* was played in the end by eccentric Scots comedian, Ivor Cutler.

The *Newcomers* job wasn't immediately followed by more TV work, the Beatles part had gone for good, and in the meantime I carried on going up for stage jobs. I was booked by a fresh-faced, young wannabe impresario to appear in the first of his productions – a summer season of four plays at the *Kenton Theatre* in the sleepy riverside town of Henley-on-Thames.

It was a good young company with a well-balanced repertoire. Simon Williams was the young male lead and 'heart-throb' in *The Reluctant Debutante*, several years before he appeared in some forty episodes as the wayward son in *Upstairs Downstairs*.

I was booked mainly for the role of *Walter*, the misunderstood German tutor in Peter Shaffer's *Five Finger Exercise*, but when the two leads in *The Knack* walked out on the Friday before the following Monday start, Lynn Rainbow and I were asked to take it on. Two days is a short time to learn any play, and this one was a string of discombobulated one-liners. Bravely we said we'd do it, before spending the whole weekend in a rowing boat on the river trying to learn our parts. We fluffed quite a bit of it, but luckily, it was in the nature of the script that no one noticed.

The Kenton was a charming little theatre where, in the light summer evenings before the performance, there was a ceremonial drawing of curtains over the three high arched Georgian windows which overlooked the auditorium. It was an enjoyable season, and remains the only occasion on which I have been employed by the subsequently stellar producer, Cameron Mackintosh.

By the time the *Sergeant Pepper* album had come out and the Summer of Love was raging in California, barely noticed by me, my own summer was occupied by worrying doubts and feelings of guilt over my marriage. While for the first year and a half since we'd wed I'd been vaguely disturbed by a growing sense of claustrophobia, through no fault of Carol's, I now found myself getting closer to Caroline Dawson, my new agent. She was an intensely vital woman, and very funny – both attractive characteristics to a lazy, twenty-five year-old performer like me. Partly, of course, I was flattered by the attention she was paying me, which had resulted in my first TV parts. And she was also very persuasive.

In the autumn I moved into the Bayswater flat she shared with a successful young casting director, Doreen Jones. It was a small and very lively domestic scene to enter. Doreen and Caroline were tremendous friends, but complete opposites in many ways, which gave rise to a great deal of sparky debate, in which Doreen, a thoughtful socialist, acted as a useful foil to Caroline's altogether Torier stance and extravagant nature.

This was all very exciting, and I knew it was the start of a new phase in my life. At the same time, I was confused and remorseful about letting people down. I tried to face up to the distress I'd caused all my relations and Carol's by leaving her in Windsor.

Her father, deeply puzzled, tackled my father over it.

'What's gone wrong?' he asked.

My dad was reluctant to be seen to be supporting me. 'Nothing's gone wrong; he's just gone off with someone else.' Sheffield folk don't mince their words.

It turned out not to have been the last time I would stumble, half seeing, into a marriage by default, which always leaves the door open for something more powerful to come along. But I hadn't done it with the remotest intention of backing out, and deeply regretted the hurt I'd created by my clumsy handling of it.

In the late sixties, when there were still half a million US soldiers in Vietnam, Israel had launched the *Six Days' War*, the *Beatles* ruled the world's charts, and shots of a skinny little model known as Twiggy had begun to fill the pages of magazines, attitudes were changing all over the world and London was an exciting place to live. It provided me with a whole lot of useful new experiences, and a few mundane ones, too, like how to exist between acting jobs, now that I wasn't permanently touring. For although I was beginning to get regular TV work (having reined in the facial and manual gestures at Paddy Russell's suggestion) there was always a lull between jobs, which weren't quite well paid enough for me to 'rest' in comfort.

One of my regular occupations around then was in the fusty, tatty environs of Portobello Road, where I had my first taste of the glamorous, if dodgy world of antiques. I worked in various shops and watched, fascinated as the dealers chiselled the punters and each other with untruths, tricks of the trade and subtle come-ons. As it happens, I'd always found the idea of antique dealing mysteriously alluring; there was something of the traditional 'quest' about it – every dealer in the land seemed constantly on the lookout and living in the fervent hope that one day they would find a missing sketch by Constable, or King Henry VIII's codpiece. It was a precarious, fantasy existence, wonderfully characterised by Ian McShane in *Lovejoy* in the 1980s.

One of the men who employed me – a shifty geezer with a nervous tick when he wasn't telling the truth (which was most of the time) – spent a lot of time fondling wads of cash, buying and selling, often to other dealers, and I noticed how a piece could shift shops two or three times, each time at a higher price before it went home with a real punter.

He gave me the task of stripping a pair of lime green louvred shutters, outside on the street, while minding the shop off Westbourne Grove. It was a really boring job, and I was delighted when a punter came in and need showing around. Unfortunately, when I went back out, the shutters had been nicked. I was mortified that I'd been so naive, and started rehearsing excuses for my boss. But he took it in his stride, shrugged his shoulders and said it was an occupational hazard in the trade.

I went off to do another TV job, and when I came back I was passed on to another dealer in Portobello Road proper, where I looked after the shop. He had a system of pricing stuff with a weird code I never got to grips with. I soon put my foot in it when a man came in off the street to ask about a small statue of a dog in the window. I didn't realise it was bronze, and translated the price as £38. Somewhat to my amazement, the punter snapped it up without even a token effort at bargaining. I put it down to my supreme salesmanship, but when the owner came back, and I proudly told him I'd sold the dog for £38, he blew a fuse. It was meant to be £238, and when I described the punter who'd bought it, it seemed he was well known for seeking out inexperienced shop staff and confusing them, in order to profit by their incompetence. My boss ran off to find him, coming back half an hour later in a fury, saying the fellow claimed he'd already sold the dog...

I realised that while I enjoyed the business, it was unlikely I would ever develop sufficient guile to succeed in it.

In the meantime, as long as Caroline sent me up, I went to audition for any TV part on offer, until at last, I found myself among the cobbles and smoking chimneys of *Coronation Street* itself, playing *George Naylor,* the first of countless coppers – uniformed and plain-clothed – who filled that stage of my career. The trend was established by my next two jobs as *Detective Constable*

Armitage in the much-loved and long-running *Z-Cars*.

Z-Cars was still a headline show then, attracting tens of millions of viewers, and I felt quite grown-up to have had a part in it. Visiting my parents in Epsom one weekend, I asked my father what he thought, hoping he might show at least a little pride in this minor success.

He was dismissive. 'I haven't got time for that rubbish.'

I was bitterly disappointed. I wanted so much for him to acknowledge what I was doing and what I had achieved, modest as it was, entirely through my own motivation and without any help from drama school or formal qualifications. But he wasn't having it – or so I thought until several years later, shortly before he retired, when a group of his office colleagues came down for a party at our house.

'He's always been so proud of you,' one of them said. 'I remember when you were first in *Z-Cars*, and we were working late, everything had to stop so we could all watch it, and he said, 'That's my son, you know.'

It seemed that he just couldn't bring himself to show *me* any appreciation of what I was doing then; I profoundly wish that he had.

One of the girls – or perhaps both of them – owned a cat who lived with us in the flat in Queen's Gardens, but when I suggested, not very seriously, that it would be good to have a dog to take for walks in Hyde Park, it was Caroline who leaped up at once and insisted that we go immediately to Battersea Dogs' Home to find one.

I'd always liked dogs, and Caroline had grown up in Sussex when it was still all country and always had animals around her; it was inevitable that we would come away with some poor abandoned creature whom we thought deserved our love and attention.

We were both attracted by a hairy beast with a smoky grey coat the texture of a well-used floor mop. He also had a curving, upright plumed tail that looked like it belonged to a much classier dog. A long fringe flopped over his face, allowing one sardonic eye to peep out. His name, we were told, was Nicky, which didn't seem right at all.

Once we'd brought him home, I started to get to know him. He was a scatty mongrel with an explosive and embarrassing sex drive which led him to treat even a soberly attired male leg as a potential object of lust. He was an interestingly moody beast who would break into sporadic mad fits, barking crazily, rushing around chasing his tail, and generally behaving in a bipolar way, a bit like me. He was, though, fundamentally a friendly chap, who got on with my mother's dog. I rechristened him The Prune, eventually La Prune, as I decided his sometimes aloof and disdainful manner suggested French ancestry. An old lady we met in the park eyed him appreciatively and announced that he was a Chinese Oystercatcher; I thought not, but nodded agreeably, while the dog became even snootier.

I soon realised that, for our tolerable coexistence, he would have to have the two causes of his uncontrollable randiness excised, although just the thought of it made me wince. The process worked, and although I sometimes felt sorry for the loss of the Prune's prunes, he never knew or, presumably, cared about what had happened, and was to be my sound and regular travelling companion on countless adventures over the next decade.

By the beginning of 1968, Caroline was getting me regular work on television – nothing big, mostly some kind of plod – and I was seldom out of work for more than a month at a time. Usually after a week or two of forced idleness I would sally out to look for employment, either in the antiques, or less contentiously, as a part-time driver – sometimes on lorries for a small haulage company working out of the docks, or as a chauffeur, wearing a dark suit, highly polished black shoes and a cap with a thistle up front.

In a gleaming Austin Princess, I'd drop people off and pick them up after funerals, or take old ladies in to the West End to go shopping. While they pottered around Fortnum & Mason, I cruised around the streets. I enjoyed driving about in big cars, and it gave me something to do. But it did have its tricky moments, like the time I pulled up in Curzon Street alongside Shepherd Market, planning to have a drink in a pub in White Horse Street. I'd barely stopped when the passenger door opened and I was joined on the front seat by a scantily dressed woman. It was hard to judge her age beneath a goodish layer of make-up and a pile of hair like a well groomed haystack. Beneath her low-cut blouse she appeared to be housing a pair of lively young puppies.

I leaned back and looked askance. 'Can I help you?' I asked, primly.

'Wotcher mean? Can I help *you*, more like.'

'Oh, dear!' I gasped like a Victorian matron, as wafts of cheap, cloying scent reached my nostrils. 'There appears to have been some kind of misunderstanding.'

'Well, what d'you expect, if you pull up in a big car in a place like this?' she demanded impatiently, letting herself out and slamming the door behind her.

When something similar happened to Jeffrey Archer some twenty years later (except for the letting herself out bit), with such dire and well-publicised consequences, leading to a bit of perjury and stir, I realised what a lucky escape I'd had.

It was during one of these fallow periods that a friend from my summer at the RSC turned up. Andrew Jack was the actor son of a well-known voice coach, Stephen Jack. Like me, Andrew had been a bit part player in Stratford in 1966, when he and I had done some singing together. I still clung to the hope that I might one day be able to make a living from singing, or writing music, and I was right with him when he suggested we follow up an idea I'd had with Jon Finch in Chesterfield. Andrew and I finished off writing *The Ten Days of Christmas*.

This was intended to be what was politely called a 'novelty' song (usually an idea so horrible it couldn't be taken seriously) – a version of the traditional Yuletide air involving the giving of gifts, in which the gifts were characterized by Goon-like grunts, raspberries, kazoos, squeals and other non-verbal human sounds. "On the first day of Christmas my true love sent to me a *'Hoink hoink'* in a pear tree," and so on. (If you think this might have sounded pretty irritating, you're probably right.)

We got into the habit of following around a band we liked who sang clever close harmonies, and often let us play our song (or two) in the interval; their manager heard the Christmas song and opined, rather unexpectedly, that he thought it could have legs. Amazingly, as a result, we were asked to meet the head of novelty records at MCA. He listened to the embarrassing demo without any outward display of emotion.

'I suppose it's funny,' he said gloomily. 'I wouldn't know; I've got no sense of humour.' Which might explain why he booked us to come in and record it, along with a suitable B-side, at the Olympic

Studios in Barnes.

While we were in the studio, between innumerable embarrassing takes with a banjo and honky-tonk piano, we were almost speechless with awe when Mick Jagger wandered in. *Mick Jagger*, for God's sake!

'Hey, man. Anyone gotta tambourine?' he asked.

We didn't have one; we yammered our regrets.

Everyone else rushed around until they found one, and he wandered off again.

Still quivering with excitement, we managed to record a final version and a B-side which was a spoof blues – '*Woke up this morning; my baby's gone....*' It was about a missing child.

We were billed on the label as *Rentaflop* and the result was let loose on a blameless public. Astonishingly, it got a few plays; Kenny Everett liked it, and Pete Murray described it as 'a real Granny Frightener', which we thought was probably good.

When we were asked to turn up and perform it on the BBC's leading highbrow show, *Late Night Line-Up*, we thought here must be some mistake.

But no, we were expected; we were introduced by a frankly doubtful Joan Bakewell, and performed our song. Ms Bakewell's reaction afterwards ran to no more than the infinitesimal raising of an eyebrow and a slight wrinkling of one nostril. Mercifully, I haven't heard the beastly ditty in years, and if you find a copy in your attic, please don't send it to me.

I was also making regular trips to Manchester, where the northern TV studios seemed always busy. I went there early in the year to do an episode of *City '68, The Old Gun* with Sonya Dresdel and former *Coronation Street* star, Bill Kenwright, who later in life –poacher turned gamekeeper – became a potent impresario and took over the Theatre Royal, Windsor. While I was in Manchester that time I was asked at the last minute to play a part in another TV series, *Judge Dee*, in which an entire cast of British actors played Chinese. I had my eyes lifted with fish scales, and a nasty scar inserted to the right of my mouth using rigid collodion scarring liquid, an experimental make-up for which I agreed to be a guinea pig, although I regretted it after when I came out in a nasty rash.

Manchester was fun, though. I used to stay in an hotel like a barn, the *Brown Bull* in Salford, which was not especially clean and tidy but oozing character, and a popular roost for any passing theatricals. There was something in the air in Manchester that seemed to encourage an unrestrained sense of fun, which matched my temperament. Here, one night, I met a hero almost on a par with John Lennon, in the form of the great George Best, then at the height of his talents. He could still put away a bottle of vodka during a night out, then go on to play First Division football next day. But I couldn't overlook that he played for Manchester United – which, to a lifelong Arsenal supporter, was almost as bad as playing for Tottenham.

Towards the end of the year, I was given a crack at the hit BBC cop series, *Softly, Softly* as *DC Rankin*. He didn't have a lot to do, but made enough of an impression for them to ask me back the following month to play him again, this time in a starring role. After spending Christmas with Caroline, I went with her to stay at her uncle's place in the country, where we watched the transmission of Rankin's second outing.

I was disappointed with what I saw. I knew the producer had been trying me out for a longer-term presence, but somehow I just hadn't pulled it off. I was still, at that stage, conscious of not overacting, and in this case, I'd understated it to the point where the character had almost disappeared. I knew it, and Caroline didn't disagree; but it did help me in the long run to find that balance between extravagant stage acting and a strong but contained screen performance.

Although I didn't suffer from the same indiscriminate and compulsive sex urges as the Prune (while still entire), my wandering eye did eventually lead to Caroline observing one evening that my vest was on back to front, when I'd been wearing it the right way round that morning. This precipitated a summary eviction from Queen's Gardens, and within minutes of the crisis, it seemed, I found myself wandering across Hyde Park clutching a small bag of personal possessions, with the Prune on a piece of string beside me, and absolutely nowhere to go.

It was my own bloody fault; I'd had a great time with Caroline, and insofar as my own indolence let her, she'd helped my career more than I deserved. I was established now as a TV actor, and sooner or later – she was convinced– I would get my break. I wished I could have been as sure. Besides, Caroline was very good company – funny, feisty (if that means what I think it does) and sexy. What was it about me that could never accept I was lucky to have any good relationship when one came my way? The trouble was, I liked being around a woman; I didn't like confrontation but I couldn't bear the thought of cutting off all other options that might – or might not – have been on offer.

I had always worked between acting jobs, but never for much money. As a result, I'd never saved anything, and early 1969 found me potless as well as homeless. It was only circumstances as dire as these that could have led me back to live with my parents in Epsom. My mother had always been interested in my career, and completely supportive; she was more than happy to have me back and gossip with me about theatre and theatricals. My father, on the other hand, seemed more distant and disapproving than ever.

I wished I could have made some connection with Dad, but it was as if he was determined to block out any approach. I'd passed through my youthful defiance phase, and it troubled me that I couldn't have anything approaching a normal man-to-man relationship with my own father. Sunnybank was not a happy household in which to lodge. I felt sorry for my mother, but I immediately set about looking for somewhere else to live.

However, one good thing came of my being at home, when my grandfather, Wallace Wyndham Harden from Bath, decided that the time had come for him to stop driving and gave me his supremely tidy, blue-grey Standard 8.

At last, with a car of my own I could roam with even greater abandon than before, and hooked up with a new friend, Chris Lewis. He was a BBC Sports OB producer living in fairly messy circumstances with two other guys in a house in Priory Road, Kew, where he invited me to join them. I was as keen as ever on sport, though I didn't play much beyond tennis when I got the chance, and I would often tag along with Chris when he was covering games or matches, which involved long sessions at Lord's and large quantities of Guinness.

Chris was also a drummer, and the others played music in one way or another, producing a lot of antisocial noise. Priory Road was not a tidy place, either, and could have been the model for *The Young Ones'* house (Rick Mayall's, not Cliff's). We existed in a state of bedlam – the kind of bedlam I enjoyed, with a constant flux of people in and out.

One visitor was Dianne Minassian, a beautiful girl with whom Chris fell instantly in love. So did I, especially when I discovered she played the guitar and wrote songs which she sang with one of the sweetest voices I ever heard. Naturally, I wanted to do all I could to help in getting her songs listened to by the right people, and recorded.

At the time, I still harboured musical aspirations of my own, and fiddled about writing songs and doing gigs with anyone I could persuade to do it. And since Dianne had first appeared in the flat in Kew, she and I had quickly become an item, which only increased my desire to help her. The strange thing about Dianne (which she pronounced *Dee-Ann*) was that although she sang like lark, she was very shy and suffered from a marked stammer when she spoke. But she also had the looks to catch the eye of a producer, and so I persuaded her that we should go ahead and record some demo tracks.

When we punted the tape around, we soon came across someone who was interested enough to take it further; it was clear that he wasn't interested in me, but he suggested that we should meet a friend of his, a producer called Tony Macaulay.

That was exciting; Tony Macaulay was a big cheese, a songwriter who'd already had a string of hits, starting with *Baby, Now That I've Found You* for the Foundations in 1967.

With some trepidation Dianne and I went to meet him for lunch in a Soho restaurant. The first thing that struck me about Tony Macaulay was that he was, in fact, Tony Instone – my former friend and musical colleague. Although I'd heard from time to time through my mother that Tony Instone was doing well in the music business, I'd no idea he'd changed his name and I simply hadn't made the connection. The last time we'd performed together was at a church fete in a vicarage garden near Epsom. Frankly, he didn't look too thrilled about seeing me again, but Dianne was offered a few more recording sessions – without me, this time. As it turned out, the producers were defeated by her overwhelming shyness and her fear of the sound studios. I tried to persuade them to give her another chance, but sadly, despite her jaw-dropping good looks, lovely voice and good songs, she wasn't taken on by any record label.

Her father, George Minassian, was a well-known film cameraman whom I met when I drove down with her a few times to Chertsey, where George and his wife lived. There was something about her family, her father in particular, which seemed in some way to inhibit her and perhaps was the cause of her shyness. I got the impression that George liked to keep close tabs on her, and she was always seemed to be looking over her shoulder to see if he approved of what she was doing. I don't think he thought much of me – an archetypal ne'er-do-well actor, in his eyes.

However, that didn't entirely squash her free spirit, and in the early spring, before the season had got going, she suggested we drive her open-topped MGB down to Treyarnon Bay, near Padstow in Cornwall, where her family kept a caravan near the beach...

There was no one much around, the grass was uncut, the shops and cafés were closed and the wind was whipping up little white horses in the Atlantic. But Dianne was an adventurous girl and a great surfer; she soon had me and the Prune in the choppy water. I had a go at surfing, without much success, but the Prune loved swimming in the sea, for the sheer exhilaration of it – although he looked alarmingly like an emaciated greyhound when he bounded ashore with a dripping coat and produced a shower ten feet all round him when he shook himself dry.

Living the gypsy life in a caravan appealed very much to my whacky romantic nature and was a great experience – if not very comfortable. Even for lithe young things who didn't mind how often they bumped into each other, it was a tight fit. Throw in the dog, and it was a shambles. In moments of intimacy, you only had to turn over and the Prune was in the way or snuffling your nether regions and had to be evicted without too much ceremony. Then he'd sit outside and howl until, philosophically, he wandered off and found a pool to play in. I was sorry for him, of course, but he wasn't my priority right then.

We had a great trip, and I loved driving the MG, but back in London I had to be content with my grandad's Standard. It was surviving surprisingly well, considering the punishment I gave it, until one summer's evening, driving to a party in convoy with

Andrew Jack and a few other friends, the poor old thing became the filling in a tightly packed sandwich between Andrew's parents' car, which he'd borrowed without asking them, and the one in front of me, which had just stopped at a red light Andrew and I had both failed to spot. The Standard was a total write-off. The Prune (a little dazed) and I couldn't get out until Andrew had prised open the passenger door with a crowbar, after which the wrecked motor was consigned to a last resting place in a West London breaker's yard.

The Standard was followed by a succession of dodgy old cars, each of which was a temporary home or dossing place for the Prune and became deeply imbued with his wet smell. There was a Triumph Herald Coupé, a Ford Anglia and a battered Renault 4, with its unique push-me-pull-you gear shift. These cars, with the dog on the rear seat, often doubled as chauffeur-driven hire vehicles when my friend Maurice Roeves and I offered our services to the public in bringing back punters from parties with *Honky-Tonk Woman* blaring from the warped and hissing cassette deck.

It was strange that in the last year of the sixties, with everything that that came to mean, I finally became aware of the significance of the times. This was brought home sharply, I suppose, by such disparate events as Neil Armstrong walking on the Moon, and Brian Jones dying from an overdose. As a long time fan, Brian's death was a big blow to me, and discouraged me from ever playing with any drugs beyond booze and tobacco.

Sadly, if inevitably, Dianne got fed up with my continual rushing around; I wasn't helping her much and we slowly drifted apart, I guess by mutual consent. Although I had no pressing urge to fill the void, I was tempted when I did a TV job, playing (oddly for me) a vicar. This was in a detective series, somewhat banally entitled *Who-Dun-It,* in which the female sleuth was played by a gorgeous, elfin faced creature, Amanda Reiss. She knew what she was doing; she'd been in a couple of sub-*Carry On* 'doctor-and-nurse' movies and quite a bit of TV. We immediately struck a spark in one another, although it turned out to be a while smouldering before it burst into any kind of flame.

In the late summer of 1969 I was booked for a couple of productions at the Mermaid Theatre in London's City beside the Thames, then run with idiosyncratic distinction by the recently knighted Sir

Bernard Miles.

In the first of these, Shaw's *Saint Joan*, I played *D'Estivet*, the lawyer who promoted Joan of Arc's trial – an interesting character and an enjoyable part to play. In the trial scene, Sir Bernard was experimenting with lighting, leaving the actors in narrow pools of light on an otherwise sloe-black stage. I had an important speech, describing who I was, what *Joan* was accused off, and what she had offered in her defence.

At the dress rehearsal, I came on to the stage to find it in almost total darkness, so I could barely see where I was going.

After a moment, I stopped.

A West Country burr emanated from the darkness of the auditorium. 'What have you stopped for?'

'I'm not lit, Sir Bernard.'

'Let me be the judge of that. It's wonderfully rare having these voices coming out of the darkness.'

And that was how we did it.

Bernard Miles was an incorrigible old showman, and charming with it, although sometimes it would backfire for him. One late autumn morning he was standing on Puddle Dock, outside The Mermaid with a gang of American tourists who'd shown up at the theatre. They were all gazing intently into the thick mist that shrouded the river.

The faint shadow of a large barge slid by.

'You can imagine,' the knight boomed, 'how that might be Queen Elizabeth, the Virgin Queen herself on that barge, on her way to visit Mary in the Tower.'

Drawing in a deep breath, he hailed the vessel, 'Ahoy there, bargee!' The echo of his greeting bounced back eerily from the piles of Blackfriars Bridge.

Through the thick mist, the disembodied voice of a cockney waterman floated from the barge across the flat river. 'Why don't you fuck off!'

After *Saint Joan*, I stayed on at the Mermaid for a production of *The Bandwagon*, an altogether lower-brow offering with the wonderful Peggy Mount. The play's writer, Terence Frisby, had had a huge comedy hit with *There's a Girl in my Soup*, which had run in the West End since 1966 and was still going strong. Sadly, *The*

Bandwagon didn't repeat this success. The producer Michael Codron, who'd done very well out of *Soup*, wanted to transfer it, but only if Frisby rewrote part of the second act, which he refused to do.

Sir Bernard asked me to stay on for a third play, but it wasn't much of a role, and in any case I thought (wrongly, as it turned out) that I had a big TV part in the offing. Instead, I responded to a call from Colin MacIntyre to go back to Chesterfield, where I'd enjoyed such a good season in 1964. It was a pleasure to be back, especially with so much more experience under my belt, and with no television roles in view, I was glad of the month's work. I played an American, *Eddie Carbone*, the lead in Arthur Miller's *A View from the Bridge*. It was a good play to be in, which I followed by being an American again – *Uncle Remus* in a Christmas show of *Br'er Rabbit*.

As ever, in a quandary about where I would work next, I drove back from Chesterfield to London where, I hoped, Amanda Reiss would be pleased to see me.

A Triumph for the Gunners

Amanda Reiss was a striking and mercurial woman with strong opinions which she was always ready to defend, and I was very taken with her. I was frankly surprised and a little flattered when she seemed to take an interest in my career. I was still living with Chris Lewis in Kew but I began to spend more and more time at Amanda's two-storey flat off Prince of Wales Drive in Battersea, where the Prune and I got to know and love Battersea Park – the rickety funfair and the threadbare little zoo.

Amanda took the theatre very seriously, and this spilt over heavily into her personal life. She loved theatrical parties and being surrounded by like-minded, arm-waving creatures of the business, such as Roland Curram, Sheila Gish or Lewis Fiander. Amanda loved entertaining, too, and would always invite a number of important agents to her parties. They would sit about, smugly aware of the power they wielded while the thespians strutted their stuff. I wasn't so keen on these gatherings and would stand on the sidelines, slightly appalled by all the gush and pose. I was confused too, as a fairly apolitical animal then, by the distinctly upper-crust flavour of Amanda's life, and the disapproval with which she and her left-of-centre theatre chums greeted the election of Edward Heath and his new Conservative government. There seemed to be something oddly bogus in these thespians drawling, 'Dah-ling, it's just too frightful having this awful little Tory in Downing Street.'

Did they really prefer the idea of Harold Wilson? I wondered.

I guessed that Amanda's mother, Ambrosine Philpotts, probably would not have; she'd formerly been married to Sir John Reiss, a captain of the cement industry. She was a formidable, uber-theatrical *grande dame* and friend of Robert Morley, and had been around a long time in British comedy movies and stage parts that called for strong headmistress types with nutcracker jaws.

I couldn't avoid the impression that Ambrosine did not approve of me and thought her daughter could have done a lot better. However, she was somewhat won round by my activities in Amanda's garden – if you could call it a garden. It was a tiny patch, open to the London sky, at the back of her flat. When I arrived it grew only weeds and, it seemed, discarded cigarette packets and other stuff that blew in. When I had time on my hands, I cleaned it up and started planting it, deriving a lot of real satisfaction from how it came out. Although as a kid I'd been dragooned into helping my father mow the lawn and trim hedges and whatnot, it was here that the seed of my subsequent lifelong love of gardening took root.

Later in the year Amanda was booked to play *Elvira*, the lead in a major revival of Noel Coward's classic *Blithe Spirit*, which was due to open at The Globe in July.

From the start it was a pretty competitive production, which involved some bare-knuckle squabbling between the two other female leads, Beryl Reid (*Madam Arcati*) and Phyllis Calvert (*Ruth*), over the ticklish issue of billing. The right spot for a name to appear on the playbills and posters can be a very contentious matter. Beryl Reid ended up with what she perceived as second billing, but had her dressing room redecorated to make up for it. The male lead, *Charles*, was played by Patrick Cargill, a popular stage actor at the time with distinctive eyebrows and an inescapably caddish demeanour.

These people were so busy upstaging one another that the show never really hung together. Amanda – naturally rather tense when she was working – hadn't been helped by the rivalry, and there was something slightly hysterical about her performance. Sitting safely in the stalls on the first night I felt really sorry for her, and just wanted to rush up onto the stage and put my arms around her.

Old Noel himself also showed up in a box for the first night, and was subsequently reported as not having been impressed. We didn't know that then; and, as often happens after a first night, we ended up sitting around all night, drinking too much in someone's flat while we waited for the early editions of the papers to hit the street with their all-important reviews. As I had privately feared, these turned out not to be worth waiting up for – or indeed, worth reading at all – for most of them gave the production a serious panning.

Poor Amanda, who took her career, and every other aspect of her life, very seriously, was distraught. But she bit her lower lip and bravely fought back the tears – at least until we got back to Battersea – and said through rigid lips, 'Oh well, I'm obviously not a critics' girl.'

I felt for her; this had been a potential big break for her, and somehow she'd blown it. It wasn't necessarily her fault; there had just been too much internal wrangling for the show to flow. Nevertheless, it did run until the following January. Nor was it by any means the end of her career, for she went on to play the Queen Mother to some acclaim in two different TV productions, and in *Crown Matrimonial,* a play by Royce Ryton at the Haymarket.

For the first few months of 1971 my own performance schedule was looking a little lean. In the absence of any better employment, and determined not to be reliant on Amanda, I went back to operating a kind of a taxi service with my chums, Maurice Roeves and Ian Sharp, with the Prune riding shotgun. But anxious not to drift too far from my core occupation, I took a job for a month or so working backstage at the Adelphi Theatre on *Showboat*, with Cleo Laine in the lead.

Another of the stagehands was a moonlighting porter from Covent Garden, just around the corner and, in those days, London's thriving wholesale flower, fruit and veg market. Les was a great character, and if a director had ordered a Cockney Sparrow from Central Casting they would have been sent something very like him. He would disappear from time to time during the evening, and always come back with armfuls of cabbages or carrots, or occasionally courgettes and asparagus.

He told me one day with great animation how he'd seen John Wayne wandering around the market very early that morning.

'I'm a fan,' Les declared, 'an' I calls out, "Allo, Dookie!", all friendly like. And d'you know what he does? Totally fuckin' ignores me! That's no way to treat yer fans, is it?'

Although I laughed at him, I never forgot Les's indignation, or the fact that, in the end, it is the fans who make the star.

I also became good friends with Cajo Kooy, one of the lighting operators, and a wacko Dutch-Canadian hippy. Clad in denim from top to bottom, with a mop of tangled hair dangling to his shoulders, Cajo had immediately caught my eye for the bizarre. He also had a great technique on the twelve-string guitar, while clutching a pipe full of permanently smouldering ganja between brown-stained teeth. He was a wonderful cartoonist, too, and was often given commissions which he seldom got round to finishing. Although he wasn't a great favourite with Amanda who, despite being with me, had a fairly fastidious taste in men, I ended up seeing him almost every night. We were soon playing and singing together, even busking in Notting Hill Gate Tube station. We thought we worked well as a duo, although my playing wasn't on a par with his, and we emerged as an act named – aptly, if not enticingly –*Drunk & Disorderly*.

More contentiously, we got a job at the Buckstone Club, off the Haymarket, where theatre people came to unwind after their show. The club needed live music in order to extend its licence, and that really was our only function; however, a lot of the clientele, after a stressful evening, considered that the last thing they needed was a duo called *Drunk & Disorderly* bellowing in their ears. There were a lot of complaints and our residency was soon terminated.

Although some of our songwriting worked, Cajo drank far too much beer and his gargantuan dope intake made him quite schizoid, with the result that we never had the discipline to push ourselves as much as we could have. Cajo had a mate, too, who played the fiddle niftily, but he drank as well, even more than we did, and spent a lot of time arguing with Cajo. Despite these hassles, I loved the music, and was glad of anything that made a few quid, especially as the TV work had gone a little quiet – in that unpredictable way it goes. The only notable job I had that summer was in an episode of *Brett*, a good but short-lived series starring Patrick Allen.

In truth, the biggest event for me in 1971 was seeing my team, Arsenal, whom I'd supported through thick and thin for twenty one years, beat Liverpool 2-1 in the FA Cup Final at Wembley on May 8th. I watched the Wembley game at the BBC Television Centre, where my friend and housemate, Chris Lewis, was one of the producers. He let me sit in the studio, seeing all the monitors and listening to all the incoming reports and commentaries.

It was a tantalising match, with all three goals coming in an added half-hour of extra time. Steve Heighway opened the scoring for Liverpool with a low drive past Wilson on his near post. Arsenal equalised with a scrappy goal from substitute, Eddie Kelly – the first time a substitute had ever scored in an FA Cup Final. In the end, the incomparable Charlie George went on and scored a dramatic winner late into extra time, when his long-range shot winged past Ray Clemence. To celebrate, in an era where extravagant

Joan, Alec & Me. Dad looks happy enough,
I look pretty unimpressed.

Aged five with Joan and 'Prince Pippin'. I've loved
horses ever since, but didn't actually ride again for 20
years

Alec in his Admiralty role.

Joan & Alec looking smart and happy.
What happens to people?

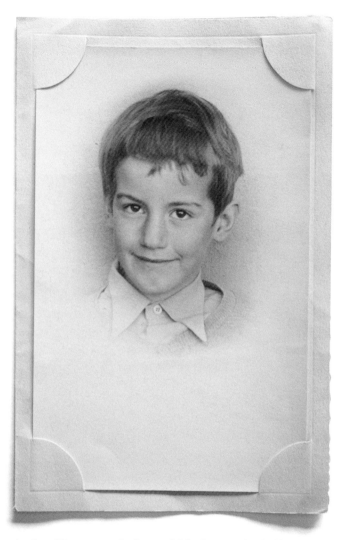

Aged six. Who gave me that hair cut? I think my mother had been at me with the pudding bowl and a pair of garden shears

Belmont School –
The model pupil, until
puberty took hold

Me – fourth from left in *Peter Pan* at Tadworth with Alan Harrin in the basket! 1950

Above: Looking very fetching as Alison Elliot in *The Lady's not for Burning* at Ottershaw School 1955
My suitor was played by Seth Gee, the relationship was doomed to failure; he turned up at the Theatre Royal in Brighton when I was on tour a few years ago, but after nearly 50 years strangely I didn't recognise him immediately!

Challis: back row, third from left at Belmont Preparatory School in
Westcott near Dorking.
With Games Master 'Foxy' Hurst and Pyne in the white jacket. He
had got his colours. I hadn't. I can remember everyone's name - It
was a happy time in spite of Foxy.

1962. My first proper acting job with The Argyle
Theatre For Youth.
The Commer van, badly parked somewhere up North.
I was the driver! But that's not my handbag! The
dangerous Bill Finlay is on the roof.

Favourite days at Chesterfield playing one of the six chords as Virgil Blessing in William Inges' *Bus Stop* with Jon Finch as Beau Decker. 1964.

Desperately trying to look older at the age of 22 at Chesterfield Civic Theatre with Jon Finch (Left) and Terry O'Sullivan (right)

One of my first film roles in *Where Has Poor Mickey Gone?* with Warren Mitchell – who went on to play Alf Garnett, Christopher Robbie on the right and John Malcolm, mercifully behind the mask.

Grandad at the Croydon Warehouse, third from left – Sam Kelly, third from right – Matthew Kelly. No idea who the dummy was on the right. Or what the dog represented

Me centre back row with Sally Farmiloe. *Dirty Linen* Arts Theatre, London, with Stoppard centre front, flanked by Richard Goolden to his right and Ed Berman to his left.

Sarah Venable (above) or Harriet Hall (below)? I liked them both,
but which one was best? Only one way to find out!

Looking out from the crown of The Statue of Liberty, NY

celebrations weren't so common, Charlie lay on his back on the Wembley turf, waiting for his teammates to lift and carry him round the ground in triumph.

What made the win trebly exciting was that just the week before I'd been at White Hart Lane to watch Arsenal achieve the First Division Championship by beating Tottenham Hotspur, making them, with the FA Cup win, the first club to score the double since Spurs themselves had done it ten years before.

Being at that match had been breathtaking, and such a joy; what was noticeable about it, compared with watching today, was how polite the rival fans were about each other's players; the real aggression that came to menace the football terraces a few years later hadn't taken hold in the early 1970s. I was near hysterical by the end of it, and I make no apologies for my continuing tribal allegiance to the Gunners, despite finding a preponderance of Chelsea supporters in my circle as I've grown older.

Later that summer I went to watch a Ray Cooney/John Chapman farce, *Move Over Mrs Markham.* This hit show had already been running for two years, and was currently starring Moira Lister with Trevor Bannister playing *Alistair Spenlow,* the camp (in fact vigorously heterosexual) interior designer who uses his 'artistic' credentials to snare unwary females.

Trevor, who later became better known in the long-running TV sitcom, *Are You Being Served?*, had made a lot of the part, and it was one which I very much fancied myself. They were due for a cast change at some point and I got myself an audition with the writers. I summoned up a nice 'Yorkshire Camp' voice and manner for it, which they seemed to like, but as time went by and I heard nothing, and someone else took over from Trevor Bannister, I assumed they hadn't liked it quite enough, so I shoved the idea to the back of my mind.

In November, I was on the train to Liverpool to star in an episode of *Z-Cars.* It went well and I had the feeling afterwards that they might want me back. I really believed I'd made more of an impact than I had when I'd had a similar chance in *Softly, Softly.* My instincts were right; a few weeks later I was called back, this time to play a more pivotal character, *Sgt Culshaw,* who went on to put in a dozen more appearances over the next couple of years, but only after a long, unexpected and deeply appreciated sojourn abroad...

I'd more or less forgotten about *Move over Mrs Markham* by the end of the year, when out of the blue, Ray Cooney rang my agent. She told me that Cooney and Chapman had liked my 'Yorkshire Camp' very much, and would I like to tour with *Mrs Markham* as *Alistair Spenlow* in South Africa, starting in Johannesburg the following spring?

Would I!? I hadn't even visited Europe since my visit to St Brevin Concentration Camp as a fifteen-year-old, let alone Africa, and I was pretty excited about the idea.

Amanda was less keen. Feisty and passionate little spark that she was, she had very strong views on Pretoria's White Afrikaner regime and the fiercely enforced system of racial segregation which supported it. Equity, the actors' union, didn't approve of its members going to work in South Africa, despite the strong demand for British actors there, but it didn't penalise them for going. A number of other friends of mine didn't like the idea; nor did I, albeit less vigorously; but I was fairly easily persuaded by talk of the value of taking 'theatre' to the vast black townships – letting them see that we, at least, were on their side – which was part of the deal most English touring companies managed to negotiate in South Africa to ease their consciences.

I came from a school of woolly liberalism which acknowledged that treating two thirds of a population as inferior human beings wasn't acceptable, but although I didn't doubt that there was an element of bogusness about the 'Culture for the African' justification, on balance I felt it would be worth going. Besides, I was desperate to see Africa, and a nine-month tour was bound to yield plenty of opportunities. So I agreed that the in following spring I would go to South Africa.

Africa

I awoke, cramped and dehydrated. I'd foolishly been drinking for the first few hours of the flight to Johannesburg; now my head ached and my feet were stuffed into nasty little slippers and wedged uncomfortably under the seat in front of me, while a large, pink, fleshy arm flopped over the armrest separating me from my nearest fellow traveller. The captain of the BA 747 was telling us that we were about to land and refuel in Libreville.

Libreville, Gabon – the old French Congo!

Bloody Hell! I was well and truly in darkest Africa now.

I'd barely been on a plane before, let alone an intercontinental flight in a jumbo jet, and here I was within smelling distance of tropical jungle, with at least six months to spend in this mind-boggling continent. I could hardly believe it.

Only a few hours before, I'd been saying goodbye to Amanda.

I really was going to miss her; she'd done so much for me and was such a unique, special person. We'd ended up with our arms wrapped around one another, soaked in tears, outside the departure gate at Heathrow.

She didn't want me to leave, and she certainly didn't want me to go to South Africa, but she'd been generous and understanding about it. She knew very well why I wanted to go – needed to go, frankly. Mine was a showy part in a very funny play which undoubtedly would be at least as big a hit in South Africa as it had been in London. On top of that, I badly needed the work. A few episodes of *Z-Cars* couldn't compare with an all-expenses-paid tour in a country where a pound went twice as far as it did in London.

Of course, I'd engaged in a skirmish with my conscience, and some of my friends had been very sniffy about my working in a semi-fascist regime. I didn't have any racist instincts in me at all; colour had never been a factor in any friendships or working relationships, and while I deplored the inherent unfairness of the apartheid system, I really believed, and still do, that it would help more to go and engage with black audiences, as well as the whites who were basically funding the tour.

The trickiest part of deciding to come had been leaving Amanda. She hadn't just been a lover; we'd been friends and each other's advisers and supporters; she'd put a roof over my head, and even let me loose to commit horticultural mayhem in her back garden. I'd been very happy since I'd moved in with her, but in my profession, I knew, you had to go where the work was.

Besides, I reassured her and myself, it wasn't going to be that long; I would be back in less than nine months, maximum.

She'd accepted that. 'If you feel you have to go, you must. It'll be a wonderful experience, and if it weren't South Africa, I'd be really envious. Anyway, I can wait, and I'll still be here when you get back.'

I thought of her as I clattered down the metal stairs from the plane into the foetid heat of the African night, and the air full of the sounds of a myriad insects rubbing their back legs together. While the pilot and the airport officials squabbled about the price of fuel, the passengers were allowed out to stretch their legs. I wandered stiffly across the open space of Libreville airport towards a flyblown bar which offered dusty old packets of Cadburys chocolate, rusty cans of Coke and bottles of not very cold African beer served by a very black Gabonese in a baggy uniform.

Still blinking in the sweaty night, once the airline and the locals had agreed terms for the jet fuel, I walked with other intrepid travellers who had braved the equatorial heat back towards the massive plane, looming in the moonlight, and looking far too big for this scrappy little coastal airport.

Back on board, I dozed again, and woke with the rising sun shining directly into the cabin. I was mesmerised by the light on the rust and sandy landscape 30,000 feet below. As we crossed into South Africa itself, and started to drop towards Johannesburg, I was transfixed by the sight of a thousand blue swimming pools sparkling like paste amethysts set in their green oases in the scorched brown veldt.

From the moment I set foot in the Republic of South Africa I was conscious that I had entered a world where entirely different standards of human behaviour applied. I was met by the show's promoter, Hymie Udwin, who whisked me through customs without any bother. Once we were on the other side, he simply clapped his podgy little hands until a black man jumped out of a queue, grabbed my bags and put one of them cautiously into the boot of Hymie's

Mercedes. He dropped the next one.

Hymie was furious. 'What's the matter with you, boy? Watch what you're doing!'

'Sorry, boss,' the man said, shame-faced.

Instinctively, I looked for some cash to tip him.

'Oh no; he gets *nothing*!' Hymie rasped. 'These munts have got to learn.'

I was shocked. I was hardly off the plane and I was already seeing at firsthand what everyone had warned me about.

The journey from Jan Smuts Airport through the outskirts of the baking city was pretty terrifying. There seemed to be absolutely no road discipline in Johannesburg, and at every junction there was a game of 'chicken' to see who would give way first, while Hymie – clearly an impatient man – swore forcefully and colourfully at every other road user.

We arrived in a well-to-do suburb and drove into the grounds of a palatial colonial villa, surrounded by a bougainvillea-clad veranda. Stepping from the cool of the Merc, I was hit by the blistering dry heat of a South African summer.

A lot of black servants were scurrying about, preparing a *braaivleis*, which is what the Afrikaners call a barbecue, while I was introduced to Rex Garner, who was directing the play, and the stage manager, Tammy Bonell. I also met a couple of expat Brits, Ian Hamilton and Ian Gardiner, local actors who were also in the show. If it hadn't been for the heat, the bougainvillea, the verandas and the cluster of black servants sloshing out drinks and managing the barbecue, we could have been at a house party in stockbroker, Surrey. Everyone was warm and welcoming; I wondered how long it would last.

Later I was driven to a flashy apartment building in High Point, one of Johannesburg's more salubrious districts. I'd been allocated a flat on the twelfth floor. It was stylishly furnished, with wonderful, vertigo-inducing views and a well-stocked fridge. So far, so good, I thought; two days later I was to start rehearsing. I was taking over the part of *Alistair Spenlow* from Geoffrey Davion, who'd decided to go back to Blighty for some reason, so I was very much the new boy in what was already a highly successful production.

At first I found rehearsals very uncomfortable and, with my rather dark, expressive face, my anxiety was showing. I heard afterwards that, had it been up to Rex Garner, I'd have been on the next plane home; but I had a champion in Ian Hamilton, and another cast member, George Little, who told Rex that it was 'all there, waiting to come out'.

Puzzled, and frankly worried that I just wasn't getting it right yet, I studied my performance in the mirror. I could see what my face was doing – sort of drooping with tension, making my eyes look beady and my demeanour distinctly evil. It was only then, forgetful as I am, that I remembered the 'Yorkshire Camp' I'd mustered for my audition in London six months before, and as if by magic, my face, and particularly my eyebrows, turned up instead of down, and eureka! *Alistair Spenlow* was all of a sudden a much jollier person and, once let loose on stage, went down a treat.

I wasn't surprised to find that there were already internal tensions in the production – there nearly always are, especially over a longish run. George Little and Rex Garner were very different; Rex was one of those brilliant 'do-nothing' actors who can suggest an idea with a mere lift of an eyebrow, while George was larger than life and extravagant in his performance, and could be very funny with it. Unfortunately, he and Rex loathed each other, and now he was leaving the show to be replaced by Ian Hamilton; I had both of them to thank for the fact that I was still there.

Now that my professional problems were under control, I had to deal with an unfamiliar domestic issue. After a week or two, I found that I had been allocated a servant of my own, and I didn't really know how to deal with him. Josh was a tall, skinny, nervous Xhosa. He had turned up with his boss, Sandy, who must have been named in a spirit of irony; he wouldn't have looked out of place among *King Cetewayo's* impis, as portrayed in the movie *Zulu*.

Josh informed me that on Tuesdays he would clean the apartment from top to bottom; on Wednesdays he would do all my washing – 'Clean the shoes, boss,' – and generally be at my beck and call to go shopping and run errands.

As a reasonable, fair-minded, twentieth-century Englishman, this was hard to accept. I was already feeling guilty enough about being in the country. I felt embarrassed about asking another individual to do my every bidding – it didn't feel natural.

'Look, Josh,' I tried to explain. 'In England where I come from, we do all our own washing, and cleaning, make our own beds, do our own shopping. I honestly don't need you. Why not take the week off?'

'But, boss, you are...'

I raised a hand, regretting it at once as he instinctively backed off. 'I'm not your boss; I'm John, OK?'

'Yes, Mr Boss, John,' he stuttered uncertainly.

I was determined to put him at his ease. 'Look, Josh, do you smoke? Here, have a gasper!' I handed him a pack of Rothmans.

Josh nervously took the cigarettes, clutching them to his chest

'Have a drink,' I offered. 'Would you like a beer?' I took a bottle from the fridge and tried to hand it to him.

I gathered from his vigorous refusal that it would be dangerous for to him to accept. I discovered afterwards that it was; black South Africans were not allowed to drink in white areas. Worse than this, offers of drinks were sometimes used by unscrupulous whites as means of entrapment.

He bowed and backed out of the apartment, still clutching his cigarettes.

When I went to the door he'd already disappeared. I walked back in, feeling that it hadn't really gone as I'd planned.

A while later I was aroused by the doorbell.

It was Sandy, looking, frankly, less sandy that ever. 'I'm so sorry about Josh, boss; he has not done his job properly. I have given him the sack.'

'You've sacked him?' I gasped, appalled at the havoc I'd wrought with my untutored egalitarianism. 'But he was fine! A very obliging chap. I just didn't have anything for him to do that I couldn't do myself.'

'He is there to do whatever you want. You told him to go away; you did not need a man like him.'

'What? Oh, God, no... I didn't mean that. Look, I'm sorry there's been a misunderstanding,' I blathered. 'He didn't do anything wrong at all. You must give him his job back; I'll find plenty of things for him to do.'

I felt a complete arse. Through my ham-fisted, well-meant attempt to assuage my own guilt, I was now responsible for the sacking of a blameless African with – for all I knew – a massive family to support.

I managed to explain to the silent but steely Sandy that I had merely indicated I didn't need any help that day, and of course, I would like Josh to come back. To my intense relief, Josh did show up again later in the afternoon, and was very pleased to be given a few jobs to do.

And there I was, subscribing to the very system I'd been objecting to. The incident was a good example – and I encountered many – of the dangers of misguided liberalism in an illiberal society.

The show, at least, was going well. *Move Over Mrs Markham* was a big hit in Johannesburg and subsequently all over South Africa. It was a great play to be a part of – not profound, but observant, witty and well written. It's always gratifying to appear in plays where audiences fill the seats and laugh at the right moments. While we were appearing at the Academy Theatre – a regular comedy venue – there was always a crowd of the great, the good, the not so good, and the not so great gathered in the bar after the show. It wasn't long before I was getting invitations to clubs, dinners and parties all over the place and, for the first time in my life, I felt a bit of a star.

There was no TV in South Africa at the time, so there was a very ready audience for live drama. There was also a great deal of radio airtime to fill, and I spent many hours giving interviews and making appearances in radio shows. I was careful not to lose sight of the fact that I was a large carp in a very small pond, but it was nonetheless a flattering experience. And, as often happens when a show is going well, I found that I could up my game to match the expectations of the audience.

On one of my forays into the clubs of downtown Jo'burg, shamefully putting to the back of my mind the lovely woman waiting for me back in London, I came across a one-time torch singer, an attractive and zingy individual called Zona Visser. She was exciting, funny and sexy, and I was a very long way from London. After a couple of encounters I found myself waking up in her bed. She understood it was a transitory relationship, and that seemed to suit her, though she was somewhat hampered by her ex-husband, an apparently psychotic Pole who was less keen on the idea of their separation.

His position as a leading medic at a major Johannesburg hospital didn't deter him from following us around, and letting down the tyres of her car, or ripping out the distributor leads and posting them back to her apartment. Nor did it stop him from sending her photos of himself standing naked beside the bed they had once shared.

It was quite alarming, and when Zona didn't show up one night for a date we'd made, I raced round to her place and found her leaving the apartment with the grumpy Pole clutching her very firmly. He did, at least, have all his clothes on.

'What's going on?' I asked, not unreasonably.

Zona answered. 'It's OK, John. Leave it, and I'll call you later.'

I watched them get into his car before I started to walk away from the apartment building. I soon heard the car creeping up behind me, until it caught up and he was leaning out of the window, shouting.

'Why don't you go back to Highpoint and get yourself some whores!'

Instead of ignoring him, I couldn't stop myself retorting rather lamely, 'So you know where to find them, then!'

At this, the car shot off up the hill in front of us; a hundred yards further on it came to a shuddering halt. The Pole got out, stormed round to the boot, and heaved what I guessed were Zona's suitcases onto the road. He threw her out too, and I sprinted up the hill to where she stood, sobbing and blubbering incoherently. I went to put an arm round her to calm and console her, only to find the Pole pointing a large pistol at me with a shaky hand.

Like any great hero confronted with a man waving a gun at him, I was terrified.

A jumble of absurd thought ran through my mind. Had I got a part in some cinema-vérité B-movie which my agent had forgotten to tell me about? Was I about to be shot dead?

A door slammed; the Pole had leaped into the car and it was skidding away up the hill again. I looked down at the shrinking, bedraggled Zona.

'Sorry,' she said in her thin, South African voice. 'It was mah fault. I never meant to get involved with you. And I have to stay with him.'

She looked very frightened.

I didn't see Zona again for some time. When I did come across her, by chance, she was working in an hotel as a receptionist. She looked cowed and terrified that we might be seen together.

Why did I get into these situations? I had a lovely girlfriend at home, and Zona would get into awful trouble if we started up again... I couldn't do it.

Besides, remembering the gun, I thought of my own health, too.

Live theatre in South Africa, as well as being active, was also very lucrative, and Hymie Udwin had a big rival in Pieter Toerien, a legendary, precocious impresario. Then just twenty-eight, Toerien was running a production of *Wait Until Dark*, a play which features a blind woman defeating a gang of three villains. They had come to her apartment looking for a doll which they believed contained a cache of heroin.

The play, a classic thriller written by Frederick Knott, who also wrote *Dial M for Murder*, had been a hit in New York, and a very big hit in London, with Honor Blackman playing *Suzy Hendrix*, the blind woman. In Toerien's production *Suzy Hendrix* was being played by English actress and '60s siren, Shirley Anne Field, whom I'd admired in some great movies – best of all *Saturday Night, Sunday Morning* in 1960, with Albert Finney, as well as *The Entertainer*, with Laurence Olivier.

The play was on at Toerien's own theatre, *The Intimate*, in Johannesburg, and it was inevitable that sooner or later Shirley Anne and I would meet. Wary after nearly making an arse of myself by cheating on Amanda with Zona, I nodded a few times at Shirley Anne across a crowded room, where she was always surrounded by a gang of attentive males. However, rather unexpectedly, she came over and asked me if I could help her with her lines. She was a few years older than me and many years more experienced in practically everything. She was also so lovely, close to, that I couldn't resist the invitation.

I spent that first night helping her with her lines, and woke up in her bed to hear the door being opened and, after a pause, closed again.

'Who was that – the chambermaid?' I asked, mildly curious.

'No, I should think it was Ian; he usually brings me a cup of tea in the morning.'

'*Ian*? Do you mean Ian Gardiner?'

'Yes, of course.'

'*Shit!*'

I was acutely aware that I had arrived wearing one of my loudest and most sartorially challenged garments – a burnt orange leather jacket – which I had left draped over the back of a chair just inside the door.

Ian, a fellow player in *Mrs Markham* wasn't blind and was, I knew, a rather sensitive fellow.

'You didn't tell me you were...'

'Oh, no, darling... It's nothing like that. We're just good friends.'

I doubted that, and when I saw Ian later that day at The Academy, he cut me dead.

I asked around and learned that Ian had indeed been squiring Shirley Anne around the place, though no one could say if they were actually lovers. Either way, I was appalled to find how jealous I was; but as I was discovering, Shirley Anne had that effect on most men.

I went to see her, of course, playing *Suzy Hendrix*, and she was mesmerizing. What she lacked in the finer points of the dramatic art, she made up for in sheer presence and eyeful.

She was witty, forceful and dangerously good-looking. The on-off, hot-cold torrid relationship that resulted from the first session with the lines and lasted for the whole South African tour could best be summed up, on my part, with the use of two words: 'lamb' and 'slaughter'.

I fell for her totally, and she was one of the most exciting, frustrating women I ever knew. She played me the way Ernest Hemingway might have played a stubborn marlin, and I sometimes had the impression that every time she wound me in, she chucked me back for another tussle, another day.

For a couple of months, we saw a lot of each other; it was a full and exciting time for me. Wherever we went, to clubs, parties and restaurants, we were treated royally. I was getting used to it; an actor from London in Jo'burg was inevitably something of a *grande fromage*. Shirley Anne was famous anyway, and together – within the always provincial context of Johannesburg – we were a bit of a celebrity couple. In restaurants, Shirley Anne was often sent bottles of wine by admirers; she didn't drink much, but I made up for it, so that every night seemed like a party. But this happy interlude had to come to an end when Shirley Anne's play moved to Cape Town, while ours still had a few more weeks to run in Johannesburg.

I had to decide then if I wanted to stay on after *Mrs Markham's* run in Cape Town. Although I'd originally planned to go back to London and Amanda after six months, I now had the offer of an extended tour for a further six months, all over South Africa, via Salisbury, Rhodesia, then coming back down to Cape Town. Knowing that Shirley Anne would also be finishing up back there at the same time, I agreed to it.

To keep myself from brooding too much while we were apart, I made a decision to see more of my surroundings and to understand better the extraordinary political and social conditions of the big and beautiful country I was staying in. I was aware that not every white South African was a hard-nosed, unreconstructed racist, and when I met those who weren't, with the greater affinity I felt, I tended to gravitate towards them.

It was at the home of one of these more liberal South Africans – from an Afrikaans family, as it happened – that I watched a performance of *Hamlet* put on by a black theatre group in a lush, white Johannesburg garden. An unexpected audience of all colours was watching, drinking tea and eating cake, until the hour came when the curfew was about to kick in, denying access to 'white' districts to non-white citizens. The whole cast and some of the audience seemed to evaporate, presumably to head for the shanty streets of Soweto.

I was fascinated and relieved to see that this degree of interaction existed, and found myself arranging trips to the townships for further theatrical contact.

Our company went down into Soweto to give a few performances, some scenes from our play, and from Shakespeare. Despite the obvious and heavy policing of these events, I was flabbergasted by the excited and appreciative reaction of the audiences, who laughed and cheered with colossal verve when they liked something, often erupting into torrents of mirth on the feed line to a joke and greeting the punchline by cheering and standing up, whooping with joy. They would wander in and out of the auditorium, swap seats with friends, clamber up the back walls to get a better view and enter into extensive participation and dialogue with the actors, rather in the manner that Mr Shakespeare himself must have experienced at The Globe, 350 years before.

The townships were pretty shocking to the first time visitor, and I became more conscious than ever of the *'Slegs Blankes'* ('Whites Only') notices all over Johannesburg – on benches in public parks, over entrances to shops and post offices – and how insulting to the majority population that must have been. I was also determined to come to a fairer arrangement with Josh, and we agreed that I would do my own washing and washing-up, he could do all the other things he expected to, while I paid him a bonus that was probably more than he was being paid officially.

My interest in the country increased when I borrowed a pickup from one of my new friends and took days out when I could go and explore the extraordinary dramatic landscape of the High Veldt. I spent many hours sitting on kopjes, marvelling at the emptiness of the place and the vast skies. At the same time, I was learning about the bizarre history of the country and the vicious territorial battles – between Britons, Boers and Zulus – which had been fought over its vast and mightily valuable natural resources.

Soon our run at The Academy in Johannesburg came to an end. Shirley Anne and I had kept in touch, and I could hardly wait to see her again in the Cape, where we were due next. But as it turned out, when I got there for our opening night in the great Nico Malan Theatre, *Wait Until Dark* had already moved on to Durban.

I felt disappointed and frustrated, especially when I heard that she'd been seen around Cape Town with another man and someone else showed me a newspaper picture of her lounging on a beach in a vast hat, looking lovely.

I tried to calm myself, and was to some extent mollified by the tremendous reception we had in Cape Town; the little farce went down a storm there, and I really did feel like a star for a while, especially when I forgot what a cultural backwater I was in. This sense of stardom was enhanced, inevitably when I was given a Chevy Charger to drive, with *'**John Challis, Star of Move Over Mrs Markham, drives U-Drive**'* painted down both sides.

Despite my anguish and frustration over Shirley Anne, I loved my stay in Cape Town. It was more liberal, more relaxed and a lot less threatening than Johannesburg. I was staying in a grand, comfortable house – a kind of Victorian villa for warmer climes –

which was one of a few that traditionally housed visiting theatricals, and was run by very amenable people. I had a lovely walk every day between the theatre downtown and my digs, behind the Botanical Gardens, halfway up Signal Hill, through parks full of birds and jacaranda trees, with views out across the bay that were very beautiful – if one could forget that the big blob out there was Robben Island, where poor old Nelson Mandela was banged up.

After a few days in Cape Town and quite a bit of tussling with my will and conscience, I phoned Shirley Anne in Durban. To my amazement she sounded very keen to see me, and I made up my mind immediately to go over there to spend a day and night with her.

'I can't wait,' she cooed. 'I'll make you a great breakfast!'

And I was off! I could hardly contain myself on the flight going over, I was in such a state of excitement, and I kept telling myself what a fool I'd been to think Shirley Anne had been swanning around with other men, when it was clear that she only wanted me.

When I arrived at her hotel, her greeting wasn't quite frigid, but it was barely lukewarm.

'Oh, hi John,' she said rather brusquely. 'I'm just going out. Shall we meet up for a drink later?'

She might just as well have socked me in the solar plexus. Within seconds, I was back to being the gibbering wreck I'd been a few days before. I couldn't understand what it was this woman was doing to me; I'd never come across anyone so determined to impose their control on a relationship – it could hardly be called a friendship.

I had thought I was grown up enough to handle this kind of thing, but I went back to Cape Town with my tail between my legs.

This was made worse by the arrival at my digs of a good-looking but quite batty red-haired woman, demanding to speak to me.

She turned out to be the wife of the man Shirley Anne had been sleeping with while she'd been in Cape Town. The woman wanted revenge. 'Here I am,' she said, 'you can have me.'

Somehow, though, Shirley Anne had left me feeling numb. I felt physically ill with frustration, and I couldn't have done anything with this woman, even if I'd wanted to.

When I next rang Shirley Anne, she was leaving for East London.

'Yes, I *do* want to see you,' she said. 'I do love you; that man in Cape Town – that was nothing.'

It was all I needed. I went off to meet her again in Pietermaritzburg. This was a more successful sortie than the Durban trip, and it gave me the opportunity to see some African life in the raw. Shirley-Anne had a daughter, Nicola, by her husband, Scottish aristo, Charles Crichton-Stuart (who seemed by then to exist somewhat in the background of her life).

Nicola was about ten and was staying with her mother for part of the tour. To help her, Shirley Anne had taken on a nanny, a lovely, cheerful black woman. While we were in Pietermaritzburg, we were not far from the nanny's home village – a real Zulu kraal of thatched mud huts, not a shanty township – and she was keen for us to go out and see the place to meet her family and the rest of the village.

It wasn't a long drive from Pietermaritzburg, and when we drew up in the cluster of picturesque native dwellings, we were greeted with a cacophony of laughter and ululation – it was a tremendous and heart-warming greeting. The nanny's own family were very welcoming and showed us into their high-status abode, which unlike the others, had a central corridor and rooms that opened off it. It was great to be treated with such warmth and appreciation, and I was very grateful. It was inevitable, then, when we stopped for some food in a restaurant on the way back and the African man serving there refused point blank to serve the nanny, that I lost my rag. It seemed too ridiculous that we couldn't simply sit down and have a meal with this lovely woman who had shown us such hospitality in her own village.

Angry at the man, although he was only responding to the fact that he could have been in big trouble for serving another African, I stormed out, leading the rest of our party with me.

During the remainder of the stay with Shirley-Anne, and our subsequent snatched week-ends together, I was conscious of the way in which she somehow kept topping up the interest, with the suggestion that we'd be together when we both ended up in Johannesburg for the end of our tours.

I even wrote to Amanda, a woman who deserved a lot better treatment than I was offering, and told her I'd fallen in love with Shirley Anne. Even as I did it, I reminded myself that Amanda was a good, genuine woman, while Shirley Anne was one of those women who liked her men dangling on a string – preferably along with a few others to choose from.

Almost immediately, I regretted sending the letter.

Before I knew it, Amanda had flown out to spend a week with me in Johannesburg, where the play had returned for a spell. It was good to see her but we were living in different worlds now, and I was hideously torn.

Shirley Anne, also back in Johannesburg, had moved into a big hotel up the road. She was damned if she going to be seen hanging around waiting for Amanda to go, and quickly rounded up Ian Gardiner and a few other willing walkers to make sure she didn't look as if she was on her own for a moment of the day. She would be seen, flirting openly with Ian, and driving me mad with it. And yet one voice was telling me I should get out now and go back to England with Amanda for a little emotional sanity, whatever the lack of work on offer for me there. But round the corner here in South Africa lay adventure, discovery, and the tantalising Shirley Anne.

Amanda said she would see me in London when she saw me, and left with a great deal more dignity than I could have produced.

Despite the ongoing crises in my love life (which, in any case, had not existed in any state of equilibrium since my introduction to the joys of sex, aged nineteen, in a hotel bedroom in Surrey), I was enjoying enormously my tour in South Africa. The play was a huge success, and my part in it had bedded in well. I'd also enjoyed meeting a great variety of people. They were mostly white, to be sure; but to the puzzlement of most of my hosts, I was determined to hear about apartheid from the black point of view, and went out deliberately seeking dialogue with black and coloured Africans as well, and had in some instances struck up genuine friendships with them.

I also made a big effort to learn more about the place, and I was developing a good grasp of the extraordinary exploitative colonisation of the naturally rich country's resources, and the millions of Africans whose parents and grandparents had come from the north to undertake the huge manual labour involved in extracting gold and diamonds, and as well as all the battles that the rush for this wealth had spawned.

I was ashamed to learn about the way the British had treated their Boer victims, creating concentration camps forty years before Hitler did, and the massacre of Zulus at Rorke's Drift. I visited the sites of these confrontations whenever I had the chance in the course of my touring around the country.

I appreciated that Cape Town, for historical reasons, had remained untouched by the more extreme forms of apartheid, and it was the city I most enjoyed.

At the end of the year, I spent a wonderful week there, over Christmas, staying in the lovely Mount Nelson Hotel, set among trees and lush gardens in the cleavage between Table Mountain and Signal Hill, looking over the city to the sparkling sea. The fact that Shirley Anne was still on the other side of the country, and there were no other women around, probably saved me from the regular domestic drama that used to dog my life around Christmas time. Like any Englishman in the southern hemisphere at Yuletide, I was struck by the strangeness of spending the day in a hot, dry sun, playing tennis, drinking ice-cold wines and eating smorgasbord while the *Broeders* sang carols and the black waiters beamed with inexplicable goodwill.

In the New Year, I took a trip out to Stellenbosch, a Dutch colonial town in the Cape, which produces some wonderful white wines. We had been invited out to taste the new champagne in one of the biggest wineries there.

Curious as ever and emboldened by the fizz, I wandered off-piste, away from the guided tour and found myself among a bunch of ebullient grape treaders. These men seemed to me to be extraordinarily accepting of the fundamental unfairness of their existence, and I couldn't help thinking this must have reflected a pragmatism or expediency which they adopted in order not to rock any boats. Once I was discovered chatting away with this jovial crowd, I was very hastily led away from the scene. The chilly reality of the regime was once again inflicting itself on me.

After Christmas, the *Mrs Markham* tour rolled on to consistently packed houses, by way of Rhodesia – now Zimbabwe. I'd driven up the N1 Road, north from Pretoria with Ian Hamilton in his car, but when we reached the border where a bridge crosses the Great Green

Greasy Limpopo at Beitbridge, it was closed for the night. We didn't have anywhere to stay, so decided to park the car among the vast groves of baobab trees out in the bush and kip in it. We were surrounded by the Marelani Nature Reserve and the noise of insects and other imagined, more predatory beasts kept us awake all night. We managed to get through the hours of darkness without providing a snack for a hungry lion, and carried on to reach Salisbury the next day.

When we got back to South Africa, I continued to seek out other views and experiences. I met hundreds of people of diverse hues, and encountered dozens of various aspects of the captivating country. Shirley Anne and I got together when our separate itineraries allowed, but I knew intuitively, as my tour was drawing to close, that our relationship couldn't last beyond it.

Three Day Week

When I arrived back in London in the early summer of 1973, deflated by this return to reality and depressed by the futility of my fling with Shirley Anne, Amanda let me move back into her Battersea flat. I didn't deserve such loyalty and I couldn't have been more grateful for that, and for the roof over my head. I tried to make up for it by carrying on the work I'd started on her sliver of a garden, which in my absence had reverted to a patch of weeds and discarded fag packets; with a dearth of acting work for the first month or two, I was able to make some progress with it. After my year of celebrity in South Africa, I was now reduced to my more familiar status of part-time jobbing actor, and I was signing on at the Battersea Jobcentre most weeks.

I'd been out of the loop for a while and TV producers had already forgotten about me, so I went to see Caroline Dawson to see if she would take me back as a client, for old times' sake, and hustle a bit of work for me. Fortunately, since she'd chucked me out of her flat four years before, we'd stayed in touch and were on good terms. Meanwhile, she'd been building a good reputation as an agent.

Strangely, not having worked on the stage in England for a few years, the first job that came up for me was at the splendid old Harrogate Theatre in Yorkshire, run by the able and well thought of Brian Howard. He was directing a new Alan Ayckbourn comedy of middle-class sex and angst, *Time and Time Again*, in which I was cast as one of the lead men. I was also booked to work in a play running at the same time in the Studio Upstairs and being directed by Keith Washington. Keith was a friend who'd been in *Saint Joan* with me at The Mermaid and he'd always been more enthusiastic about directing than acting. Now he'd got this gig with an experimental piece called *Lovers*, in which I appeared with Jean Fergusson (whom I worked with years later in *Last of the Summer Wine*). It was a lively, cerebral play, written by Carey Harrison, an emerging young playwright and son of Rex and Lilli Palmer.

I was sometimes doing the two plays on the same night, which was both challenging and fun. Harrogate itself was a fastidious old spa town, full of well-educated wrinklies who liked going to the theatre, making it a very satisfactory venue in which to appear – especially in an Ayckbourn.

While I was there I shared a house in the north side of the town with Keith, his wife, Joan, and Jean Fergusson. It was a cramped little two-up, two-down stuffed with furniture and we were all a bit on top of one another. Jean and I came in together late one evening to find that Joan had gone out and was driving her car round and round the block, presumably in an attempt to express her frustration. The Washingtons' marriage, I knew, was fairly volatile; but this looked like the last throes, and in the morning we found she'd gone for good, while poor Keith had to get on with the job of directing *Lovers*, which struck me at the time as being acutely ironic.

My own love life, as usual, was in some turmoil. When I'd returned from South Africa and moved back in with Amanda, I hadn't intended to see Shirley Anne again, but she was so embedded under my skin that after a few weeks I stupidly rang her. I knew she was seeing someone else, but when she said, 'Come on over,' I loped round to her top floor flat in West Hampstead like a hound on a scent. Even though I knew it was fanning dead embers, I carried on, and she didn't stop me. I hadn't told Amanda and I felt bad about it.

My mind was taken off my guilt a little while I was in Harrogate when I came across an interesting actress. Suzanne Bertish, distinctive and beautiful, was a feisty creature in her early twenties who'd already done a stint with the RSC; she was the kind of girl who was bound to catch my eye. In the end not a lot developed between us, but she kept me from brooding over my own hopeless situation. On my thirty-first birthday, she agreed to come on a moonlit picnic with me. We drove into the country and sat in a field in the Yorkshire Dales, where we witnessed a stallion servicing a mare – a pretty alarming sight. I don't know what effect it had on Suzanne, but she went off to London soon afterwards and became a serious classy actress.

When my two plays finished their run, Brian Howard asked me to stay on for the rest of the season, but, always seeking greener grass, I wanted to take up offers for a couple of *Z-Cars* and a small part in a TV movie with Jack Palance.

Palance had been a hero of mine since I'd first seen him in *Shane*, all dressed in black and peering meanly through slitty eyes at Alan Ladd, and the chance to be in a film with him was too tempting to pass up (although, in fact, I was never in shot with him.)

He was here to make an American TV feature length version of *Dracula* (there have been an astonishing eighteen films made about the old bloodsucker) and we were filming on a location purporting to be Whitby, the port where *Dracula* came ashore, and I had a scene with Nigel Davenport and Simon Ward.

It was only a day's work, and when I turned up I found I hadn't been allocated a changing room. A little wardrobe chap bustled up and pouted at me. 'I'm so sorry, dear, we haven't got anywhere for you to change, but Jack's not in today, so you can use his caravan.'

I was sorry that I wouldn't get to meet Jack Palance, but childishly thrilled that I was to use his caravan. I was let in, and wardrobe turned up with a Victorian Shipping Clerk's outfit. I'd just clambered into the kit when the caravan door was tugged open and up stepped Jack Palance to fill the small space.

'Hello, what are you doing here?' His eyes narrowed and his cheekbones gleamed. 'You had a drink?'

I almost panicked. Did he think I was in here raiding his booze cupboard? It was only nine in the morning. 'No, honestly,' I protested. 'Well, not yet, anyway,' I added breezily.

'Then it's about time you did!' He rummaged around for a bottle and glasses, poured a couple of shots of bourbon and handed one to me.

Although generally ready for a drink, I wasn't used to drinking on set, in the morning. Nevertheless, I tilted the glass and knocked back the whiskey with a noisy, unintentional grunt.

Palance did the same and grinned.

'You in the movie?' he asked mildly.

'Ah... well... yes...' I yammered. 'Wardrobe didn't have anywhere for me to change. They thought you weren't coming in today.'

'I wasn't going to, but I had to drop by for a couple of things,' he answered, completely relaxed about my being there. 'But listen, feller, that's OK. I'm not coming back again, so you feel free to leave your clothes here. No problem.'

A moment later he was gone.

What a nice, friendly guy! I thought. No prima donna bullshit.

Being Boycie

I never saw him again, and I never saw the film shown in the UK.

Meanwhile, *Sergeant Culshaw*, the copper I'd created for *Z-Cars* just before I went off to South Africa to be a faux-gay interior decorator for a year, had wormed his way back into the script, presumably with a little help from my agent, Caroline. I was booked for several more episodes, pleasantly interrupted by Keith Washington asking me to come and do Carey Harrison's *Lovers* again. The venue this time was Sam Walters' Richmond Fringe Theatre, which Sam had founded a couple of years earlier in an upper room at the Orange Tree pub on Kew Green. This initiative had been a success from the start, and The Orange Tree already had a strong name for demanding, cutting edge theatre.

It was great to work with Keith again, and although the project didn't put much money into my empty coffers, it gave my confidence a boost. I saw a bit of Keith, and was optimistic about his marriage when he told me that Joan, after driving off into oblivion when we'd been in Harrogate, had come back to him. But I soon realised that communication had not improved. At dinner there, with their ten-year-old child sitting between them, they sniped incessantly in a way I vowed should never happen to me. In the end, the marriage didn't last much longer, and this was one of those times when you wish people would save themselves a lot of misery by recognising when a relationship was truly beyond repair.

For the first three months of 1974 the whole of Britain seemed to grind to a halt. Despite sitting around with Ted Heath in smoky rooms in Downing Street for hours on end whilst munching large quantities of sandwiches (and, I dare say, suffering nasty attacks of indigestion as a result), the leaders of the coalminers' unions decided to bring their members out on strike, and heavily picketed the delivery of coal into the nation's power stations. The result of the power rationing that followed was the infamous 'Three Day Week', when shops, offices and restaurants, sporadically deprived of electricity, had either to close or light themselves with candles and oil lamps in order to go on trading.

It was a gloomy period, but in their characteristic British way, people rallied and got on with it. When they couldn't watch TV, they went to bed and increased the population a little, or headed out for candlelit pubs, which seemed able to function without electricity. And once there, they even talked to one another.

An old chap at my local, the Latchmere on Battersea Park Road, told me he was very impressed with this revival of human contact. 'I've voted Labour all me life,' he declared over a frothing pint of Young's bitter, 'but them Tories 'as really got us all together with this three day week malarkey, so next time, I'm voting Tory.'

Being a gregarious, pub sort of chap myself, I knew what he meant about the value of people talking to each other again. And, despite the general gloom and doom, I wasn't doing too badly anyway, as a string of TV copper parts came my way.

My personal life, on the other hand, had hit the rocks, again. After failing to revive the vibrant times Shirley Anne and I had had in South Africa, I admitted to Amanda what had been going on.

It was a sad end that followed. Our own relationship had run out of steam; she needed a man who better understood her theatricality. But I had loved her, and I knew she still cared about me.

I deserved what was coming when she threw me out of the Battersea flat.

It wasn't the first time I'd found myself in this position, but now, at the age of thirty-one, I wondered if it should still be happening.

This time, Caroline Dawson came to my rescue, perhaps to make up for chucking me out herself so peremptorily five years before. Her sister Anna had recently hooked up with a new man – a fifty-year-old actor called Eric Lander. She was younger than Eric, but he was very good-looking and charming, and still famous for his role as *Det. Insp. Harry Baxter* in Associated Rediffusion's *No Hiding Place*. Between 1959 and 1967 he'd appeared in 140 episodes as the thrusting younger detective always at odds with his more conventional boss, Raymond Francis's *Detective Superintendent Lockhart*. His was one of those faces that everyone recognised, and he'd worked consistently since then on television and on stage, until fairly recently. His penchant for booze had exposed him to the destructive mood-changing power of whisky, and his last woman had left him a couple of years before.

I hadn't worked with him, but I'd met him a few times, and like everyone else had been taken by his charm. Caroline suggested it might suit us both if I moved into the spare room in his pretty

Georgian cottage down by Kew Pier. It was a wonderful spot, overlooking a small green, with the river towpath a few dozen yards away, and a set of good tennis courts opposite.

We met to discuss it in the Greyhound on Kew Green – a pub where I was to spend many long hours over the next year or so – and agreed a rent. We both felt we'd done a good deal. The truth was that Eric, having been in constant demand for ten years, wasn't getting so much work now; he was drinking more since his last girlfreind had gone, and he needed the extra money.

When he was drunk he was unpredictable. He could be uproarious and genial; he could suddenly become deeply maudlin, or – especially with whisky – he could be very grumpy. I learned how to accommodate his moods, and when not to try, and made the most of his company.

There were some colossal sessions in the Greyhound, especially when there were a few like-minded actors around. Nigel Green, who'd been in the great movie, *Zulu*, and Ian Hendry were regulars, with whom Eric and I would get very drunk and noisily humorous. Ian, still sore over losing the lead part in *Get Carter* to Michael Caine, was, like many in our profession, a very extravagant drinker.

After mammoth sessions, we would have to talk Ian out of driving himself home; not easy when we were all drunk too. On one occasion we failed, when he woozily declared that he was 'perfickly sober'nough to drive', staggered out of the pub and zoomed off in his car, weaving along the road across Kew Green. As he went, I thought of Alex Munro, ten years before, announcing with such pride how his daughter, Janet Munro, had just married the international film star, Ian Hendry. They had divorced in 1971, and a year later Janet, only thirty-eight, had died of heart disease, leaving their two young daughters behind her.

We heard later that Hendry had written off his car on the Dick Turpin roundabout above Putney. The following week he was back in the Greyhound, ragging Eric about his double, Lyndon Brook, a lesser-known actor deemed to be more accomplished than Eric.

At home, I never knew how I was going to find Eric. One night I came back and he was particularly morose. He'd been out with Anna who, like her sister, could be pretty forthright.

'What's the trouble?' I asked.

He looked up at me bleakly. 'Anna's just said why didn't I make a man of myself and learn to drive.'

Eric had never driven, and as I don't suppose the level of alcohol in his blood had been below the legal limit for several years, that was probably a good thing. But Anna, it seemed, had questioned his masculinity, and that made him very miserable. She didn't stick around for long after that.

I quite often had to rescue him from his own vagaries; one time, coming home, I found him on all fours at the edge of the small ornamental fish pond in the front garden, leaning across it precariously and dipping his hand in gingerly. For some reason never clearly explained, he had thrown his house keys into the pond; I guessed it was a fit of whisky pique.

Soon after I moved to Kew, I had a call from Cajo Kooy, the Dutch Canadian lunatic I'd met on *Showboat*. 'Hi, John! How are you, man? How about a few beers?'

I knew it would lead to all sorts of shenanigans to see Cajo again, but I hadn't seen him for a while. I told him to meet me in the Greyhound right away.

Nothing had changed – the flop of wavy, chestnut hair down to his shoulders, full set of facial hair, horn-rimmed glasses, full denim outer layer and lingering musky whiff of ganja.

'OK,' he said. 'What're you doin'? Let's make music!'

Within minutes of meeting, we were planning the revival of *Drunk and Disorderly*. With a little persuasion we got a booking to play lunchtime sessions at the pub. This produced mixed results – on the one hand we pulled in quite a few loyal (and quite possibly deaf) followers, while on the other, we drove away a number of regulars who, like the thespian clientele at the Buckstone, had come in to relax with a quiet drink. In a clear case of hope overcoming experience, and despite the buzz the South African tour of *Mrs Markham* had given me, I still hankered after a career in music. I still loved doing it, and we started trying seriously to write more of our own material.

Somehow, though, like before, we didn't push hard enough and never seemed to get anywhere with our songs.

Eric could be very scathing about our efforts, depending on his booze intake, but he didn't mean to be malicious. He and I were getting on well, although he would castigate me for mistreating women. In fact, that was usually a result of misunderstandings when he would end up entertaining girls who had dropped in on their way back from the tennis club opposite to see me. If I was out with another woman, he would take it as a cue to sit them down and engage in a long, intimate exchange of ideas.

Towards the end of the year, Eric announced that he was going to take off and spend Christmas with friends. I was not in any particular relationship at the time, so far as I knew, and I asked my parents if I could come down to Sunnybank for three days over Christmas. Since my grandmother had died, my mother's father always came up from Bath to spend the holiday with us. I liked to keep in touch with him, and I still had fond memories of my own childhood Christmases at home.

As the Prune and I loaded up my car, I was looking forward to the visit.

The minute I was inside the house, I detected an atmosphere. Recently, I knew, my parents' baiting each other had become a regular activity as my father drank more and became sourer about his own life choices. But this was worse than usual. Their sparring tended to be triggered when my grandfather was there. My father, out of a sense of his own social inferiority, used to get a kick out of saying things that underlined his Sheffield background. Over Christmas dinner, he leaned back in his chair – something which always annoyed my mother

'Coom on, soop oop, it's Christmas! Oh, I do like a bit of browsin' and sluicin', me,' he announced in a much broader Yorkshire accent than normal. He knew my mother loathed him doing that, especially when her own father was there. She kicked him sharply under the table.

'Bloody hell, loov, what were that for?' he demanded, to make her embarrassment more acute.

My grandfather would pretend it wasn't happening, and whistle quietly to himself, which only made things worse. When they weren't scrapping with each other, my parents were vying with one another for my support, which drew me very unwillingly into the fray. When it became too much over Christmas, I could stand it no more. My already raw nerves were irritated beyond tolerance and I suddenly flipped.

'What the hell are you two doing?' I asked. 'Just going on and on at each other? I mean bloody hell you've been married over thirty years; surely you must have got used to each other? And this is Christmas!' I was practically in tears by now. 'We're supposed to be happy, for God's sake!' I leaped to my feet and stormed out into the garden. I called the Prune to come with me to defuse my frustration and to calm my anger at their behaviour.

Dogs listen, they don't answer back or swamp you in phony sympathy. They don't mind too much about your mood; they think they're out for a walk.

Sun, Soil & Sin

By the spring of 1975, I was still living in the cottage in Kew with Eric Lander. I loved the house and the area, and I'd gained some satisfaction in sorting out the small garden at the back of the cottage. The taste for horticulture which I'd picked up doing Amanda's garden still lingered.

Eric had proved a generous cohabitant. I enjoyed his company a lot and he presented no serious obstacles to my currently free-wheeling love life and social activity. He was, sadly, not really winning his battle with the bottle, while his TV work, unlike him, was drying up; I sometimes felt almost guilty about going to the pub with him.

By then, there were no theatre prospects in sight for me either, although earlier in the year I had a goodish part in the final episode of a short lived Granada TV series, *Nightingale's Boys* with Derek Farr, and I'd made what turned out to be my last appearance as *Sgt Culshaw*, who'd been popping in and out of *Z-Cars* for the past three years.

Shortly after this I was booked at short notice for a part in a feature movie, *The New Spartans*. The film was being directed by Jack Starrett, a gung-ho Texan actor/director in his late thirties. Best known for directing down'n'dirty, low-budget action movies, as an actor he'd been in *Blazing Saddles* the year before, and went on to play a biggish part with little Sly Stallone in *First Blood* a few years later. A tough-looking, heavily tanned individual, with a strong, un-American sense of irony, he wore a T-shirt boldly printed with the words, '*I'm not Lord Lucan*'.

We filmed on location around an old castle in the West Country. *The New Spartans*, as far as I could tell, was about a group of people who had formed themselves into a gang of mediaeval vigilantes to go around righting wrongs and meting out justice. There was a strong cast: Oliver Reed, Harry Andrews, Susan George, Toshiro Mifune and a Chinese kung fu artist.

I had a decent little part as a manic terrorist who has to lead an ambush on the heroes. Starrett called me over. 'John – you're John, right?' He told me roughly how he wanted to shoot the scene, but left me more or less to set it up and direct it.

This was highly irregular, and we were all a little baffled. However, I did my best to work out a scenario and got people in place, while Starrett bellowed from a hundred yards away that I should get a move on. We burst into action and I felt we'd played the scene quite effectively, although obviously I wouldn't know until we'd seen the rushes. In any case, Starrett seemed happy when we'd finished and came back up.

'OK,' he said. 'That was great! We're going to do the close-ups now, so just do it again, exactly as you just done it.'

None of us had the slightest idea of what we'd just done; Oliver Reed was standing watching, with a bottle in his hand, leering and roaring with laughter, as if he knew something we didn't. Inevitably the reprise was a complete shambles; I couldn't believe that anyone made movies that way.

Off the set, at nights, in the unfortunate hotel housing the cast and crew, there was constant bedlam. On the first night, Oliver Reed cornered the kung fu expert.

'You're no kung fu wizard,' he leered in his most irritating way. 'You're nothing but a Chinese poof.'

After that there was a mad sort of tag fight. The kung fu chap, frankly, didn't excel himself while Oliver pranced around, flapping limp wrists, throwing out the occasional kick, like a girl trying to step on a worm. There was a lot of noise from supporters, and large sections of the public rooms were partially destroyed. All in all, it was a rather alarming experience; I wasn't particularly surprised when none of us got paid, and the movie sank without trace, never to be released. It's surprising and quite depressing, after all the effort and money needed to get a film shot, how often that happens.

When I got back to Kew in a slightly disoriented condition, I was taken completely by surprise when I received a visit from a woman who looked familiar, but whom I couldn't place. I recognised a kind of wild-eyed unpredictability which rang a few alarm bells. Their volume increased when I realised the woman was Carmen, who'd been in the Argyle Theatre for Youth. I hadn't seen her since I'd been in Cambridge, where she'd turned up at my digs and involved me in some demanding sexual activity for a few days before announcing her pregnancy.

I wondered what had happened after I'd given her the hundred pounds.

'Was that all alright, then?' I asked.

She looked at me as if I were mad and brushed the question aside with an impatient gesture. I thought it wise to get her out of the house by taking her for a drink at the Greyhound. We talked a little; she abruptly announced that she had to go, and I never saw her again. It was strange to think back to the intensity of the youthful sex we'd shared fifteen years before and how not a vestige of that connection remained.

As summer advanced something sparked in me the idea that it was time for me to put down roots. I'd been wandering around from one theatrical digs to another, from one woman to another, for the past fifteen years, and I'd reached a time when a little stability looked an attractive idea. I'd also accumulated just about enough money to put down a deposit on the purchase of a modest abode of my own.

I found a good two-roomed basement flat – what estate agents like to call a 'garden flat' – in a late Victorian brick terrace at No. 65, St Margaret's Road, Twickenham. As it happened it did have a long garden, which was all mine. This contained a desolate ornamental pond, and a strange home-made wall about 150 feet long, which looked as if it had been built from the remains of a shattered Byzantine basilica, containing shards of broken ceramic pots, chunks of marble, bits of mosaic, splinters of glass and fancy brickwork.

To make my mark for posterity, I planted a cherry tree in the tiny patch of front garden. It took off right away, and to my pride every time I drive along St Margaret's Road, it's still there, thirty-five years later, huge and flowering.

The evening after the Prune and I had moved in, we set off on a long walk to get to know our surroundings. While the Prune wanted simply to gallop from lamp post to lamp post to mark out his new territory, I wanted to mark mine by sampling the local pubs. We set off through Marble Hill Park, down towards the river. It had started to rain quite heavily so there was no one else around. The Prune and I got thoroughly soaked, but it didn't matter; we were relishing our freedom.

We were rewarded with the discovery of a good crop of field mushrooms, then again by stumbling on the White Swan, a wonderful riverside pub. From there we walked to Twickenham through York House Gardens with its own splendid water feature of a troupe of life-sized stone ladies disporting themselves in the tumbling water, one with a heron perched on her head. From there, through little cobbled waterside streets, we came upon another fine old boozer, the Fox, for a quick pint of Fuller's London Pride. As we wandered back to our new home, I relished the feeling of being on my own at last and not accountable to anyone else – not to any of the several women who had housed me over the last few years, or housemates of any kind. It was, for as long as it lasted, very liberating. So was the gardening.

After planting the cherry tree, my first task was to clear away the rampant unwanted wild shrubs, the thick matt of neglected grass and overgrown beds until I had the 'blank canvas' I needed to start planting from scratch. To help with this I engaged the services of a strange little character I found selling plants from an alleyway at the back of his wife's hairdressing salon in Crown Road, just around the corner.

In fact, I'd first met Leslie Churchill, with his domineering and impossibly brassy wife, at the St Margaret's Hotel, a gaunt, red-brick Victorian boozer on the corner of Crown Road. This was just a short stagger from my new flat, making it my favourite watering hole. It is a fact that those you meet in your favourite pub will, if you spend enough time there, become your most intimate chums – or so it seems when you're in their company. It's a unique and special aspect of the English pub that it's a great social leveller. In a pub bar, all the inmates are there on a more or less equal footing; it's like an informal men's club, where birds of a feather will flock.

Leslie was an engaging individual of about fifty, with an indefinable aura of dodginess about him and an implausible history. He had flown bombing missions during the war, had subsequently become a high-powered chartered accountant and had been working in New York for the past few years.

Or so he said.

As I got to know him it emerged that his life story had been much edited and embellished. He had in fact been invalided out of the RAF because his nervousness had led him to overcook the bombers' engines, earning him the nickname 'Revs', and, rather than having emigrated to the States to practise his particular form of creative accounting, he'd been banged up for fraud in England.

He came to help me clear out my garden, we got to know one another, and after that, when I wasn't working, I used to help him do it for other people. My part-time career as a contract gardener had begun.

I was, though, still acting sporadically. Douglas Camfield, a prolific TV director who worked a lot for the BBC, cast me as a heavy in an episode of *The Sweeney*. I was henchman to Peter Vaughan's character, a Mr Big who went round leaning on people and beating them up when they didn't cooperate. For this I had to learn how to fight and how to hit people.

As a peace-loving man, I'd spent most of my life avoiding violence, either by trying to joke my way out of it or, if that failed, by running away. Not surprisingly, I had no idea how to hit anyone in an effective or realistic way. By the time the fight director had finished with me, I could have gone eight rounds with Janet Street-Porter (although I'd have probably lost on points).

I hadn't worked with Peter Vaughan since 1965, when he'd played *Gladstone* in *Portrait of a Queen* at the Vaudeville. Peter was especially good at looking threatening and seemed to enjoy the physical stuff, perhaps more so since he and Ken Hutchison (also in this episode of *The Sweeney*) had worked together on *Straw Dogs*. They used to stand together, sneering at us novice heavies. Despite this, we both got shot to pieces backstage at the Wimbledon Theatre by Dennis Waterman and John Thaw.

At least Douglas must have been happy with my performance, because he went on to cast me in similar heavy roles in several more shows after that.

Back in Twickenham, I was settling into my flat, getting to grips with my long garden and working regularly with Leslie. We would clear people's gardens, dig their borders, prune trees and shrubs and do more or less anything anyone asked us to.

'Can you lay crazy paving?' punters would ask. 'Can you create a lake and waterfall?'

'Oh yes!' Churchill would reply, like that eponymous insurance dog, although our efforts at paving were so crazy, they could have been sectioned.

To my surprise, though, Leslie turned out to have an encyclopaedic knowledge of horticulture, and I began to learn a lot from him. I also earned a bit of money to top up my meagre-ish acting income. Most of this, inevitably, was spent in the St Margaret's Hotel. The place had become my second home, populated with a bizarre but fertile mix of film people from nearby Twickenham studios, and locals – most of whom seemed to be involved in some sort of criminal activity.

Towards the end of the year, I had a break in my gardening activity when I went up to a castle in Cheshire to play one of the *Merry Men* in a TV mini-series of *The Legend of Robin Hood*. While filming in and around Peckforton Castle, an impressive but bogus mediaeval fortress (built in the 1850s by a flamboyant businessman called Tollemache) I had a wonderful opportunity to perform one of my 'deaths', much as I had done to amuse my schoolmates as a child. I was shot in the chest with an arrow while standing on the ramparts, from where I had to tumble 100 feet to the ground. Rather unsportingly I was only recognisably in the shot up to the point where the arrow struck, presumably to penetrate my chest and heart. From then on the 'death' was taken over by a stunt double... probably a good thing.

The incredibly resilient TV drama series, *Doctor Who*, was well into its thirteenth season (and its fourth *Doctor*) by 1976 when I found myself with a role in it. Although *Doctor Who* was originally – and is still – pitched at an audience of children, as a result of its high creative standards it always sustained a large adult following, subsequently bolstered by former child fans. As a result, the lead character's embodiment became almost as burning an issue as the identity of the next *James Bond*. I found it exciting to work on an iconic series which had long possessed a reputation for good writing, clever effects and imaginative plotlines.

Tom Baker, the *Doctor* at the time, had succeeded William Hartnell, Patrick Troughton and John Pertwee and, in a couple of years, had already become the most popular *Doctor* yet. He had somehow managed to add an extra quality of mystique to the character, and for most people his deep resonant voice (much parodied since), long knitted scarf and floppy hat made him the most memorable as well as the longest lasting *Doctor* (appearing in over 170 episodes).

On this occasion Douglas Camfield was directing. He was a

veteran at *Doctor Who*, ultimately clocking up fifty-two episodes, and was now working on the series for what would turn out to be the last time. He was an intelligent and experienced maker of action TV, with whom I liked working very much. Once again, he had cast me as a villain, *Scorby*, who was henchman to the *Doctor's* nemesis in a six-part story called *Seeds of Doom*. *Scorby's* boss *Harrison Chase* was played by Tony Beckley (who'd played *Peter the Dutchman*, the camp villain, along with Ian Hendry in *Get Carter*). At that time, Elisabeth Sladen was the *Doctor's* assistant, *Sarah Jane Smith* – another iconic role which she played in over eighty episodes, and reprised thirty years later in the *Sarah Jane Adventures*. She was still going strong when, very sadly, she died in the spring of 2011.

Seeds of Doom portrayed members of the *World Ecology Bureau* discovering a centuries-old seed pod buried deep in the permafrost of the Antarctic...

It seems to be still alive, growing without soil. The *Doctor* is sent photographs by the *WEB* and, suspicious of what it might be, he immediately flies down with *Sarah*. They don't know that a leak in the bureau has tipped off the discovery to *Harrison Chase*, a rich plant fanatic. *Chase* sends my character, *Scorby,* to get hold of it by any means possible. But before anyone arrives, the pod hatches and the tendril-like life form within attaches itself to one of the men, turning him green. As the *Doctor* feared, it's a *Krynoid*, a Triffid-like, man-eating plant hell bent on world domination.

A lot of *Scorby's* action was filmed in and around Athelhampton House in a part of Dorset where the villages are all named Puddle This and Piddle That. It's an attractive enough spot, but it was the middle of winter, so we spent a lot of time sitting in an outhouse, huddling around a roaring log fire, until I had to undertake a long scene up to my neck in a lake that felt like frozen gazpacho. In what was promised to be a single take, I had to wade out towards the middle, and be drowned and gobbled up by a huge rampant weed. Once I was assumed to be drowned, I had to swim out of shot for the other shore, where I clambered out, covered in weed and goose pimples, with my teeth chattering like a pair of castanets. I was rewarded with a bottle of brandy, and the news that I had to do it all over again – which at least earned me a second bottle of brandy!

In acute contrast to my part in *Doctor Who*, my next job was playing *Bread Man* in an episode of Ronnie Barker's wonderful sitcom, *Open All Hours*, where I had the pleasure of working not only with Ronnie, but also his young sidekick, *Granville*, played by up-and-coming comedy star, David Jason. Such is the serendipity of the acting profession, I had, of course, not the slightest idea how much time I would spend working with David over the next twenty-five years.

Although 1976 had got off to a good start with *Doctor Who,* other TV jobs were only trickling in and I'd steered away from any long runs in the theatre, because they tied one up and made the TV work difficult to fit in; besides, frankly, the stage work paid a lot worse on a per hour basis. However, I was beginning to become aware, at the age of thirty-three, that I still wasn't doing enough to accumulate much of a surplus bank balance and, although I'd always been pretty carefree about money – not to say spendthrift – I thought maybe I should start planning ahead a little.

Ever since I'd started acting people had warned me I'd be out of work for long periods; I'd never worried about it too much, partly because in the early days I seemed to have bounced from one repertory job to another, and partly because months of unemployment had sounded, in my youth, like an idler's dream. Nevertheless, once I started doing more television and less theatre, I'd got into the habit of filling time with my various menial jobs, like minding the antique shops in Portobello Road or hanging around outside funerals in large cars, waiting to chauffeur grieving old ladies home. More recently, as a result of the interest in gardening I'd developed tending Amanda's patch of a garden in Battersea, I'd drifted into the horticultural business with Leslie Churchill as a sideline, almost without thinking about it.

At that time, although I was keen on gardening, I really didn't know a lot, putting me in mind of the great American writer and cynic, Dorothy Parker, who, when asked about the subject said, 'All I know about horticulture is that you can take a whore to culture, but you can't make her think.' Witty old thing.

At the same time, like many (perhaps most) actors, I also suffered from periods of severe doubts about my value as an artist. I sometimes felt that my whole acting career had been founded on an elaborate con trick using smoke, mirrors and sleight of hand, and that I wasn't really an actor at all – just pretending to be one.

Being Boycie

It wasn't so strange, then, that by the spring of 1976, with no acting job on the horizon, I was more or less ready to give up the whole thespian dream and treat horticulture as a serious alternative to acting. I'd also gathered a new drinking companion at the St Margaret's Hotel that winter, an entertaining chancer called Michael Slater. A tall, good-looking Lothario who was kept very busy by the large number of women in his life, he was about my own age, and so far as one can judge these things, not from the upper echelons of society. He introduced himself to me as a former racing driver, now a skilled public relations man, who was being head-hunted all over the place for his special talents. His real ambition, he admitted, was to get back into motor racing and become a Formula One driver.

'Right now,' he told me, 'I'm just boogieing about until I get offered the kind of deal I deserve.' He was an untrustworthy scoundrel, but he made me laugh and I enjoyed his company.

In the meantime, he came and joined Leslie and me in the garden contracting business.

Drinking at the St Margaret's Hotel had become very much part of my life, and I recall – probably inaccurately – dozens of gargantuan, hysterical sessions there. Leslie and his wife Helen were the protagonists in sustaining this culture. She was a vast wobbly woman with blonde, highly coiffed hair and a loud and spectacularly foul mouth. Anyone who got on the wrong side of her towards closing time knew they'd been in a fight.

It was in the pub that Leslie first mentioned that premises had become available on Crown Road, just around the corner – opposite the Egg Man and next to Ches's Diner.

'We should get it, dear boy. It's a bloody cheap lease. Ridiculous not to grab it while we can.'

'What about the money?' I asked. 'We'd still have to pay for it and stock it with plants and things.'

'No problem,' he declared with characteristic machismo. 'I'll take you round to my bank and we can take out a loan. Listen,' he leaned in towards me, smothering me in whisky fumes, 'it can't bloody fail! We're already doing well down the alley, and with a shop like that we could do a helluva lot more – exotics as well, orchids, and everything!'

I was enthralled by the idea, and, as always, ready to look at what might be lurking on the other side of the fence. I told myself that I'd never taken the acting that seriously, the garden business was booming and with the right partner – i.e. not another actor – I'd always be able to get away and do those jobs in Hollywood when they came up.

We went off to Lloyds Bank in Richmond, where the manager seemed delighted, and to my mind suspiciously eager to throw the money at me. That was after he'd been subjected to Leslie's powerful sales pitch, convincing him that everything we sold would carry a 100% mark-up – if we bought a box of 60 bedding plants for 60p, we'd be sure to sell the same box for £1.20 – it was a doddle!

Leslie and I set ourselves up as partners in the *St Margaret's Garden Centre* and we were in business. Michael Slater was taken on as part of the deal, to help out when we needed him. Despite his claim to be a sought-after PR operator, he seemed very glad of the work. Leslie had been right about the profit on the bedding plants and in the spring, the little African marigolds, petunias and busy Lizzies that people seemed to want for instant bedding display flew out of the shop at double what we'd paid for them, while our outside work was paying well – until Leslie started taking on larger and more complicated jobs which needed more people and more wages to carry them out. Slater and I did several big jobs, including the gardens of the Pope's Grotto Hotel, a massive red-brick lump of a boozer by the Thames in Strawberry Hill, and named after a meeting place of Alexander Pope and his fellow-travellers, where we landscaped the riverside grounds.

Shortly afterwards, the great drought of '76 set in.

If you were around at the time, you'll recall that April and May had been ridiculously dry; June was even hotter, with not a smidgen of rain. Richmond Green looked like the Transvaal and the park resembled the foothills of the Atlas Mountains. It was so hot in restaurants that even the candles in bottles started to droop. Slater and I lived in shorts and sandals with bare torsos for three months. By the end of it, we thought we were a couple of bronzed Adonises; so did others, it seemed.

There had, in fact, been an element of competition between us all through that hot, lusty summer. One of our clients, a hairdresser with a salon in Notting Hill Gate, had recommended our gardening services to her neighbour, who ran a legitimate massage parlour.

Being Boycie

We laid a patio for her, with *Saturday Night Fever* blaring from the radio, and after a while she began to make suggestive noises to me about the openness of her marriage. It wasn't long before she was telling her husband, whom I never met, that she was going out for an evening's shopping, and she would end up in my flat. I didn't discourage her; it was somehow exciting to be meeting in these clandestine conditions, although I'd never really been keen on the additional complications that attach themselves to married lovers – or perhaps I'm just plain old-fashioned.

Slater, of course, had to turn this into a competition, and he took great delight in telling me, a few weeks after the first encounter, that he had visited the massage parlour for a sunbed session, where our client had obliged him with what he termed an 'oral massage'.

After that long, hot dry summer, our fledgling business was knocked for six. There was a hosepipe ban, the ground was so hard you couldn't get a pickaxe into it, and if we bought a box of marigolds at eight in the morning by midday they were a foot tall. By teatime they had flowered and were past selling.

No day went by without some new disaster.

One of our customers, the casting director Mary Selway (who depressingly declared that she thought, on balance, that I was probably right to focus on gardening rather than acting) kept buying plants for her window box, but the plants always died. This was embarrassing for us, until she realised she'd been sprinkling Harpic over them, thinking it was plant food.

Another customer, a startling woman with scarlet hair and eyes like an ostrich, bought some seed potatoes from us in early spring. Three months later she came back in a state of considerable dudgeon, demanding a refund.

'Why?' I asked.

'Well,' she raged. 'I planted the potatoes the way you told me; the stalks and leaves came up, then they flowered – I waited and waited, and no potatoes came up – and now the plants are dead!'

'Have you looked *under* the plants?' I asked.

'No.'

'Well, that's where you'll find them.'

She rushed back home, to return an hour or so later with a large crop of spuds. She still wanted her money back, she said, because most of them were green.

We gave her some late potatoes with written instructions on how to grow them.

By August, I was beginning to despair over what I believed to be the demise of my acting career; I hadn't had any jobs since early in the year, and only one small TV part booked. It was high summer, and with no sign of sustained rain, Leslie and I were both getting fairly desperate. Leslie, of course, would come over all optimistic and constantly remind me that it was bound to break soon, and it was unprecedented for England to go without rain for such a length of time.

It may have been, but it was precedented now, while the overdraft was growing like a bamboo in a monsoon as we struggled with the rent and our bloated wages bill.

When a customer asked if we could supply him with ferns, Leslie wouldn't entertain the idea of buying them from a nursery or a wholesaler when he knew that Richmond Park at that time of year was stuffed with ferns. I wasn't so sure this would work, but we drove into the park in our battered Transit van and, behind a cluster of trees, dug up half a van full which we took back and potted up. When the punter next came in he saw them and shrieked. 'I said *ferns*, not bracken!'

Another punter wanted a Christmas tree out of season for a commercial they were making in Twickenham Studios. That was easy. In the middle of the night we drove up the Isleworth Road in the Transit and pulled up near a roundabout. We snuck out and nicked a handsome eight-foot tree from the middle of it – a victimless crime, if ever there was one; you couldn't even see a gap where it had been.

While the business was already heading inexorably towards the buffers before it was even a year old, I wasn't entirely in control of my love life either. I'd always had a tendency to home in on unusual women who seemed to need help in some way, and then take them back to my place, like a small boy taking home a bird with a broken wing. This had led to my inviting Bethan Owen to come and stay with me in St Margaret's Road while she got herself together.

Beth was a lovely girl who'd been in the company at Chesterfield with me. Then she'd been known by her birth name, Hazel Williams.

Being Boycie

As Hazel, she'd launched herself into the beauty contest circuit at a young age and in 1962, she competed in the *Miss Universe Beauty Pageant* in Miami Beach. She didn't win the overall title, but tied with a contestant from the Dominican Republic for the title *Miss Amity*. This was awarded, apparently, for friendliness – admittedly a quality perhaps not easy to find among a pack of beauty pageant contenders. The following year she won *Miss Wales*. Since then she'd had parts in a few not very distinguished films and TV shows during the '60s before becoming a *Playboy Bunny*, and for some reason I never gathered, Beth Owen.

Her career by the time I re-met her had lurched into the long grass; she was broke and living in Talgarth Road when I encountered her again and I rather optimistically offered to take up her case. How or why we agreed that she would move in I simply don't remember, but once she was there, of course, I found myself straining at the leash to get out and get on with life the way I usually did, deliberately *not* looking after her, to the point where she became very morose and a little vino-dependent. And by this time (and this had led to a lot of difficulty) she was no longer a lover – more a non-rent-paying flatmate. Almost as if too compound these tricky conditions, she had brought with her two cats, of which I was not especially fond. This led to the poor old Prune being billeted down at my parents', where my mother took him on with great affection. But it meant my time with him was restricted to the occasional visit or long weekend.

I don't know why I did these things. Why, after so many misjudgments and false starts, hadn't I learned how or when to say 'No'? But I hadn't. And I didn't learn for many years. It's a matter of judgment; it's a matter of not wanting to make other people think you're unkind, which leads to being far more unkind than if you'd simply said 'No' in the first place.

I couldn't tell what had brought Beth down so much, but it was quite out of character, and I guess I brought it on in some way. Before she did any damage, she broke down one morning and declared that she might harm herself. I didn't know what she meant, and in any case, I had to get to an audition and I left her there. When I came back, I found her in a state of almost uncontrollable depression.

Meanwhile, I was getting a lot of angst and blame over Beth's unhappiness from Gordon Macintosh, a strange, mournful individual I knew from the St Margaret's bar. From time to time Gordon would take a sudden, unexpected interest in a woman whom he would pursue doggedly, quite oblivious to their indifference. Now he'd become fixated on Beth.

When Gordon turned up at a party I'd arranged on a friend's river cruiser, I saw him glaring at me and ogling Beth fiercely as he got more and more pissed, and came to a climax with a declaration of his love for her. At her inevitable peremptory rejection, he stripped off most of his clothing and dived over the side of the cruise boat, forgetting that the tide was out, and ended up wallowing in the thick green muddy goo that flanks the River Thames at low tide in Richmond.

Having fallen so deeply – and, it should be said, unrequitedly – in love with Beth, he went on to castigate me frequently for being a complete bastard to let her get into such a state.

He was exaggerating, of course, but his impassioned, relentless tirades did make me stop and think. I knew I hadn't handled Beth's condition well, but I guess at that stage in my life, I was fairly vulnerable myself. I hadn't been in a relationship that made any sense since Amanda had chucked me out and I was beginning to believe that my acting career was over. Added to that, not coming from a business background and with the indefatigably hustling Leslie on my back, I didn't really know how to cope with the mounting money problems.

I had realised by now that whatever Leslie – and to some extent Michael Slater – might have earned out of the business, they weren't going to have to carry the can with the bank. Foolishly, I'd added my name to Leslie's on the bank guarantees, and I was beginning to suspect that he was a man of straw, with nothing to back up his undertaking, while the bank, knowing I owned my own property, would look to me first.

Caroline Dawson did find a little more work for me towards the end of '76 – a part in two episodes of a series called *Cedar Tree*, and a bit in an episode if the *New Avengers* at Pinewood, with Patrick Macnee and the lovely Ms Lumley. I was playing a soldier, one of a group sitting just below her with a wonderful view of her spectacular legs protruding from a miniskirt, which was the point of the scene.

We were supposed to look awestruck; I didn't need to act. The job was fun, but it was going to do nothing to avert a looming meltdown in the Challis finances.

Wind of Change

The year 1977 opened for me in a state of deep gloom, perhaps reflecting the national mood in one of the worst years of our lifetime. The heyday of punk fashion, race riots and the anti-music of the Sex Pistols, it seems, in hindsight, to have hit the rock-bottom in the prevailing popular culture, in whish nastiest was best.

I was trying to field the heavy correspondence being fired at me by my bank, while already struggling to keep up payments on my mortgage. Leslie Churchill had niftily ducked out of sight, leaving (with his big blousy wife) a distinct gap in the bar of the St Margaret's Hotel; he was clearly not going to throw any of his own money – if he had any at all – into the sinking ship of the *St Margaret's Garden Centre*.

I was getting fairly desperate, and was even grateful to star briefly in a single episode of *Coronation Street*, as yet another copper – a detective sergeant who blunders into the murky side of *Corrie*. While I was in Manchester, I found myself in the bar after work, sitting beside the iconic Julie Goodyear, every man's dream pub landlady as *Bet Lynch*. I bought her drinks and took the opportunity to chat her up. Tentatively, I asked her if she'd like to come out and have dinner with me later.

'Oh,' she said, 'let's not bother, love. Why don't just we go to bed?'

I was impressed – a direct and forthright lady who knew what she wanted.

Of course, the fee for the part did little to ease my current financial pain, and I was still wondering what the hell I was going to do. The gardening business which had been intended to replace my flagging acting career was now about to fold. In an attempt to salvage something from the wreckage, I'd started to chart the adventures and disasters that had befallen me in my gardening career as the basis for a possible sitcom – preferably a sitcom that would include me.

I'd done some landscaping for James Saunders, a likeable, talented man and a prolific playwright with whom I'd worked at The Orange Tree. I gave him my stories of the misadventures and erotic encounters in the business which Leslie, Slater and I had experienced. He loved them and slickly turned my tales into functional scripts. They looked promising to me; he said he'd give them to his agent, but in my current gloom, I didn't expect anything to happen soon.

I had pretty much reached a nadir of unemployment, impecuniousness and depression when, almost out of the blue, Sam Walters offered me a part in the first English production of *The Memorandum* by Czech playwright (later President) Vaclav Havel. Sam was a great supporter of Havel and had already produced several of his plays at the Orange Tree Theatre, where I'd done *Lovers* with Keith Washington three years before. Although not much money was involved, it promised to be a prestigious production, and an awfully long way from being a copper in *Coronation Street.*

Mine was a good part in a fine play by a man who had become world-renowned for his strident opposition to the hard-line communist Czechoslovakian government. Along with a number of writers, actors, musicians and political activists, Havel had signed the highly influential *Charter 77,* a blueprint for a free state and a critique of his government's human rights abuses.

The Czech government responded by imprisoning or restricting the movements of all the signatories. Under this oppression, writers and actors had developed a culture of putting on clandestine plays in each other's flats and houses, scurrying through the streets of Prague with props and costumes in suitcases to dodge the Secret Services and the penalties that inevitably followed detection. The Orange Tree, through its connection with Havel and his plays which it produced, became a significant factor in promoting *Charter 77,* which in the end saw most of its aims realised twelve years later, after the Velvet Revolution of 1989, when Havel was declared President. In March 2009, the theatre was the venue for a great reunion of the signatories and a twentieth anniversary celebration of the achievements of the Charter.

Havel wrote the play in 1965 as a satire to take a potshot at the absurdity and iniquities of communist bureaucracy, and it's generally considered one of his best. Mine was a key part – a bureaucrat who reminded me of a typically smug, self-important

Inland Revenue chap who'd once turned up to investigate my tax affairs.

When the tax inspector had finished going through my accounts, he looked at me disdainfully. 'Well, you don't seem to be very successful at what you're trying to do. Why don't you give it up and do something sensible?'

'What? You mean become a tax inspector like you?'

His lips pursed as he drew himself up. 'There's no need to be offensive,' he sniffed.

There was something about his pomposity and ridiculous sense of self-importance that fascinated me and, as always, I'd stored away his particular characteristics in my personal archive. The mindset and demeanour of a bureaucrat was, I guessed, the same from Vladivostok to London and, with no specific instructions on how play my part in Havel's play, it seemed a good idea to base it loosely on my taxman.

When I was confronted with these kinds of dilemma, I would think back to the time when my mother had wanted me to try to get into LAMDA, and I had opted to dive straight in at the deep end with the Argyle Theatre for Youth, rather than going to drama school.

Since then I'd encountered numerous actors who had come through drama schools, and in general, I had the overriding impression from the younger ex-drama students that it tended to flatten individual ability and homogenise acting talent. It's axiomatic that a widely taught skill or technique will tend to produce sameness in its practitioners. At the cruder end of the scale, I've noticed an irritating similarity in the way most BBC reporters, when standing (or, often, walking) and speaking to camera, will use a very recognisable gamut of hand movements and gestures – to such an extent that they sometimes look like they're doing the hand jive in the crush of the *2i's* back in the late 1950s.

Sam Walters was rehearsing our play in Matthaie's Café & Bakery (which had a rare surviving Art Deco shopfront) in Kew Road. I was still feeling very pressured from the negative influences of the past year and though I knew I was being hypersensitive, I was raw and vulnerable at the time. While we were rehearsing there had been a lot of news coverage of the trial of the Balcombe Street Four, all members of an IRA unit who in 1975 had been tracked down after bombing and firing gunshots through the window of Scott's Restaurant in Mayfair, killing and injuring several people. They'd been chased back to a block of flats in Balcombe Street near Marylebone Station, where they took two hostages.

In the end they'd surrendered and the case was now being heard at the Old Bailey. Their lawyer was claiming that the four other Irishmen convicted of the earlier severe bomb attack in Guildford were innocent.

I had always been very angry about the IRA bombings that terrorized England in the mid-'70s. They were pointless, brutal and utterly callous acts of murder. I didn't see how anyone could justify them. Shaking with impotent rage when I got to rehearsals that morning, I found a few other members of the cast voicing a liberal point of view that these atrocities wouldn't have happened without Britain having first created the situation in Northern Ireland.

I wasn't prepared to temper my views; I became very angry, and the argument flared up into some nasty exchanges.

Sam Walters took me to one side and told me to go home for the rest of the day – like a surly schoolkid – to cool off. In confusion, and cursing my own lack of self-control, I went back to my flat and put myself straight to bed, where I lay and wondered if I'd just blown my last serious chance as an actor.

But I was allowed back, and the effort we'd all put into the production paid off. It is, in any case, like most of Havel's plays, a beautifully constructed piece; but we felt we had done our part in making it work, and we were thrilled when Irving Wardle in *The Times* declared it 'a masterpiece'.

Inevitably, with news of the heavy-handed actions of the Czechoslovakian government and the jailing of Havel for subversion, the play attracted a lot of attention, and the tiny auditorium was always packed.

One night, a short time into the run, I was having a drink in the pub downstairs after the show, when an arty-looking bloke appeared by my shoulder.

'I've been watching your performance,' he said. 'I'd like to buy you a *dthrink*,' he added, with a strange roll of the 'r' which struck a faint chord.

I couldn't place him, though he looked familiar. 'That's fine,' I agreed. 'Anyone can buy me a drink... as long as I don't have to buy one back,' I added, regretting my flippancy at once.

We sat, and when there were a couple of full glasses between us, he sat down and looked at me across the table. 'I very much enjoyed your performance.' He paused. 'My name's Tom Stoppard...'

I squinted at him, on the brink of retorting, 'Yeah, they all say that....' But then of course I realised he *was* Tom Stoppard and, in my confusion, leapt to my feet, and sat down again feeling rather foolish.

Stoppard flashed a strange grin. 'I wondered if you'd like to be in one of my plays,' he went on.

'W...What?' I blurted, before recovering my dignity and continuing, as blasé as I could manage, 'Well, I'll have to check my availability...' I could hardly contain my excitement. A Stoppard play, after all, was a Stoppard.

He nodded. 'The only trouble is, it's to tour in South Africa. How would you feel about that....?'

He left the question hanging.

At the time apartheid was still very much in place in South Africa, and it was considered by many to be a major social crime to have anything to do with the regime. I knew all about that – when I'd toured South Africa for over a year in *Move Over Mrs Markham*, back in 1972, apartheid had been even more rigorously enforced. But there were moral justifications for taking art to this oppressive regime, where television had only recently been allowed and public discussion of the issues was still severely limited.

I explained this to Stoppard. 'How do *you* feel about it?' I asked.

'Frankly,' Stoppard admitted, 'I was uncomfortable, of course; but I spoke to my friend, Athol Fugard [the South African playwright] and he was insistent that I should allow it to come. "Send it," he said. "Do it, because information is light".'

After we'd talked a little about South Africa and his play, Stoppard left, saying he would speak to the director.

A couple of nights later Peter Bowles turned up. He'd been playing the lead in Stoppard's new play since the original production in London, in April '76.

Peter Bowles had already agreed to go on the South African tour, with the proviso that he would also direct the play. This had been agreed when he turned up to watch me in *The Memorandum*. I knew him slightly; we'd worked together on an episode of a TV show, *Brett*, in which he'd starred and I'd played a species of renegade terrorist sniper.

I recalled what he'd said at the time. 'You're a very good actor. What are you doing in a small part like this?' He'd asked the question with characteristic frankness.

'That's all they offered me,' I'd shrugged, without embarrassment.

Now he invited me for a drink after the Havel piece. 'I want you to be in my play, and there are some good parts,' he said expansively. 'I gather you've met the writer, but I'll be directing it in South Africa, and I want you to be my assistant director.'

I was surprised, never having seriously directed before – and chuffed – but I did my best to take it in my stride.

'Yes,' he went on, without waiting for my agreement. 'I'll need you out there with me a couple of weeks early to audition the local people.'

There would be four British actors going out, he explained – himself, me, Charles Hawtrey and Richard Warwick – and the agreement with the South African actors' union was that we would cast the rest there, much as we had done with the *Mrs Markham* company.

I went home from The Orange Tree that night with a big new bounce in my stride. Now I was almost relieved that the gardening business had gone belly up. Otherwise I might not have grabbed so eagerly at the chance to do any acting, however meagre the fees. Once it was running, I realised how lucky I was to have got the part in *The Memorandum*. It was a serious, quality play, and exactly the sort of thing I'd really wanted to do before I'd almost given up acting. And it had led to my meeting with Stoppard.

Beth Owen was still living at 65, St Margaret's Road, and partly reacting to Gordon's chiding and partly because I knew I bore some responsibility for her, I was doing my best to look after her. In fact she was improving and seemed to be getting herself together again, and knowing that I was going away soon, I didn't want to risk upsetting her by asking her to move on. In any case, it was probably just as well to have someone in the flat while I was in South Africa, and I told her it would be fine for her to stay. I tried not to think about what would happen when I got back.

Dirty Linen and *New-Found-Land* effectively combined two one-act plays which Stoppard wrote to celebrate the British naturalisation of Ed Berman, founder of London's *Almost Free Theatre*, where the work was first performed as part of the theatre's season celebrating the American bicentenary. *Dirty Linen* is a farce based on a House of Commons Special Committee appointed to investigate reports that a large number of MPs have been having sex with the same woman. Its subtext is a commentary on the government, how it works and its relations with the press and public. Inserted within *Dirty Linen, New-Found-Land* is a short interlude in which two government officials try to decide whether to give British citizenship to an eccentric American (based on Ed Berman). At the end, it contains an extraordinary virtuoso piece of writing, a long soliloquy that is a rhapsody to America, movingly delivered in this production by Richard Warwick.

Peter Bowles was playing *Withenshaw*, an unashamedly bluff North Countryman and chairman of the Committee, which he'd played at the Arts Theatre in London, and I was to play *Cocklebury-Smythe MP*, an old-fashioned Tory who looked down his nose at *Withenshaw*, and these days probably wouldn't even get in front of a constituency selection committee. The key role was *Maddie Gotobed*, a female character who is secretary to the Commons Committee. She's an alluring woman with a talent for plain speaking while the MPs waffle, obfuscate and tell ridiculously implausible porkies about their sexual shenanigans. For this, she must be naive and unsophisticated, and at the same time highly sexually charged. This was hard to cast in England; it would be harder in South Africa.

Working with Peter Bowles at close quarters was an extraordinary experience. Looked at objectively, Peter could be a somewhat preposterous individual, like most actors, but he was also brilliant, inspiring, paranoid, self-doubting, and hilarious – and I loved working with him. He took the theatre in general and our play in particular very seriously. Any perceived slight or hint of a suggestion that our production of *Dirty Linen* wasn't being treated with the proper respect would have Peter stamping his foot and demanding that it be accorded due deference.

From my perspective, as someone who always wants to get things right, but usually compromises in the face of strong opposition, I could only admire Peter's unrelenting stance on behalf of the play and its performers.

'We will *not* be playing in your theatre tonight unless we have sandwiches and coffee during our dress rehearsal. We have come a long distance to be with you tonight, and we deserve some respect for that.'

'Hear, hear!' I muttered, although the good *Broeders* of Port Elizabeth and East London had never been spoken to like that by a mere theatrical performer. Usually, most actors were too grateful that someone had agreed to allow them to perform for them to complain much.

As Peter had promised, I'd gone out early to South Africa with him, as his lieutenant – a role which suited me. I'd happily sort things out, deal with any fallout, and offer second opinions. This became most critical when we were trying to cast the rest of the play beyond the four Brits represented in *Dirty Linen*. The crucial casting was *Maddie Gotobed*. As the play unfolds, *Maddie* sheds items of her clothing, always in circumstances in which it isn't noticed until she once again becomes the focus of attention, so she had to look pretty good in scanty underwear. Matching this quality with the ability to play a complex part wasn't going to be easy. She needed to be savvy with a no-nonsense attitude, as well as looking great in her underwear.

Peter and I quickly concluded that the applicants should not only read the part, but should also be prepared to be seen in a bikini, as if we were auditioning for a very different sort of show. Neither of us had ever had to cast in this way, and there was no doubt that it was embarrassingly tricky for two red-blooded males who were trying to be serious about casting a difficult and key role.

Our reactions ran from 'Phwoar, this is all right!' to 'Should we really be doing this?'

Nevertheless, it was fascinating for me to be on the other side of auditions for a change. Until then I hadn't appreciated the variety of approaches that people adopt in promoting their talents. Some would swagger in, bursting with apparent confidence, which often evaporated the minute they opened their mouths on stage.

Others, more interestingly, would creep up diffidently and then produce, as if from a magician's topper, a belting performance.

But however bad or unsuitable they were I found it very hard, rather like Leslie Garret on *Comic Relief Fame Academy*, to utter blunt words of rejection. Fortunately, Peter had no such qualms.

In the casting of *Maddie*, the problem was, broadly, that those with the best bodies couldn't speak, and vice versa. None contained all the requirements in one package, as it were. One girl – a great actress, with a body and boat race to elevate the limpest of libidos – just didn't have the overconfident chutzpah that the part needed. After seeing around thirty women, we ended up deciding that the one who best combined the disparate qualities we sought was a South African actress, Moira Downie. She wasn't the best actress we'd seen, she didn't have the outstanding poitrine and hourglass figure we should have liked, but she had the sharpness of mind, she looked terrific, and she was naturally very sassy and forthright.

We told her she'd got the part. 'Yah! Ach man,' she declared in a virtuoso display of Afrikaner English, 'Ah am going to give you guys some stick, you know!' And she wasn't lying.

At the same time, with a British background she had no trouble playing *Maddie* with the appropriate upper-crust English accent.

Soon we'd cast the most of the show, but we still hadn't found anyone to play *McTeazle*. I had been tagged as *Cocklebury-Smythe*, a Tory MP on the Select Committee, with a healthy contempt for any liberalising compromises. *McTeazle* was more of a wishy-washy Lib-Dem type, who liked to see all points of view and whose attitudes shuffled from side to side – a difficult attitude for most South Africans. To overcome this problem, I offered to play *McTeazle*, and we gave *Cocklebury-Smythe* to Sandy Robertson, an expat Australian actor with some stock Australian characteristics.

'Jeez mate, you're not gay, are you?' he asked me, after he'd introduced me to some extraordinary and unfamiliar herbal substance which led to my passing out on the floor of his hotel room.

It was very stimulating for me to be back in South Africa, four years after my first visit, and to observe all the small changes that had already taken place – the absence of apartheid signs on park benches, and the increase in open dialogue about solutions to the inherent inequity of the regime. It was also exciting to be part of a successful tour of a Stoppard play, which inevitably attracted the thinking, liberal sections of the population – more numerous than most Europeans would have guessed – and to take the play into the black townships.

It was fun, too, to meet up with some of the local actors I'd got to know on the *Move Over Mrs Markham* tour – Ian Hamilton in particular, a big friend from that tour, who had married an actress called Erica Rogers. He'd moved more into the agency business, and was busy with *The Wild Geese,* a big action movie with Richard Harris, Richard Burton and Roger Moore and a massive cast of extras, being shot on locations around South Africa.

Rex Garner had become quite a star on the new South African TV in the last few years, and had married Tammy Bonell, the stage manager on *Markham* who'd met me off the plane last time with Hymie Udwin. Rex was full of beans and keen to show me his grand new house on the outskirts of Jo'burg. I went up there to watch the Cup Final on TV, between Liverpool and Manchester United – a corker of a game with all three goals scored in a five-minute period, two of them by MU.

My English colleagues in *Dirty Linen* made a strange bunch. Apart from Peter Bowles, who went through his own periods of bizarre confusion during the tour, there was the well-known skinny and fragile Charles Hawtrey, whom I'd laughed at and enjoyed over two decades of *Carry On* films. He was a source of great puzzlement to the citizens of Johannesburg, who would watch him mincing down the street with lips pursed and eyes darting like a nervous rabbit, while his twig legs protruded from baggy safari shorts, ending in knobbly sandal-clad feet. He wasn't at all sociable with the rest of the company, but complained that no one came to see him in his flat. He admitted that once he'd thrown his keys from his eighth floor bedroom window in the hope that someone might bring them back up and talk to him. He didn't tell us if the ploy had worked.

Richard Warwick was a remarkably good-looking and experienced actor whom I liked very much. I admired him for his talent and his brilliant rendition of the great soliloquy in *New-Found-Land.* He'd been prominent as the camp *Grand Duke Dimitri* in *Nicholas & Alexandra*, and was one of the many pretty young chaps scampering around in Franco Zeffirelli's *Romeo and Juliet*. He was still dithering about his sexuality, and often distressed by the confusion this caused him. Moira Downie adored him, which confused him more.

He had a great sense of humour, though, quick and waspish, and would always refer to Peter Bowles as 'Sally', after Christopher Isherwood's *Cabaret* character.

His moods could swing very swiftly and led to some strange and alarming situations. We were on the beach in Cape Town, on a perfect day, looking up at Table Mountain, when we decided it would be good to get right up there and gaze down on the beautiful city. The trip was like a boy's adventure for Richard, who teetered right on the edge of Table Mountain, thousands of feet over the city, and pretended that he was about to jump. For a few awful minutes I thought he really would. I never worked with him after the *Linen* tour, but always enjoyed seeing him perform until he died, sadly young, in 1997.

With no real commitment to anyone back in London, it was inevitable that I would quite soon find myself entangled, and indeed I did, with an English expat I met in Jo'burg through old friends there.

Another chap in the company, quite inconveniently, became besotted with Moira. It wasn't surprising – she played such a key, seductive role in our play, and she was very beautiful. However, she didn't reciprocate her admirer's feelings, and I ended up hearing both sides of the story, unable to advise either on what they should do.

After a couple of months of getting on well with Moira myself, and really responding to her skills as a mimic, and her good grasp of her part in *Dirty Linen,* we found ourselves being drawn closer together. When we got to Durban, she shared a remote and lovely beach house, buried in the dunes on the edge of the Indian Ocean, with Richard Warwick. They weren't lovers; Richard by then seemed clearer in his own head that he was gay, but he loved the company of sassy women like Moira, once he'd got to know them.

A whacky friend – one of the local actors – and I decided to play a prank on them, and crept up to raid the house in the dunes in the middle of the night, when we found them both asleep, in separate rooms, of course, and pretended for a few unkind moments to be burglars.

As soon as we owned up to being who we were, Moira was so relieved she collapsed in a state of high excitement. Quite suddenly, she and I found ourselves in a relationship, which lasted for the rest of the tour, and beyond. Moira was a very stimulating woman to be with. She had a strong, funny personality and we spent hours conversing in thick Afrikaner English and Bantu pidgin, which, in time and with her help, I made good use of in a series of sketches I had started to write, based on my experiences of two visits to South Africa under apartheid.

I had to take over as director of *Dirty Linen* when we went up to what was then illegally governed Southern Rhodesia, a diplomatic no-man's-land since Ian Smith's government had issued its Unilateral Declaration of Independence (or UDI). Peter Bowles had refused to go there, on the grounds that 'my government does not recognise the regime', so I'd also had to take on his role of *Withenshaw*. It felt strange to be in this maverick nation, and once there, I wasn't sure I should have come; but there was a lot I wanted to see in the short time we had.

While we were in Salisbury, I mentioned to Naomi Buch, one of the South African actresses in the company, that the last time I'd been there, doing *Mrs Markham* in 1973, I'd met Sam Westmacott, a well known female journalist, later a PR consultant in London.

Sam was a tall, rangy, challenging sort, with a well-developed sense of fun. Soon after I'd met her I found myself swimming in the pool at her villa on the outskirts of Salisbury. It was after midnight, and – darn it – I'd forgotten my swimming trunks!

As far as Naomi was concerned, I couldn't have uttered a more toxic name than Sam's. She was apoplectic; Sam was *not* her favourite person, and she accused her of all sorts of anti-conjugal behaviour. Strangely, though, many years later, my fourth (and final) wife, Carol was introduced to her by Bruce Gyngell, the charismatic head of TV-am for whom they worked together on PR, when they got on very well, in one of those bizarre, serendipitous connections that life throws up.

I flew back from Salisbury (now Harare) to Johannesburg on August

16th at a time when the tension within Rhodesia was growing uglier. Nevertheless I was sorry that the African tour was ending, despite the political discomfort, for I loved the beautiful country for itself. It was also my 35th birthday, and I was indulging in a little airborne celebration with the rest of the company when our mood was shattered by the pilot's announcement that Elvis Presley had died.

I took a while to register how much that shook me, but I guess although I'd never been a great fan, Elvis had for so long represented a major watershed in the evolution of rock'n'roll, he'd always been an inescapable presence. The announcement instantly quashed any birthday excitement and, like Kennedy's death fourteen years before, seemed to underline the great upheavals that were taking place in the country I was in. This sense of looming doom was heightened when just four weeks later Steve Biko was murdered in police custody, becoming a true martyr to the cause of African freedom.

Besides the experience of working and living in South Africa, I'd come back with several other arrows in my quiver. The first of these was the potrfolio of dramatic sketches I'd written about people and circumstances I'd encountered in South Africa. I'd been very struck by the huge enthusiasm for our play shown by black audiences, and the gales of unrestrained laughter that greeted the humour of it, and I'd tried to get closer to understanding the outlook of the black South Africans, and how they dealt with the indignity of apartheid.

Under the surface of white society, too, there were many stories of people eager for change. There was, for instance, a celebrated couple – a white girl and a black journalist who had fallen in love. Quite openly, he went to stay with her in Johannesburg, and she would stay with him in Soweto, both of which arrangements were banned under South African law. Bravely, they put two fingers up at the authorities and carried on, until eventually he disappeared, never to be seen again. This really moved me, and it was taking place when Steve Biko, who did not believe in violent protest, was saying a lot of things the regime didn't like. He was arrested and transported hundreds of miles to the other end of the country, where he died from injuries inflicted by the police. This was a time when optimistic liberals had been beginning to think that the end of the system was in sight, and the Biko case caused a great deal of grief. I followed the story closely, and used it in the stories I was putting together.

I'd also got involved with some illicit black and white theatre groups that would meet in the smart white suburbs of Johannesburg. As a result of this, I soon sussed that I was being followed. My apartment was turned over. The police came round and treated me with suspicion and deep disdain, which was entirely mutual; as nothing had been taken, I guessed it was they who'd ravaged the place anyway.

It was experiences like this and the many long and fairly profound discussions I'd had with South Africans, black and white, that prompted me to start writing what I hoped might become a stage play dealing with the whole complex question.

It started out not so much as a structured piece, more as a group of vignettes – all delivered by one man and a woman. Before setting out for this second trip to South Africa, I'd naturally had serious doubts, but Stoppard's careful reasoning had swayed me; besides, I needed a job. When it came to it, I never felt entirely comfortable about being there, though it was clear we were giving some solace to those whites who wanted change.

Moira Downie continued to help me with my writing too, showing me the other side to being born a white South African, and explaining her reactions to those who castigated people like her for still being there. And of course she was wonderful at playing the parts of the South African women in the sketches.

While I was still in South Africa, Moira announced that she was going to leave her husband and come to England to audition for the part of *Maddie* in the London production of *Dirty Linen*, still playing at the Arts Theatre. She would also be able to work with me on my play, which, even in its rudimentary form, had evoked interest from Sam Walters at The Orange Tree.

Stoppard – Both sides of the Pond

It was quite alien to be back in cold, noisy London after an exhilarating three months in South Africa. I'd put the whole gardening company fiasco behind me, and my confidence in my ability an actor had been substantially restored by being part of *Dirty Linen's* successful tour and the strong critical acclaim the production had attracted. The financial mess I'd been in before I'd left had been eased by my dear old mother volunteering to pay off the business overdraft, although I vowed to pay her back as soon as I could. There was no sign of Leslie Churchill and the brassy Helen, but I heard later she'd dumped him, and he'd been left sitting in darkness in a flat where the electricity had been cut off. It didn't sound as if I would recover a halfpenny from him.

What the hell! I was an actor again, and I was to join the West End production of *Dirty Linen & New-Found-Land*.

Tom Stoppard had written to me to thank me with genuine warmth for taking over the part of *McTeazle* when we couldn't find a local to play it, and for directing the tour in Rhodesia when Peter Bowles had refused. Now he offered me the choice of three main parts, from which, naturally, I opted for *Withenshaw*, the largest and most robust of the male roles.

However, knowing that Moira would be turning up in London at some point, I had to find some solution for Beth, who was still living in my flat. I had been a bit uneasy about how she would react when I returned. As it turned out, Beth had sorted herself out and was in much better shape emotionally. When the woman I'd had brief affair with in Jo'burg turned up in London, she came to see me in St Margaret's Road. To help me out of a spot, she told Beth that she was intending to move in. This wasn't true but it galvanized Beth, who in any case was ready to move on, so we were able to part on good terms. The only downside to the arrangement was that she had nowhere to take her cats; I agreed, in the feeblest possible way, to keep them at 62, St Margaret's Road, thereby delaying the Prune's return indefinitely.

It was confirmed that I was to take over the part of *Withenshaw* in the London production of *Dirty Linen,* which had already run for two years at the 350-seat Arts Theatre, off St Martin's Lane (and went on to complete four years). I was thrilled to be back on a West End stage, especially as a lead in a very successful play. I was rather excited to find that the key – and very sexy – female role of *Maddie Gotobed* was being played by a twenty-four-year-old West End ingénue, Sally Farmiloe. Although Sally had been born in South Africa, she had all the attributes of a posh English ex-debutante, which, combined with a lusty glint in her eye gave her a lot of allure for me.

While we were on the same stage, it was inevitable that there was some chemistry between us, and that we should have carried that chemistry out of the theatre on occasion. Sally was an electrifying girl with an extraordinary body which she knew very well how to use. I wasn't massively surprised when some twenty years later she had a three-year affair with Jeffrey Archer who, while evidently not always fussy about the women he consorted with casually, was fond of telling people what a good eye he had for a work of art.

On the 16th November 1978, we celebrated 1,000 performances of the play. The most widely used publicity shot was of Sally in a pair of camiknickers, setting, as it turned out, something of a precedent; even now, thirty years on, she's not averse to a lingerie photographic shoot.

She was no philosopher but she was always fun. One weekend she threw me the keys to her snazzy little open-topped car and asked me to drive. With her long hair whipping in the wind, in the time-honoured fashion of a thousand advertisements for women's consumer goods, we shot down to her family's place in Sussex.

That seemed to go all right, and when her family were asked to a smart society wedding, they agreed that Sally could bring me. This very formal event was to take place in one of the City of London livery halls near the Bank. I asked Sally what I should wear – I imagined traditional morning suit, but she had other ideas. My favourite garment at the time was a smart new fawn suede jacket. She thought I should wear that.

I was frankly doubtful and aware of Sally's penchant for not doing the obvious and I wasn't surprised to find every other male at the gathering clad in black or grey tails. However, I wasn't completely ostracised, and some people even talked to me as if I were not an alien, until after the cake had been cut, when a liveried toastmaster, with military bearing and moustache marched up to me.

'Excuse me, sir. The host and hostess have asked me for your name.'

After a little prevaricating, I owned up, and the quasi-soldier chap strode off in a ceremonial way to the hostess. After a brief council of war, and hooded glances at me, he returned.

'The host and hostess say you have not been invited and they have asked me to ask you to leave.'

I thought of making a stand on behalf of suede-jacketed interlopers everywhere, but thought it wiser not to.

Sally protested that I was with her. That cut no ice.

I was surprised, and rather impressed when Sally's family – my official sponsors, as it were – all marched out with me.

During the course of my run in *Dirty Linen* in London, a number of people I hadn't seen for years showed up at The Arts Theatre, including a few I hadn't expected to see, like my father. I was sitting at the kitchen table with him in Sunnybank after lunch on the Sunday after he'd been. He was quite pissed by then and, very unusually, allowed his guard to drop for a few minutes.

'That play...' he said, slowly nodding his head. 'I was so proud of you.'

I burst into tears. Since I'd first told him I was going to be an actor, he'd never, *ever* said anything like that.

Still nodding, he went on. 'How do you get up there on stage and do that?'

I shrugged, elated by this unprecedented show of approval. 'It's my job, Dad.'

'Fantastic,' he said, now shaking his head in wonderment at his own son's achievements.

I was amazed and massively grateful for his reaction. I guessed that the subject of the play – the activities of a Parliamentary Committee – was something that he was familiar with and appreciated. And I think that at last he'd accepted that I had moved on to a more serious, respectable level of acting. This went a long way in reinforcing my own new belief in myself. I gave him a copy of *Dirty Linen* which I later found by his bed when he was staying away.

Disappointingly, he never communicated his approval to me again.

On another evening, a familiar face from a long time ago appeared in my dressing room at The Arts; I just managed to place her before she told me that she was Frances, the woman in the Argyle Theatre for Youth company, who had been kind enough to give an eighteen-year-old novice his first lesson in the rudiments of sex. It's a lesson one never forgets, and I was still grateful to her.

After a short, intense love affair with Sally Farmiloe, during which I think she spotted we weren't ideally matched, my ardour waned when Moira Downie arrived in London. Moira and I were both as eager as each other to pick up and run with the fairly powerful relationship we'd had on tour in South Africa, and she was soon living in my flat in St Margaret's Road.

I was encouraged to find that she'd done more work on the play I'd started writing in South Africa and had even added to it. The material we had now was packed with an insider's experience of life for the black and white populations of South Africa, revealing aspects that outsiders had never seen. I had started simply by writing my account of the dozens of bizarre situations and encounters I had witnessed, like the confusion over my servant on the first trip, and the visit with Shirley Anne Field's nanny to her home village, and the shock of her not being able to sit with us in a restaurant run by a black South African. I'd also expanded on the awful story of the white girl and black journalist who had the temerity to fall in love, then paid for it when he disappeared and was never seen again.

I went to see Jeremy Paul, a friend and a playwright with a number of outstanding TV credits to his name, a co-founder and kind of 'house' playwright at The Orange Tree. He lived with his wife, actress Patricia Garwood, near me in St Margaret's, where I went to show him the material. He disappeared into another room to read it; he didn't come back until an hour or so later.

'The bad news,' he announced, 'is that I can't make a play out of it; it's too rich, too full of information, but I love it, and the way you tell it – as a series of stories – is fascinating, and I think you could present them on stage as simply as that.'

He agreed to help me collate the stories into a more cohesive, chronological collection with an identifiable thread running through them.

We showed the new work to Sam Walters at The Orange Tree, and he loved it. He put on *Cut the Grass, so We Can See the Elephants* (named from an old African saying) at lunchtime every day for a fortnight, with Moira and I playing all the parts.

Moira was wonderful at depicting a great variety of South African women, and the audiences – as I'd hoped – were intrigued by this perspective on South Africa and its recent history.

The piece got a great reception at The Orange Tree and a strong write-up in *Time Out*, which pulled in a lot more punters. It was also seen by the people from The Croydon Warehouse, who booked it and where it ran for a week or so.

Here, once again, it found appreciative audiences and reactions, although one night I was alarmed to see a large block of black faces in the auditorium, and was nervous about how they would react to my portrayal of some of the black characters, and their African English accent that I'd tried to develop. They were from a London-based black awareness group, and they came back to see me afterwards. They thanked me for painting some of the realities surrounding apartheid – the white man's view of the black 'problem' – and told me they appreciated that I was airing these aspects of apartheid and how much they'd liked my characterizations.

The play was also picked up by a Dutch producer for a two-week run in Amsterdam as part of a Third World Festival, for which Jeremy Paul came over as producer; Moira couldn't come, though, and her place was taken by an electrifying actress and woman of extreme views called Sarah Porter.

Sadly, it hasn't had a showing in Europe since, but I was thrilled that it got as far as it did. And it was to resurface in New York some four years later.

During the terminal months of my first attempt at commercial entrepreneurship with the St Margaret's Garden Centre – which, thank God, already seemed like a lifetime ago – I'd written my account of all the disasters and occasional triumphs I'd experienced with Leslie and Slater, as well as a number of predatory, highly-sexed female clients, as an act of catharsis as much as a serious wish to see it turn it into anything profitable. When a friend and gardening client, James Saunders, had taken it, promising to work on it, I hadn't expected much to happen with it.

I went to see him when I got back to London to find out how he'd got on.

'I like it,' he said, 'but my agent can't see it.' He shrugged philosophically. In the scribbling game, an awful lot of speculative material ends up collecting dust until the mice have eaten it. 'You may as well take it and see what you can do with it.'

I took the manuscript away with me and showed it to my new agent, Marina Martin.

She was thrilled. 'This is *exactly* what I'm looking for, for you. I'll take it to the BBC.'

The BBC liked it, but not for me. They were looking for a vehicle for the massively popular, talented and likeable Richard Beckinsale, and offered him the part of *Stan*, an out-of-work actor turned gardening-shop-wallah, based mainly on me. Richard had already had terrific success with Ronnie Barker in *Porridge*, and Leonard Rossiter in *Rising Damp*, and he was absolutely right for the role in *Bloomers*, as it became known when it was launched in 1979.

In any case, I did get to play a small part in it, a great scene based on the time Leslie and I had nicked a Christmas tree from the roundabout on the Isleworth Road.

In this embellished version, *Stan* and his partner, played by David Swift, get caught by two policemen on the roundabout as they're chucking stolen trees into their knackered old Transit. One of the coppers – played by me – goads *Stan* into tripping himself up in a ridiculous, convoluted excuse for being where he is. That was fun, and Richard even had the good grace to apologise. 'I'm sorry mate. I'm playing you, really, aren't I?' he said, and presented me with a large bottle of malt whisky.

After that he worked on more of the planned six episodes. But for the sixth, incredibly sadly, he didn't show up for filming – he had died the night before of a major heart attack.

He was very much missed, although his talent lives on in his beautiful daughters, Samantha and Kate.

In the spring of 1979, I left the cast of *Dirty Linen & New-Found-*

Land at the Arts Theatre to become part of Ed Berman's British American Repertory Company.

This had been set up by Berman to be a kind of democratic, egalitarian group of theatre people, in which input at all stages was encouraged from all the members. It was intended to be as unhierarchical as possible. There were no stars, and parts were shared round on a Buggins's turn principle rather than on absolute merit.

This would have been fine, if only one didn't at the same time want to get the best possible reviews, and for that matter give the best possible performance. There was no escaping that some players were better at some parts than others. In the end, in practice, that became the overriding criterion.

The BARC was in turn an offshoot of an organisation which Berman had set up in the UK called *Interaction*, a trust whose purpose was to develop a range of innovative approaches to urban, social renewal, like the creation of City Farms and Community Arts projects for unemployed youth.

As a direct result of my involvement with the two Stoppard plays, I'd been selected as one of the English actors in Ed Berman's experimental company that was going to tour a Stoppard play in the USA. The company was, by definition, composed 50/50 of American and English actors. They were an easy-going crowd and I was happy to be working with them. Once we'd started rehearsals in London, I found a strong affinity with one of the Americans, Sarah Venable – an experienced stage actress from New York who'd also been in a couple of movies. She had a lovely soft voice and old-fashioned, dark good looks which rather reminded me of my mother. She seemed to reciprocate this interest, and we started enjoying each other's company. After a few weeks, I was in love – again!

This was complicated by the fact that Moira was still living in my flat in St Margaret's Road. For, although I had been very excited when Moira had chosen to come back to England to audition for *Maddie Gotobed* at The Arts and work with me in the African play, like most who have tried to consolidate their holiday romances (which are very similar to theatrical tour romances), we had rather drifted apart – at least, I had, once my attention had been well and truly hijacked by the gorgeous Sarah Venable.

Moira and I had found, as is so often the case, that the magic of our on tour relationship had dwindled, mutually – although we were still good friends. She was disappointed when her audition in London hadn't led to her playing *Maddie* in the Arts Theatre production of *Dirty Linen*, but, resilient and always a pragmatist, she went out and looked for work elsewhere.

Ed Berman had intended to take Tom Stoppard's new play, *Dogg's Hamlet, Cahoot's Macbeth* – which he considered a major work – to the States, with an American play to balance it; but to his frustration, nothing from the US had presented itself, and for want of anything else, he decided to take *Dirty Linen* as well, which suited me as I knew the play inside out by then.

Dogg's Hamlet, Cahoot's Macbeth is in fact a pair of interlinked plays, as complex as anything Stoppard has written – based he explained to me, on a section of the philosopher Wittgenstein's investigations into language. It was not easy to watch or to play (though, with his acid wit, Stoppard had named my character *Easy*). On the page, parts of it seem almost incomprehensible, but with the kind of direction Ed Berman was able to bring to it, it did work. Stoppard, who is a perfectionist, never really believed he'd got it right and privately considered it an unfinished work.

I enjoyed the challenge of rehearsing these difficult plays, all hours every day, but I admit to having been distracted from the job on May 12th, when my team, Arsenal, was playing Manchester United in the FA Cup Final. It was showing on a TV in a room adjacent to the Interaction rehearsal area, and I couldn't tear myself away from it. Ed Berman clearly didn't understand the significance of the event, and called me back into the rehearsal.

'Challis,' he said, 'we are rehearsing a major work by one of the world's greatest playwrights, but obviously there are more important things in your goddam life at this moment. Get outta here and come back when it's over!'

I did, like a shot. Arsenal led 2-0 and were cruising, but in the 86th and 88th minute, Manchester United scored two lucky goals to equalise. Three minutes later, and a minute before Full Time, Alan Sunderland popped one in, to win the game for the Gunners, 3-2.

'To hell with Hamlet, Macbeth and Stoppard!' I whooped. 'We've won the Cup!'

It was only then that I realised the referee was called Ron Challis,

Tom Stoppard seated fourth from left with Ed Berman third from left. In Grosvenor Square sitting on a bouncy castle which represented Elsinore - we were playing in *Dogg's Hamlet*, *Cahoot's Macbeth* on tour in England and afterwards in the USA

Left to right:
Alison Fraser, David Hall and Sarah Venable

South Africa 1972. Hair and shirt epitomise the era.
I even fancy myself! No seriously, with that nose?

The Arsenal Supporter.
Just what you need on the
terraces at The Emirates -
it seemed to be more fun
in those days.

McTeazle in Tom Stoppard's *Dirty Linen* with Sarah
Venable, the object of my affection, as Maddie Gotobed
- Somewhere on tour

With Moira down at The Orange Tree in Richmond 1978, rehearsing *Cut the Grass*. Moira later married the Actor and musician Mervyn Stutter with whom I worked many years later on his own radio series *Forty Love, New Balls Please* and *Getting Nowhere Fast* and I met up again with Moira.

With Julie Goodyear as Bet Lynch and me as Detective Sergeant Somebody or other in *Coronation Street* in 1975. I think the '70s were quite stylish, certainly in my case I was better dressed on screen than off. Picture courtesy of ITV Photo library.

My favourite picture of me and the Director Douglas Canfield. We worked together on *Dr. Who* and *The Seeds of Doom*. One of the only Directors who ever employed me twice.

DOCTOR WHO

AND THE SEEDS OF DOOM

PHILIP HINCHCLIFFE

Book cover from *Doctor Who and The Seeds of Doom*.
Courtesy of Chris Achilleos

Scorby in *Dr. Who and The Seeds of Doom*. Wrestling with Liz
Sladen over the gun that never fired. Liz had a resurgence
in *The Adventures of Sarah Jane* thirty years later. She is sadly
missed. Picture courtesy of BBC Photo Library

With Caroline Dawson and The Prune in Brighton. I never did manage to turn Caroline onto football or any other sport come to that. The Prune looks a little doubtful about being forced to sit on an elephant.

Brighton 1979. Me Puzzling about how one actually felt
about these momentous questions.

Slater! Looking suitably serious and
sympathetic after my break up with
Sabina.

Publicity Shot!
Just who did I think I was
trying to be? Probably had
no one to sew buttons on
to the shirt.

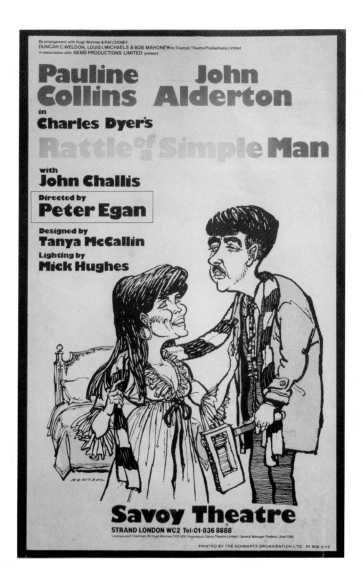

Pauline Collins   John Alderton

in

Charles Dyer's

Rattle of a Simple Man

with

John Challis

Directed by

Peter Egan

Designed by

Tanya McCallin

Lighting by

Mick Hughes

Savoy Theatre

STRAND LONDON WC2 Tel: 01-836 8888

Licensee and Chairman: Sir Hugh Wontner CVO GBE Proprietors: Savoy Theatres Limited General Manager Frederic Lloyd OBE

With the Alderton Brothers. My name on the poster for *Rattle for a Simple Man* at the Savoy. Directed by Peter Egan whose wife Myra Francis, introduced me to my present wife Carol!!

This was the show that deflected me from going back to America and led to *Only Fools and Horses*

Only Fools and Horses in the Nag's Head. We always looked forward to the pub scenes – it was where the series really lived. Picture courtesy of BBC Photo Library

Only Fools and Horses – A losing Streak. We had to find out how to play poker – nobody knew which hand beat which. Picture courtesy of BBC Photo Library

DI Humphreys in *Citizen Smith*. The Boycie prototype
- with the best hair I ever had. Picture courtesy of BBC
Photo Library

which made me feel vicariously responsible for the win.

On the way home from rehearsal that evening, I stopped off for a beer in a pub I didn't know in West Hampstead. Standing in the bar was a man I dimly remembered from an old TV show I'd done.

'Hullo mate, how the devil are you?' I greeted him exuberantly, still high on my team's win.

'Not bad,' he said – a little gloomily, I thought.

'Come on, cheer up! We just won the cup! Isn't it great? What a game! I thought we'd blown it – but wow! Isn't it the best when it's so unexpected? What are you drinking?'

He was looking at me rather squiggly-eyed. 'Do you mind if I don't? I'm a Man U supporter.'

By the middle of '79, arrangements were all in hand for the US tour starting in September, and I was thrilled to be going on it, not least because it would allow me some respite from the difficulties of my tangled love life. Until I finally grew up, around the age of fifty, I always lived in mighty dread of a female's quivering upper lip, and this often led me to shirk telling it like it was to those with whom I had – always regretfully – fallen out of love.

Now that Sarah and I were going to the States together to grapple with *Dogg's Hamlet, Cahoot's Macbeth*, it seemed inevitable that what was left of my relationship with Moira would finally falter, or so I thought...

My first few days in Washington were extraordinary and life-changing for me. Apart from my two trips to South Africa, I hadn't travelled much, and never to the States. The intensity of being there was increased by my lifelong interest in American movies and, by extension, American culture. I suspect that most Brits – if they're honest – are a little overwhelmed by America when they first go there. It's hard to reconcile the familiarity, gleaned from TV and the movies, with the very great differences, as well as the sheer scale of everything, and the overwhelming evidence of abundant wealth.

To begin with I wandered around looking at the White House, the Lincoln Memorial and the Pentagon – all familiar images, but much more impressive in the flesh. I enjoyed watching the locals and the way they interacted with one another and dealt with foreigners, like me, for the most part with busy friendliness.

Being Boycie

It was in the esplanade in the middle of the Watergate Complex, next to the Kennedy Center and by the banks of the Potomac that I witnessed a strange scene that's stayed with me all my life. I'd stopped at a little open air café to have a beer and a sandwich. It was a warm sunny day, and I was musing on the extraordinary events that had taken place in these very buildings only seven years before and led to the downfall of President Nixon.

A few yards away, an old fellow sat at a table, tended by what I took to be a nurse – an efficient and solicitous black woman. As I watched, he picked up his glass of beer, leaned back his head, and, with the sun full on his smiling face, took a long draught. Abruptly, his head and torso fell forward on to the table, his glass fell to the ground and shattered. I could tell at once from his motionless upper body, flopped on the table, that he'd passed out; his nurse was instantly panic-stricken, and yelling for help from anyone.

'Oh my God! He's dead!' she shrieked.

And he surely was. I'd just witnessed the very last, evidently happy moments of an old man, before it took him a split second to die. It was an eerie, unsettling, but at the same time, reassuring image, which I've vividly retained ever since.

Generally, though, at this stage of the tour, I wasn't at my most receptive. Just before we'd left England, Sarah had told me that when we got to the States, she was going back to her husband – a scenario I hadn't remotely contemplated in the full throes of our affair in London.

Now it was hell seeing her every day, working with her in rehearsals, when we'd been sleeping together most nights in London, and all the while knowing she was going back to stay with her husband. My pride was bruised, and I badly missed her company.

To compensate, I was drinking too much. At the Kennedy Center where we were working, I'd identified a suitable companion in one of the local stagehands – an off-the-wall bin-case called Gary. He was a man who enjoyed excesses, and that just suited my mood. He drove around on a great hairy motorbike, and lived in a dangerously tatty houseboat on the Potomac. The vessel was well stocked with booze and dope, and a lot of my free time was spent there playing the guitar, rolling spliffs, and watching Gary shoot flies with a high-powered air rifle. He quite often hit them, but the iron walls of the boat were peppered with small dimples.

Sometimes a friend of his would come round. He was even nuttier and a Vietnam veteran. They would relax by throwing knives at each other, very occasionally failing to avoid the target, in a painful game of 'chicken'.

When rather self-indulgently I told Gary what had happened with Sarah, he was sympathetic. 'Shit man, you gotta have a woman!'

I nodded.

'Listen,' he said, wanting to help. 'You want a woman? I'll get you a woman. There's this great chick I know, Charlene, a Mountain girl, works in a restaurant downriver; she's good, real good. Knows what she's doing, know what I mean?'

I wasn't entirely clear what he meant, but I was missing female company just at that moment. I nodded slowly.

'Jest tell her Gary sent you,' he instructed.

When I found Charlene and told her Gary had sent me, I had the impression it wasn't the first time he'd done it. She was a good-looking girl, if a little too rustic in outlook for my taste; but she was fun, she was a woman, and I was feeling pretty bereft. We got together in a small way for the couple of weeks I was in DC.

I told Sarah about her; Sarah looked grumpy and demanded more details. As I couldn't think of any more details, I didn't volunteer any, and Sarah's eyes darkened. Very discreetly, within myself, I bucked up at the sight. Sarah, it seemed, hadn't completely jumped ship.

Ed Berman came over from London to see the show. The tour manager who'd rescued me from the zeal of immigration officials when we'd first landed must have told him about the problems I'd been having. He and Ed came looking for me.

'John, are you OK? Or are you drinking too much?'

The tour manager answered for me. 'Yeah, he probably is, but it's not affecting his performance.'

I thought that was loyal of him, because I knew he was worried about me; he was constantly telling me what I should be careful about while in the States. The way he put it, the whole country was full of drunks and hustlers, just waiting around to do me damage.

He certainly wouldn't have approved of my friendship with Gary. But, as it turned out, Gary was a big help in taking my mind off my troubles. I'd always been interested in the American Civil War and knew quite a lot about it, so it was great to be near so many scenes of action. When I told him I wanted to take a trip out to West Virginia and see some of the sights, Gary rustled up a friend who owned a great beast of a Pontiac Firebird, with a gas-guzzling 7.5 litre engine. With a couple of friends we took off for the Blue Ridge Mountains and the Shenandoah River, both significant in my own version of American mythology as the setting for some of my favourite James Stewart films.

Other more dangerous pursuits occurred to me, involving maybe white water and rednecks, but our tour manager vehemently advised against them. 'John, *John*, you just cannot do these things; that's too crazy. There are too many risks; too many folks out there ready to take advantage of you!'

He had very much taken me under his wing now, desperate not to lose a key cast member. But I still managed, soon afterwards, to find myself in the midst of a hurricane like I'd never seen before, where roofs were blown off and trees uprooted; that was exciting.

We were in Washington for little more than two weeks, but it had done a lot to prepare me for what was to come, although it turned out that Washington was tame compared with New York, where we went in October.

I was booked into an hotel of alarming scruffiness, up by Central Park. A faint aroma of dodgy drains hung around the place; the lift creaked as if it were about to collapse in a heap of brass and mahogany at the bottom of the shaft, and my room, which was furnished with faded, slightly grimy old world tat, looked out onto a sunless inner well cluttered with rusting fire escapes. My room also contained a small hotel of its own – a cardboard contraption labelled '*The Roach Motel – they check in, but they never check out!*'

I never did dare look to find out how those check-ins were going.

From the day the company arrived in *La Grande Pomme* there was a big buzz around the play. On the whole, audiences in New York are more sophisticated than in Washington, and Stoppard was a big name there. I responded happily to the dynamism of the place and the great vibes around the show. When New York takes you to its bosom, it does so with mighty bear hugs, and although I recognised a fair helping of bullshit about it, I reckoned I'd do well to make the most of it while it was on offer.

After our first performance in New York, we sat around for hours, drinking nervously in the Algonquin, the legendary arty hotel and bar, where Dorothy Parker had spent many days of her life hanging out, while stylishly slagging off her rivals with much-quoted bons mots. Stoppard and the whole company were there, waiting for the all-important newspaper critics' verdict on our show.

We'd had good reactions in DC; here the response was ecstatic.

My role, *Easy* the removal man, was quite complex, in that it was saying a great deal more than just the spoken lines suggested. I even earned a personal accolade from the all-powerful Clive Barnes, long-standing *New York Times'* theatre critic, a man capable of closing a show overnight if he gave it the thumbs-down.

It produced a tremendous rush in all of us to find that we were in a New York hit, albeit in a small theatre for a short run.

Stoppard's reaction was ambiguous. He confided in me that he was worried because his next play – *Night & Day* – was following hard on our heels into Washington soon, and he thought it a better play. It was more mainstream, but still clever, and had done very well in London with John Thaw and Diana Rigg. And he was sure it would succeed here, where *Dogg's Hamlet* was sort of getting in the way. This was disheartening for me, who thought I was involved in a minor triumph, while it became to clear to me that Stoppard felt he hadn't pulled it off with *Dogg's Hamlet*, and he was worried that it was just too inaccessible and thus might hamper *Night & Day*.

I pointed out the great reactions of the America audiences. After periodic discussions with him about it I came away with the impression that he didn't feel American reactions were necessarily reliable. It was as if he were worried that our show was doing *too* well.

As someone whose life was strongly driven by the enjoyment of female company, I found myself frankly confused by the quantity and quality surrounding me in New York.

Sarah Venable – back with her husband, sort of, but still around

– in some bizarre ploy had got me together with a friend of hers, a flaky blonde who was fun, sexy and quirky in a way that intrigued me. This had led to a short uncomplicated sort of relationship, while, hot on its heels, one of the Americans in the company, Davis Hall from Atlanta, Georgia, introduced me to his sister, Harriet. She was a good, intelligent actress with chestnut hair and striking, individual looks who attracted me strongly right from the start. She was a whacky woman, though, and heavily into Sufism, which I didn't understand at all, although I realised it was fashionable in New York at the time. She coexisted with her fellow Sufis in a kind of commune – although, as far as I could see, on her own terms – in an open floor of a warehouse above a happy-clappy Christian church. She'd appeared for a while in a big American soap, *Somerset*, but a rebellious streak in her had meant that she didn't react well to NBC and the producers telling her what to do as if they owned her. She refused to have her lovely mass of auburn curls cut off.

When it was clear that our show was the hottest in town – at least, among the intelligentsia – the cast were asked to parties every night. At one of these I felt myself almost suffocated by own tendency to want to be in love with every attractive woman I met.

It was a big party in someone's massive apartment not far from the theatre off Times Square. We'd come on from Sardi's, where we earned a bit of applause for the great notices we were getting.

The day before, Moira Downie had rung from London – from my flat, in fact, where she was still living – to say that she was coming over to New York to see what was going on, slightly as a result of my own guilty suggestion.

I told Sarah, who reacted succinctly. 'I don't give a flying fuck what she does!'

Sarah was at the party; her flaky friend, whom I'd spent a few evenings with, was there; so was Harriet, whom by then I'd fallen for completely.

I arrived there with Moira, and when I saw these other three women there too, I could only lie back on a sofa, close my eyes, grit my teeth and wonder what the hell I was going to do. Perhaps, I thought, castration was the answer...

They all knew about each other. Sarah's friend soon left with a toss of her head. Sarah was studiously ignoring me now (which made it harder to work with her). Harriet was looking confused and pissed off. Moira sensed at once that she had stepped into an already complicated set-up, and made up her mind to go back to England pretty quickly.

When I saw her in London the following year, she told me how she'd soon landed a part in a provincial tour of a then hardy perennial, *No Sex Please, We're British* – a ridiculous, critically panned farce that had become a massive hit. She'd had an affair with the star of the show, Robin Asquith, and when the tour came to an end, found herself a houseboat on the Thames, upriver from Richmond.

I'm glad to say that Moira and I worked together again, in great harmony, about twenty years later, on a radio comedy drama – *Getting Nowhere Fast*, which her husband, Mervyn Stutter had written.

While I was in New York I was determined to go and seek out some of the African-American music that I loved – the blues and jazz in their natural habitat. Within the first few days I snuck off to Harlem to see what I could find.

Getting off the subway at 125th Street, I wandered up past The Apollo, the venue for several great James Brown albums, and in and out of a few bars, looking for the kind of music I liked. I was very conscious of being, most of the time, the only white person around.

I didn't feel particularly threatened, and generally, if I wasn't ignored, I was greeted with friendliness. Nevertheless, I had a sort of feeling at the back of my neck that I might not be in the right place. I didn't want to feel this; since my trips to South Africa, I felt, somewhat naively that I'd met enough Africans for it not to be a problem here.

What seemed to interest most of the people I spoke to was my accent. It was remarkable to me how few Americans have ever really encountered an English accent – a lot evidently didn't watch English films or TV programmes, and only ten percent of the population even possessed a passport. I found that when I got talking, people gathered round as if I were an exhibit in a museum. I had a crack at my version of a Southern US accent, which just made them laugh. They were much more interested in cockney. I tried to explain all the great variations in accent and dialect that existed in the UK, how there were regions where I couldn't understand even half of what was being said. In a country like the US where regional variations are not so pronounced, they could hardly believe there was so much diversity in such a compact island as Britain.

Over a bowl of chilli and beans, I got to talk about music, but found for them it was such an integral part of life it wasn't so special. I danced with a couple of girls, which evoked more laughter, and one of the men took me off to another bar.

After a few more drinks, he showed me the way back to the subway and I headed downtown.

When I got back to my hotel, the tour manager's face paled.

'*Where* did you go?' he gasped. 'You shouldn't do this!'

'But why not?' I shrugged my shoulders. 'I'm fine.'

I was being a little disingenuous, but I'd guessed that, having gone down to Harlem without any desire to challenge anyone I met, the loclas had been prepared to accept me at face value.

After we'd opened, Tom Stoppard still wanted to change things and was endlessly tinkering with the script, wrestling with problems he perceived in the play; he seemed to think that the great New York notices were irrelevant.

My character, *Easy*, linked the two plays in a crucial way. Although I believe in general Stoppard preferred working with actors who didn't attempt to intellectualise and lay their own interpretations on characters, allowing him to act as puppeteer, in this case he seemed pleased with the way I'd handled my part. When we were rehearsing, I'd often come up with suggestions to achieve what he wanted – practical ideas mainly derived from my own longish career in rep and the ingenuity that often demands.

He was always grateful. 'Thank God you're in this show,' he said.

It was true to say that apart from the American leading man, there wasn't an overwhelming amount of talent in the company. 'You at least are completely in tune with what I'm trying to say, and the way I want to say it. Either I'm a Challissian playwright, or you're a Stoppardian actor.' He said it with his most enigmatic grin – half smile, half smirk.

I never completely understood him and I didn't believe that I could significantly provide the kind of help he was looking for. However, he appeared very glad of what I had done.

It was a strange period for me, brought on, I guess, by Stoppard's own uncertainties at the time. I think he already knew that *Night & Day* was going to lift his career and standing as a world-class playwright up several levels, and he was preparing for it.

After one of these rehearsal and tinkering sessions, he told me he needed somewhere to sit and think. Would I mind if he came back to my hotel room with me so that he could do that?

I thought of the rickety elevator, the smelly inside well, the Roach Motel; all my instincts were to say 'No', but he seemed to need this escape quite badly.

I agreed and we headed up uptown to the hotel.

When we got there, it was clear that he didn't want to talk; he dropped himself into one of the creaky old easy chairs and just sat, deep in thought, staring at the lank grimy curtains as if I weren't there.

He certainly didn't want to chat, while I sat there bursting with the urge to say something helpful and, if possible, profound.

Having been involved with Tom Stoppard now for over two years, I was accustomed to his way of doing things with quite unselfconscious quirkiness. But, if asked, he would give reasons for it. When I was playing in *Dirty Linen* at The Arts in London, he turned up once at a weekday matinée with barely half a houseful. I asked him why he had come to a performance that would inevitably be flatter than normal.

'Because the audience reaction won't get in the way of the script,' he said. 'Because actors will play up to a busy, receptive audience, and I can't hear it so well.'

He was right, of course; all actors are to some extent whores who will play to the laughs. Nevertheless he certainly acknowledged actors who he believed interpreted him well.

When I'd come back from South Africa, having switched parts to accommodate the local talent in the *Dirty Linen* tour, and he'd written to thank me, he'd also asked me if I could come to Cambridge with him to help him with a lecture he was giving there. He had asked Jean Fergusson, a colleague from my stint in Harrogate, too. He was talking to the university about the development of his work, and wanted us to deliver passages from various of his plays to illustrate points he was making.

In November 1979, the Stoppard bandwagon rolled on to the Wilbur

Being Boycie

Theater in downtown Boston. It was a fine old theatre, not much changed in fifty years; even the dressing rooms had received no more than the odd lick of paint. I was glad of that when I found I'd been allocated the very room used by Marlon Brando thirty years before in the pre-Broadway run of *A Streetcar named Desire*. It seemed to me almost unbelievable that I should be sitting where the great Brando had sat, looking into the same tarnished dressing mirror, and leaning back to see the same cracked ceiling and cornices. As I responded to my call each evening, I left the room muttering, 'I coulda been a contender!'

For living quarters I was billeted in an hotel with all the hallmarks of cheapness situated, although I didn't know it, right on the edge of the red-light district. Harriet was back in New York and I was feeling a bit sorry for myself.

The first evening we were there, I thought I'd go out and get a little of the flavour of the city and drifted into one of those big circular bars that are part of Boston's Irish legacy.

Harriet's brother, Davis Hall, was with me, while I jokingly asked the barman where one found women in Boston.

'You want a woman?'

'Well, you know, just to meet, sort of bump into.'

The barman, unfamiliar with British circumlocution, gave me a knowing wink and went off to make a quick, muttered phone call from the back of the bar. I vaguely thought he might be ringing one of his regular female customers whom he knew to be unattached at the time.

He strolled back, looking smug. 'OK, I've got somebody coming to meet you; isn't that what you want?'

I wasn't sure quite what he meant, until a woman with short legs, very high heels, beehive hair and half a pound of make-up on her face made an entrance into the cavernous bar.

The barman greeted her with a nod in my direction and she walked over. I was feeling embarrassed now; this was not remotely what I wanted, and Harriet's brother was with me watching the whole pantomime as she walked up, waggling her arse and substantial breasts. As soon as she reached me she leaned up, kissed me on the lips and started chattering inanely in a way that demotes a grown male into a small boy who has expressed a desire for a cream doughnut.

'What'll you have to drink?' I invited her with, I thought, exemplary politeness.

The girl did a double take at my unfamiliar accent.

Davis Hall giggled. He thought I'd *meant* to order a hooker.

I shuffled from foot to foot, answering her small talk in monosyllables, until, with more frequent glances at her Liberace watch, she sensed that a deal was not in the offing and excused herself with a trip to the 'powder room' – never to be seen again.

The show did well enough in Boston, though we didn't get the eagerness of the New York audiences. We expected better on the final leg of our tour in the altogether more reflective ambience of San Francisco.

I knew I was going to like San Francisco, but not as much as I found I did. The laid-back, unfettered charm of the city enchanted me and I naturally warmed to the place.

My always complex love life was confused by the distance between Sarah Venable, here in San Francisco, and her husband, left behind in New York. For the last two months, Sarah had moved herself to the sidelines of my life, occasionally firing a warning shot across my bow to remind me of her prior claim. I hadn't stopped admiring her free spirit, nor had I forgotten the depth of our visceral relationship back in London; but when Sarah had told me it was over, Harriet had moved into the space she'd left. I hadn't the strength – some might say the sense of honour – required to fight off the temptation to see Sarah again. Besides I didn't want to be a source of hurt to her, and for a brief period, our affair resumed.

From the secure place where I am now, I can ask, why did I do these things? Why, when a few moments' reflection would have told me I was going to cause more hurt by reviving a semi-terminated relationship, didn't I walk away from it? These dilemmas had become a recurrent feature of my life, and I seemed to have no strategy for dealing with them.

While I wasn't occupied evading these issues, in the three weeks we were there I had time to get to know San Francisco. I would wander around observing people, marvelling, as ever at the astonishing array of humanity on offer in this cosmopolitan city. By day I'd take buses and little cable cars that climbed halfway to where the stars would have been at night. On one trip, a man dropped into a seat in front of me, looking very respectable, with a neat haircut and glasses, conventional in every way – except for the pair of large bear's ears with which he had supplemented his own. Why was he doing this? No one paid the slightest attention to him, besides me.

Down by the waterfront I found a human jukebox, a large oblong cardboard box painted appropriately with buttons and knobs which one could press for a tune. A bored, hollow voice from inside would say, 'Yeah? What do you wanna hear?'

'Could I have *Good Vibrations*?'

'Sure.'

After a pause and a big intake of breath from inside the box, followed a top-notch slightly muffled performance of the Beach Boys classic, played on the trumpet. Delighted, I tried a few more. It seemed he could play anything I threw at him; I thought about exporting him to London.

At night, after our show, I liked to trawl the bars and clubs for the best music. One night I found myself with one of the Americans in the cast in a Tiffany shaded joint somewhere near Polk Street. I was sitting up at the bar – always the best vantage point from which to launch a conversation – when a fairly deranged-looking woman lurched in and slumped on a stool between us. She seemed to want to engage us in some kind of incoherent conversation. I offered her a drink, which she accepted eagerly, then, seeing some dice and a dice box on the bar, challenged me with wild eyes. 'I wanna play dice.'

She won a few throws, hurling back the bourbon I'd bought her, and became more deranged. I won a throw, and she started getting scratchy.

'You fuckin' Limey bastard,' she snarled. 'You've got no fuckin' balls! You think you're so fuckin' great coming over here, thinking it used to be your fuckin' country.'

I lifted an eyebrow like Gregory Peck and won another throw. 'Aha,' I said. 'Look at that – good old England, we win again!'

She leaned towards me. I thought, Christ, she's going to kiss me! Instead, she bit my right ear – very hard indeed.

I felt a warm trickle down the side of my neck, but it was too dark to see clearly what she'd done.

The barman came round to deal with her. 'Hey, come on! Get outta here,' he said and aimed her out of the bar through a pair of swing doors.

He was apologetic. 'Gee, I'm sorry about that. She used to come in here a lot, but she's just got out of jail.'

'God, what was she there for?' I asked.

'You know, drugs and shit...'

I somehow got back to my hotel and went to bed; I woke with my pillow soaked in blood. When I met Sarah in the morning, she gasped and insisted that I go and see a doctor. She booked me into the nearest specialist, and I shot off in a cab, praying on the way that it wouldn't cost too much.

The doc took one look. 'My God, why didn't you come to me last night?'

He told me that a bite on the ear by a human being was one of the most dangerous bites that one could suffer, second only to a bite from a chimpanzee. How did they know? I wondered. How many people get bitten by chimps?

He showed me pictures of people who'd had ears bitten and come in too late. I had to stifle a gasp. There were great cauliflower aural extensions, impossibly distorted lugholes – the ugliest I'd ever seen.

'You're an actor; this is the last thing you need.'

While I panicked, he stitched up the ear, dressed it and gave me some lotions. 'That should be OK.'

I wasn't so sure.

A few days later, though, the ear was healing nicely – no sign of a cauliflower. I arrived back at my hotel in a cab and, just as I was walking up the steps and the cab was disappearing round the corner, I realised I'd left my wallet inside it. Everything, every document vital to existence in America was in that wallet, and I had no idea how to identify the cab or its driver. All I could remember was that the driver spoke English with a strong French accent, because we'd talked about being an alien in the States.

For practical purposes, the bottom had fallen out of my world, and I was due to leave in a couple of days!

Without much hope, I went desperately round every cab company I could find in the phone book to ask if they had any French-speaking drivers. Most of them had one or two but had no way of identifying the cab I'd been in.

But the gods were smiling. Next day, there was a note waiting for me at my hotel, telling me that if I had lost something, I should ring a certain number.

I pounced on the phone and made the call. After I'd described what I'd lost, a woman told me someone would meet me with the wallet at the theatre before that night's show. I was massively relieved, but wondering how much she would sting me for her trouble.

I recognised the driver when he turned up at the stage door, bringing my wallet and everything that should have been in it.

He had, he said, discovered my identity and my address when he found my doctor's appointment card. There was nothing else there that could have led him to me. I tried to give him a $50 bill, but he wouldn't take it.

'Listen, you saved my bloody life!' I said, hurling the note into the back of his vehicle.

He drove off, happy enough.

And I thanked God that the dopy woman had bitten me.

I'd never have got the stuff back otherwise.

I flew out next day, singing to myself, *'I left my ear... in San Francisco.'*

The tour had ended in San Francisco, and I was confronted with the need to make a decision. I wanted to see Harriet again; I'd been in touch with her regularly while I'd been on the West Coast. I also did not want to go back to London, where there was nothing very much waiting for me. I was beginning to think, in that paranoid, actors' way, that my agent had completely forgotten my existence.

By happy chance, she rang me just as I was thinking how much I didn't want to go back and witness my parents' seasonal infighting. I asked her what she was doing for Christmas.

She was, she said, planning to stay with her parents in Des Plaines, on the outskirts of Chicago. Her brother, my friend and colleague, Davis, would be there too

'Why don't you come and spend Christmas with our family?' she suggested.

It was a brilliant idea. I agreed at once.

Reluctant Homecoming

Christmas 1979 in Chicago was a great experience. It was wonderful to spend it with Harriet, whom I loved, Davis who had become a good friend, and their easy, down-home parents. Chicago was exciting, too, even with the icy winds blowing through the famous skyscrapers on the shores of Lake Michigan. There was glamour, dynamism and a lingering air of the lawless days of Al Capone about the place – and the big, bold skyline that confidently challenged New York.

Mr Hall, not the least bit theatrical, was a big, bluff Irish American, who, once he knew of my love for British football, was determined to tell me all he could about the American game. I sat glued to the TV with him, fascinated as he told me all about the 'Rush', the 'Blitz' and the 'wide receivers', as well at the joyous splendour of the great running backs.

He was a very likeable old fella, who called me 'Good buddy' – tremendously heartening in an alien land – and I was very happy to sit and listen while he told me why the Chicago Bears were really the premier team in the US.

When the holiday was over, I went back to New York. Without planning it, and without much choice, I found myself back in Harriet's weird set-up on East 14th, where she and her Sufi chums drifted in and out of each other's lives and space, and the happy-clappy guys in the ground floor were still at it. She continued to possess a bizarre and, to English eyes, unfathomable blend of religious mysticism and carnal lust. However, although the Sufism was beyond me, I had no problem with the lust aspect. Regrettably, no amount of physical love was going to change the fact that I was broke, and even if Harriet had been much richer, I wouldn't have taken any support from her.

Being in New York now was strikingly different from the first time round, when *Dogg's Hamlet* had been doing a good tour. As a piece of fairly arcane British drama, it had attracted plenty of attention among Manhattan's self-proclaimed intellectuals and their followers. Actually being part of it meant I'd been touched with the same ephemeral glory.

Having been feted to the heights at the time, now I had to learn the harsh but essential truth that in the States (far more than in Britain), if you'd been up and then made the mistake of coming down, they didn't forgive you – not, at least, until you were up again. Now I was in no show, and no more than a very skint, out of work (actually, *legally unable* to work) actor with pretensions to being a playwright.

As often happens when you have absolutely nothing, you start dreaming the impossible dream – in my case a quite banal impossible dream, like buying a Red Pontiac Transam and heading across the US by road (taking in Route 66 on the way) with the lovely, scatty, sunset-haired Harriet by my side by day, and in my bed by night.

This was never going to happen, and I also had more practical dreams, like marrying Harriet and getting a green card in the process.

In the meantime, in between doing the odd illicit voice-over, I touted around my South African play – now known as *Cut the Grass* for short. There was some interest in it.

'I like it,' people would say, 'but I can't quite see it working here – not just at the moment, you know, with everything else going on. But, listen, I'll get back to you.'

I found that Americans seemed to promise a lot when first you met them; they issued lavish and apparently heartfelt invitations for you to visit their homes, but when you called to take them up on it they were busy. However, with one good Clive Barnes crit to my name, others would make encouraging noises about my acting. 'You could do OK in LA; you're quirky – that's good.' But no one came up with any mouth-watering offers. Despite the obvious bleakness of my position, I lulled myself into believing that if I only waited, I was sure to catch a good tide sooner or later.

Inevitably, I kept running out of money. In England, the monthly mortgage payments on my flat came round relentlessly, and I'd neglected to rent the place out to cover it – because I'd only planned to go to the States for a ten-week Stoppard tour. But I wasn't prepared to give up yet. Even Sarah Venable reappeared, and reiterated the view that I should move to LA, where she was sure I'd find work.

But I didn't want to leave New York. That would feel like giving up, so I hung on there, partly to go on pursuing the unrealistic aim of wangling a green card and partly to bring some kind of conclusion (or at least order) to my confused love life. Neither of these was a turn-on for the local glitterati, and the party tickets that had been flooding in only a month or two before all dried up.

I'd been in New York for all of January, making no headway as an actor or a playwright, and was close to penury when I had a phone call from Marina Martin, my agent in London. This was the call about a small but good part in an episode of John Sullivan's *Citizen Smith*, the BBC sitcom that had launched Robert Lindsay's career as *Wolfie Smith*. I knew it had been running since 1977, was well established and now into its fourth series.

I dithered. I didn't want to leave the States yet, not while there were still a few vague promises hanging in the air. And Harriet didn't want me to go; she assumed – quite wrongly, as it happened – that I wanted some space between us for a bit, that the Sufism had finally got the better of me.

After a couple of days' agonising, I called Marina and said I'd come back to London.

My character, *Det. Ins. Humphreys*, only makes a couple of appearances in the episode *The Letter of the Law*, but they're key to the plot, which, like most Sullivan plots, was pretty convoluted. *Humphreys* is in the bar of *Wolfie's* local, chatting to *Ronnie Lynch*, a known local villain and friend of *Wolfie's*. *Wolfie* comes in and sees them. He doesn't know *Humphreys* and beckons *Ronnie* over. Not too discreetly, he tells *Ronnie* he knows where he can put his hands on a load of pocket calculators, for very little. He doesn't need to tell him they've been nicked. 'D'you know anyone who'd take 'em?'

Ronnie thinks he'll have a bit of fun, and indicating *Humphreys*, he says, 'I've got just the bloke for you!'

He tells *Humphreys* to join them. 'Wolfie, this is Colin...'

Humphreys nods meaningfully, 'Pocket calculators?'

Wolfie's straight on the case. 'Listen, Colin, I've got this great deal – a whole bunch of pocket calculators going very cheap.'

Ronnie goes on. 'Wolfie, this is *Detective Inspector* Colin Humphreys.'

Wolfie jumps back. '*What*?'

Humphreys raises a supercilious eyebrow. 'You were saying?'
'Saying what?'
'Something about calculators going cheap.'
'Oh yeh, that! Down at Woolworths. They're flogging 'em cheap.
You got to get there early, mind.'

It turns out that *Humphreys* has recorded the whole thing, and it all comes out in court when *Ronnie Lynch* is being tried for something else.

Once I'd read the script a couple of times, I thought I could do worse than base *Humphreys* on Gordon Macintosh, the supercilious drinking acquaintance of mine who had fallen in love with Beth Owen. I'd spent many hours – far too many – with him in the bar of the St Margaret's Hotel in Twickenham, where he would pontificate relentlessly to a generally docile audience. He was usually dressed in a drab suit of faintly stained eau-de-nil, a grey-white shirt, a grimy fake regimental tie and a pair of worn-out but well-polished black brogues. He always had on a lead beside him a small grubby dog of unfathomable parentage. He gave the impression that he thought he was pretty smart, when in fact he was a kind of Walter Mitty whose fantasies were blindingly obvious to anyone listening to them. But he expressed himself with such absurd self-importance that it was clear he believed his own bullshit, and as a result was very hard to discourage. Whatever topic cropped up in the bar – the history of the Balkan Wars, the life cycle of the Great Crested newt, the prospects of the Richmond Heavies rugby team, or even, once, the details of Margaret Thatcher's love life – he always insisted he knew more than the other (admittedly not always well-informed) regulars, and would drone on at all of them, brushing aside any suggestion of alternative views. He always sounded plausible and might even have been right, for all we knew.

He also liked to make highly improbable claims about his past, which I deliberately encouraged, without letting on that no one believed a word of them. However, somewhere along the way, he'd learned the value of hugging a mystery to himself, and when asked what he did for a living, his eyes would narrow as he touched the side of his nose and say, 'I can't really talk about it because a lot of what I do is *very 'ush-'ush*. Suffice it to say it is in the field of electronics.' I discovered later that he'd been a traveller for an electrical equipment wholesaler.

He turned out to be one of those people who feature in one's life for a year or two on the grounds of a shared watering hole, never to appear again. Nevertheless, although I've no idea what happened to him, I've always been grateful to him for providing the mould for *DI Humphreys*.

It was fun playing *Humphreys*, and a challenge to get the nuances right; I enjoyed the few days' work. I felt that the character had worked well, and Ray Butt, the producer, was certainly pleased with him. After the shoot, Johnny Sullivan, who'd written it, came over to congratulate me.

'I really liked your Humphreys,' he said. 'I'll find another part for him somewhere – just you wait.'

Oh, yeah? I thought. *I've heard that before.*

After the *Citizen Smith* job, I was planning to sell my flat and get straight back to New York in order to push on with my campaign to be allowed to work there, but before I left I had a few things to sort out, like earning some money to pay for the return journey. Strangely, the person to help me most was my former girlfriend and co-habitant, Beth Owen. Since she'd gone on and found her own feet, with a lot of tenacity and grit, and using all the knowledge of the trade she'd gained over the past fifteen years, she set up an agency for voice-over artists with Hywel Bennett, called *Talkies*.

Now up and running and totally revitalised (and without me to drag her down), she'd made a great success of it, right from the start of a big boom in voice work. Determined to refill the coffers, I found myself very busy – in a good week almost running from studio to studio to voice advertisements, trailers, anything where experience and a little versatility mattered. In the same week I could be the voice of *Mintos,* the white hot mints in the blue wrappers, or of Sony, or Pizza Hut. I could be *Head Germ* for Domestos, or the voice behind Henry Winterman's cigars. Working for Nick Angell at Angell Sound, we would often find ourselves confronted by dodgy scripts which just didn't work, and we would have to go in and sort them out – never getting a writer's fee, I might add.

This was a period of rich pickings for v/o artistes; there were nothing like so many chasing the same jobs as there are now, and it was a sellers' market. Once I earned £15,000 for saying two words

– 'Top floor' – for an actor who was delivering pizzas, but couldn't say 'Top floor' with sufficient authority.

While this was going on, another TV job came in – the first of a series of *Play for Today* called *Number on End* – and I was offered a part in a stage production of Charles Dyer's *Rattle of a Simple Man*.

I couldn't make up my mind what to do. With a tour and a residency at The Savoy, the play would have a longish run, and I'd already been away from the States longer than I'd planned. While I was dithering I had a letter from Harriet – a *Dear John* letter, so to speak – telling me she was sorry I'd left, but now she'd found someone else.

I was surprised how much it affected me. My relationship with her, though volatile and, perhaps built on shifting sand, had been very exciting and inspiring. I was confused and disappointed that it had just petered out this way.

However, Harriet's letter at least had the effect of making me decide to take the part in *Rattle* and the TV play.

The episode of *Citizen Smith* with my Gordon Macintosh-inspired *DI Humphreys* was broadcast in June. I was pleased with the character I'd created for the part, and wondered if anything would come of John Sullivan's promise to use him again. At the time, I was working on the TV play, *Number on End*. This was directed by Douglas Camfield, whom I'd got to know and like very much while we were doing the *Doctor Who, Seeds of Doom* series four years before.

Around then, I'd been voicing an ad in which I'd featured as *DrainClear Repair Man*, a superhero with specialist skills in the field of waste-pipe blockage. I was on my way out of the studios when I met Debbie Arnold coming in – a brilliant little brown-eyed blonde who immediately caught my eye. It turned out she was with Beth's agency, *Talkies*, as well, which led to us often working side by side.

She was just twenty-three, fizzing with confidence and already a trouper. At the age of seventeen she'd appeared as Marilyn Monroe in the TV impersonators' show, *Who Do You Do?* I'd never known anyone quite like her, and although I was fifteen years older, I couldn't help being impressed and entranced. She was bold and brassy, a Geordie from a variety theatre background, and brimming with Jewish chutzpah. Her mother, Mary, was a successful agent for variety acts, including Debbie's dad, Eddie Arnold.

Eddie, born Maurice Koffer, had died young, before I'd met Debbie. He had been a well-known impressionist who specialised in American stars and hosted the London Palladium's *Show Time* in the late 1960s. The family were from Sunderland but had come south to seek their fortunes. Debbie and her mother then lived off the Edgware Road in a swish flat, crammed with bling and photos of variety stars, where they led a much racier life than I was used to.

As part of her career development, Debbie made herself a successful groupie – and was even a girlfriend of David Bowie's, to the extent that he would ask her to go and check out venues he was due to play for security and ease of access. As a result she'd become amazingly confident at blagging her way into anything, and was friends with a gang of unruly actors and fringe variety performers whose idea of fun was drinking and playing uncomfortable pranks on other people. It was a world I didn't know until she took me along to meet them at Morton's in Berkeley Square, and the Stork Club – a slightly dodgy milieu with a whiff of danger to it which intrigued and appalled me at the same time. It was obvious that a lot of the men fancied Debbie because she was so zesty, funny and sexy, with a lot of front.

And it didn't take much to make me fall for all that front. Debbie was great to be around, and her colossal confidence seemed to make up for my own lack of it. She was also a lovely warm physical woman, with absolutely no need of the alarming rock-like breast 'enhancements' that I'd encountered in an affair a few years before.

The only obvious downside to being with Debbie was that it took me a while to adjust (and I never entirely did) to some of the people she liked to mingle with. There was always a group of good-looking girls, who could have been described as 'Mayfair Mercenaries', hanging around with the actors, and accepting extravagant 'presents' from the Arabs who'd started to come over to play in London. Despite their apparent sophistication, these girls' function was fairly obvious, though Debbie herself was ambitious in a different way; she had great ideas of what she wanted to do and, I came to realise, was already grooming herself for stardom.

I rather envied her certainty, but she hadn't much idea of the straight side of the theatre. I thought I could help her by introducing her to the serious end, and I encouraged her to go after better quality jobs.

Since I was a kid I'd loved the countryside and English landscape, but I could never persuade her to come on long walks in the country with me, or talk about the history and beauty to be found there. She was never entirely comfortable out of London – an urban girl in high heels and leopard-skin leggings – but she did try to respond to a more sophisticated approach to the theatre.

In general, her world was a real eye-opener for me. So was the way she was able to make the most of every celebrity encounter by putting on a show of chutzpah that was hard to ignore, and sometimes thrust her and me (often against my better judgment) into uncomfortable positions.

In August we started rehearsals for *Rattle of a Simple Man*. First produced in 1962, it was a three-hander with the very popular Pauline Collins and John Alderton – as tightly bound a theatrical couple as you could find. Married for over ten years by then, they'd appeared in innumerable shows and TV dramas together, and both had made their names in the massively successful 1971 TV series, *Upstairs Downstairs*, and then eight years later, in their own spin-off show, *Thomas and Sarah*. I'd first come across John in Bill Norton's, *All in Good Time*, and I'd seen then what a good comedy character actor he was. Married in 1969, he and Pauline had worked together dozens of times and had made themselves a pretty formidable double act.

The play opened in August at the Theatre Royal, Windsor, where I'd spent so much time hanging around in the late '60s, when my then wife Carol Robertson had been working there. After a short tour, on September 17th we opened at The Savoy. It was good to be in a beautiful London theatre, in a good play and a pivotal part. I played *Ricard*, the brother of a prostitute who has come back to remonstrate angrily with his sister, *Cyrenne*, in the end causing her to search for redemption and a change in her way of life. I guess it was inevitable that I felt a little excluded being in a three-hander with Pauline and John, who were so much involved with one another – the Alderton Brothers I used to call them. Pauline was lovely, but John by then was quite aware of his own standing, and didn't let you forget it, making sure you hadn't missed his latest car or pointing out the more obvious trappings of his success. The only other people in the company were two understudies, and to be fair to John, while we were touring he would often take us all out to dinner.

We worked well enough together, and despite some obvious weaknesses in the play's construction, our production had some good reviews. *Punch* said it was 'all a bit slow, though, admittedly, the play perks up a bit when *Ricard* appears'.

I'd kept in touch with my old friend, BBC sports producer Chris Lewis, since we'd shared a house in Kew, and we still met up now and again for a drink at the St Margaret's Hotel. Through him I came across Dennis Waterman, who was a friend of his. Dennis was a very keen footballer (and Chelsea supporter) who ran a team of his own. One weekend Chris persuaded me to come along and give a commentary on a big charity match Dennis had organised. Chris thought it would add a bit of fluffy blonde glamour to the occasion if I brought Debbie along to kick the game off.

Somehow the gig got out of hand, I seemed to end up on the wrong side of Dennis and there were a couple of ugly moments. In the Turk's Head in East Twickenham after the game, he spoke to a friend of mine while I was out of the bar. It seemed that he still felt vindictive towards me because I'd had a short but exciting affair with Penny Dixon, when I'd worked with her at the Chesterfield rep, before she'd even met Dennis or become his first wife. It didn't make much sense, and besides, he'd divorced Penny five years before anyway.

The truth was that Dennis was on a great high at the time; he'd made a big name for himself on *Minder*, as well as having a hit with the theme song, which his wife had co-written and he'd sung. He wasn't the easiest of people and it suited him to surround himself with a gang of quite dodgy characters who found their pleasure in drinking like whales, teasing and bullying any easy targets who swam across their path. Dennis was currently touring a big concert, and now Debbie had met him, she latched on to him, determined that we should go to one of the shows and get backstage.

Being Boycie

So we went, of course, and next to us in the audience was *Duran Duran* drummer, Nick Rhodes, whom Debbie seemed to have come across. After the show, she easily wangled her way into Dennis's entourage with me. She still didn't really know him, though, and he didn't look at all pleased to see us.

This kind of thing happened a lot with Debbie; she was young, easily impressed and more interested in celebrity than talent, and loved the flamboyant, noisy folk we came across – Jim Davidson, Ken Huchinson, Lindy Benson, Nick Rhodes and (a young) Chris Tarrant; I didn't really feel I belonged in this crowd. Nevertheless, I'd always admired comics and stand-ups who can pitch themselves at an audience with nothing but their own script and a talent to captivate. They and their techniques fascinated me, and prompted me and Debbie to develop a kind of stand-up routine of our own.

Using what we thought were our complementary talents, she and I tried to rig up an act loosely inspired by a pair of great American comedy actors, George Burns and Gracie Allen. I'd always loved their style of laconic wordplay:

'Sorry I was late home last night, honey – I got held up.'

'Yeah, I heard you got held up all the way home.'

The act didn't last long. We tried it out at a charity gig, where it died on the spot, pole-axed by audience indifference. Nobody got it, nobody laughed – except Barry Cryer, who told me afterwards he thought if we really tightened it, we could have something. But Debbie's mother, Mary, never one of my premier fans, was faintly scathing. 'It was OK, but it's not an "act".' And this was her job. I admit, I was defeated, and I didn't persevere. I simply didn't possess the rhino hide needed to launch a new stand-up act.

A few months into our relationship, I sensed that Debbie was keen to see it through to the next phase, and was talking wistfully about our getting a bigger place, a house of our own.

Towards the end of 1980 I was still living in my flat in St Margaret's Road where, on the morning of 8th December, I turned on the radio, to hear them playing one of my favourite tracks, John Lennon's *Imagine*. I had to go out for an hour or so and when I came back I was surprised to hear they were still playing it.

I was puzzled, with a hint of suspicion, until it finished and the presenter started talking about the shooting that had taken place outside the Dakota Building in New York the evening before, when John Lennon had been shot dead.

I flopped onto the sofa, huddled up and wept. His music had been part of my life since 1963. He, more than the other Beatles, had been a permanent presence in the culture of my youth. When I'd met him he'd been charming and generous, and said he wanted me to be in the group's *Magical Mystery Tour*.

When I'd recovered slightly, I felt the same kind of impotent rage I'd felt after the IRA bombings of the mid-'70s; furious that the unhinged, maniacal tendencies of a few individuals could do so much harm. I felt like I did after I'd been sent home by Sam Walters from The Orange Tree rehearsals. And I did the same thing – I went straight to bed, and straight to sleep, as the only way to deal with my anger and frustration.

There was no particular moment when I decided to marry Debbie, but the subject had cropped up regularly towards the end of 1980. We'd joke about it and Debbie would say, 'If we did this, we could do that,' with the effect of easing one into a commitment without one realising it. I even found myself agreeing to visit a register office – just to see what was involved! And somehow, susceptible as I am to female suggestion, over Christmas (always a dangerous time) I found we were definitely making plans for a wedding. I sold my flat – scene of so many rumpuses, with Beth and then with Moira – and bought a house, a Victorian semi two streets away at 13, Alexandra Road, where Debbie and I would live.

I was attracted to Debbie, for sure, and loved her in a protective way; she had a good heart and I felt I might be able to help her to become an altogether superior kind of actress – like *Higgins* and *Eliza* in *My Fair Lady* – and perhaps a more circumspect sort of woman. By then I certainly felt responsible for her, though she was well able to manage her life in the way she wanted.

In any event, it seemed that somehow an unstoppable momentum had built up, pushing me with frightening inevitability towards a second unsuitable marriage, and I simply didn't know how to deal with it.

My own friends were bemused. Of course, they could see that Debbie was fun and attractive – but to *marry*? Her mother, Mary, was pretty suspicious, too; for one thing, I was a goy, and for another I already had one failed (if distant) marriage behind me. As our proposed wedding drew nearer, I grew more certain that I was making a mistake. But I've always hated causing awkwardness and hurting people – whether out of cowardice or gallantry I can't say – and despite being beset by strong feelings of doubt and guilt, I went through with it.

I was still appearing nightly in *Rattle of a Simple Man* at The Savoy when, on March 16th 1981, Debbie Arnold ('formerly known as Jeannette Deborah Koffer', it says on the certificate) and I were married at Richmond Register Office. It was a short, unconvincing ceremony, compared with all the Roman Catholic elaborations of my first marriage. It was followed by a reception which Debbie had arranged at an Italian restaurant in Sheen. The entertainment was provided by Toni Dalli, a sub-Mario Lanza crooner, accompanied by an old accordionist who could have walked straight off Montmartre. It was an eclectic gathering, with my parents, Debbie's family 'doon from Soonderland' and the Alderton Brothers, all rubbing shoulders.

The whole tenor of the event did nothing to quieten my misgivings. As I delivered an inept and frankly disingenuous wedding speech, I heard the continuous hiss of air rushing between my mother's teeth, while the crackle of tension between her and Mary Arnold was palpable; neither of them was happy and nor, absurdly, was I.

My father looked as if he were present under sufferance. As it happens, he looked as if he was suffering most of the time now. My mother told me he spent more time than usual staying on up at the office.The Department of Energy, for whom he worked, had rooms to put up people whose work had caused them to stay late. He had also routinely been arriving home late and drunk, and my mother told me she was beginning to feel something of a victim. He announced shortly after the wedding that he would be taking early retirement that summer.

Once the wedding was over, I did my best to settle into our marriage. I'd always been comfortable about moving from one environment to another, which perhaps is why I've always been happy acting – being in someone else's world – and I didn't have any great problem with married life as such. To begin with I thought maybe it would turn into something more real than it was feeling then.

At the same time, I needed to be with someone I admired, and I did at least admire Debbie for her obvious talent, and her sparkling good looks. She had inherited her father's ability to impersonate – had learned the techniques either through example, by osmosis or through her genes. She knew how to do a recognisable Marilyn Monroe or Jayne Mansfield, using all the raw drive she reckoned it took to be a star, while I continued to encourage her, no doubt with a little wishful thinking, to direct her talents in a more serious direction.

My own career, in a stop-start, feast-famine sort of way, had moved up several notches since Stoppard had approached me in The Orange Tree after the *Memorandum*, and the low point of 1976. The tour and West End run of *Rattle of a Simple Man* had gone well, and I'd even earned a couple of decent notices. The voice-overs were still coming in, and I had to admit – a little reluctantly – that returning to England had been the right thing to do (notwithstanding my continuing unease over my marriage, and sporadic memories of the whacky, carefree life I imagined I'd been leading in New York).

Less than a month after we were married, I was sitting in the drawing room of our house in sleepy Alexandra Road, moodily drinking coffee, wishing I felt happier now I was married and thinking about what I would do when *Rattle of a Simple Man* came to an end, as it shortly would. It had run for over six months, but although it was a good production, the play was evidently not strong enough to maintain the momentum needed to carry it on much longer.

The phone on the floor beside me rang. I answered, and perked up like one of Pavlov's dogs at the sound of my agent's voice. Marina Martin, who'd been handling me for the last year or so, seldom wasted time in ringing unless she had something useful to say, which meant that a month or two could go by without my hearing so much as a small white lie from her.

'I've got a nice little job for you. Remember that *Citizen Smith* job you did for Ray Butt and John Sullivan last year? They want you for a new show.'

I wondered what for; I hoped it wasn't another ruddy policeman.

Being Boycie

Citizen Smith had run for four series and finally come to an end the previous summer, having clearly established the duo's reputation and that of its lead, Robert Lindsay.

'It's called *Only Fools and Horses*,' Marina went on.

The title didn't mean a thing to me, although I recalled later that it had been used before for an episode of *Citizen Smith*. It was, I gathered, a cynical old cockney axiom suggesting that only half-wits or dumb animals would actually graft for a living.

I knew that Butt and Sullivan were good at their job; and Sullivan had promised me the previous year that if he could use my *Inspector Humphreys* again, he would.

Another copper, after all? I thought. Oh well – what the hell.

'I'll tell Ray to send you the script,' Marina was saying.

As soon as I'd torn the wrapping off the bundle of text that arrived and read the part they wanted me for, I was very happy; the character, *Boycie*, suggested a lot more scope than the copper I'd last done for them.

I was in just one scene in Episode Two of the first series. It was a short appearance, but from the start, I tried to make *Boycie* distinct from any other comedy character on British TV. Sullivan had written him, and I played him, a long way from the nation's most recent comedic car dealer, George Cole's inimitable *Arthur Daly*, who had launched some memorable phrases into the English consciousness – ''Er indoors', 'The world's your lobster'.

Sullivan had been careful in his drawing of *Boycie* not to rush to occupy that ground. In time I came to realise that I had to develop a persona that would make the most of the dry aphorisms Sullivan could put in his mouth. In his first outing, discussing the qualities of the car he'd bought for his 'bit on the side', *Boycie* pontificates, 'It's only Sebastian Coe and E-type Jags make me feel proud to be British these days.'

This is a deliberate counterpoint to *Del Boy's* equally distinctive (and even more inexplicable) misuse of French sayings – '*Son et Lumiere*, wouldn't you say?' expressing his admiration for something.

I enjoyed filming my scene. John Sullivan was such a fun-lover that David Jason, Nick Lyndhurst and I were having a great time and squeezing everything we could from it. The crew had been highly entertained by Nick's performance with a terrible tatty old rag-top Cortina they'd brought from *Boycie*. It was spewing smoke, roaring, banging and skidding wildly over an area of ground between a few rows of lock-up garages, made extra real by the fact that Nick in real life hadn't yet passed his driving test.

Although the opening episode wasn't due to be aired until the following September, the live audience reaction to the studio sequences had been terrific, and there was already a bit of a buzz about the show.

When Debbie asked me how the shoot had gone, I tried to curb my enthusiasm. Often shoots that look very funny at the time don't seem to work out that way on screen. Nevertheless, although nothing had been even hinted at about a second outing for *Boycie*, and I was cynical enough not to hold my breath, I did have some hope that it might lead to more. In the meantime, my episode wasn't due to be aired until the autumn, so I was just going to have to wait until then to see what the public thought of it.

Casting around for a new project, I'd heard about a new Stoppard play in the offing – his translation and reworking of Austrian playwright, Johann Nestroy's nineteenth century farce, *Einen Jux will er sich machen*. It had also been the source of Thornton Wilder's *The Matchmaker* and, from that, *Hello, Dolly!* Tom Stoppard, with his love of English at its most expressive, had titled his version *On the Razzle!* It was to be directed by Peter Wood at the National Theatre.

Having already worked in two Stoppard plays I was a big fan and I wanted very much to be in another, especially as *Night & Day* which had followed *Dogg's Hamlet* into new York had heaved Stoppard right onto the top tier of the world's dramatists.

I hadn't seen much of him for the last couple of years, but I still had his number and I thought that with the ideas we'd shared when we'd been in New York he wouldn't object if I gave him a ring.

'So, you'd like me to put in a word for you with Peter Wood about *On the Razzle*?'

'Well, no, not if you don't want to....' I protested as weakly as I decently could, not wanting to appear a brazen self-promoter.

'So you *don't* want me to put a word in for you then?' he asked.

I wanted to kick myself. 'Well, no, well, not exactly....' I blathered in a way I hoped he would understand to mean that I did want him to.

In any event, he did and I went to The National to see Peter Wood, whom I'd never met before.

Peter looked at me speculatively. 'Mmm. I've heard a lot about you; I've been told you're very versatile. The trouble is – I'm not sure I've got anything for you. Would you care to understudy anything?'

'I'd rather not.'

There were a couple of small but enjoyable parts unfilled.

'Would you consider playing these and understudy one other?'

'For an extra consideration,' I said.

'Oh.' Peter arched an eyebrow and turned to his assistants. 'I think he wants more money!'

I had my two small but enjoyable roles – *Hupfer, the tailor* and a rather slovenly old *Italian waiter*. Peter Wood said my *Hupfer* reminded him of 'the darker corners of Jack the Ripper's Whitechapel'. Sadly, though, I never did get to play my understudy part, that of the *Coachman* – a robustly enjoyable role which was being played for some complicated internal reason by Harold Innocent, a sweet man who had been promised a series of roles at The National but really wasn't butch enough for this one.

Stoppard, who was often at rehearsals, said to me once, 'You know, *you* really ought to be playing this part.'

I agreed, but there it was. In any case, it was a joyous, hilarious play to be in and I loved working at the National.

On the Razzle was launched at the Edinburgh Festival – which tends to produce fun-loving audiences – on September 1st 1981.

A week later, at 8.30 pm on September 8th, the catchy strains of the title song....

> *Stick a pony in me pocket,*
> *I'll fetch the suitcase from the van*

announced the first airing of *Only Fools and Horses* on BBC 1.

The thirty-minute episode, *Big Brother*, introduced three characters, *Del, Rodney* and *Grandad*. Just half an hour long, it was filmed largely in studio and had the look and feel of a small scale comedy drama where the characters were still feeling their way around each other. Nevertheless, the dialogue was robust and confident, and knew exactly where it was going; in addition, there was an obvious, strong chemistry between Nick Lyndhurst and David Jason.

With the characters now so firmly fixed in the public consciousness, it's impossible to consider anyone else playing the key roles. Nevertheless, it's rumoured that nobody wanted David Jason for *Del Boy* except the director, and even then he'd been third choice for the role. Ray and John had already tried to get Enn Reitel (long-faced, then little known but brilliant impressionist) for the part. Then he tried Jim Broadbent, but neither he nor Reitel could commit to a series of six at the time.

It's quite possible that either of them could have delivered Sullivan's fast, witty lines just as well as Jason. However, that's hypothetical now, and perhaps the physical contrast and the instant interaction between the two stars has been the key element in the success of the series. We'll never know otherwise.

The first episode attracted 9.2 million viewers – very respectable at the time – although it was almost completely ignored by the critics. In theory that shouldn't have mattered, and in the end it didn't much, as a large proportion of the audience were viewers who didn't rely on reviews to choose what they were going to watch.

John Sullivan had been a brewery worker when he saw a story in the *Sun* about Johnny Speight earning £1,000 an episode for writing *Till Death Us Do Part*. He showed a friend, who laughed. 'We're funny guys. We should do that.'

Sullivan looked for the quickest way into the television end of the BBC, and got a job as a scene shifter. He was told that on no account must he harass the stars. But he did, at every chance, and managed to show some of his writing to Ronnie Barker, who liked his ideas and encouraged him.

Sullivan moved into the job with no formal education and no training of any kind, but he was able to extract from his own memory vivid pictures of mates who tried, but never made it.

By the time he started work on *Only Fools*, he had written thirty episodes over four seasons of *Citizen Smith*, and some sketches (with writers like David Nobbs and Barry Cryer) for the *Two Ronnies*. Both Ronnies famously demanded very high standards.

Being Boycie

Sullivan started by basing his *Only Fools* characters on his own youthful friends who had the confidence and ambition to make something of themselves, but neither the education nor the nous to do it. However, they usually had an overwhelming self-belief. They were like an awful lot of ordinary guys going about their lives in the certainty that with just the tiniest helping of luck, they too could have become millionaires.

In the early series, Sullivan created the classic comedy trio of the old fool, the young fool and the fool in charge; but, as he said himself, it became a community rather than a mere family, with a Dickensian breadth to the dramatis personae in the later, bigger episodes.

The following week, as the *Razzle* tour hit the Bristol Hippodrome, *Boycie* made his debut TV appearance. I was quietly pleased with his all too brief appearance as one of Peckham's leading pre-used car dealers, but the viewing figures dropped to 6.1m and some witty BBC executive remarked that the show was doing about as well as *Trotters Independent Trading*. The head of comedy was heard to describe the figure as 'rather disastrous', though luckily, I didn't hear that until many years later; otherwise I'd have convinced myself it was all my fault.

As it was, and not just with hindsight, I felt that the cleverness of Sullivan's writing was obvious. It showed his ability to establish *Boycie's* personality in just a few lines, and I was confident the character had worked and wouldn't be just a one-off. The plot in *Go West, Young Man* had shown *Del Trotter's* principal defining characteristics and his relationship with the world around him, and I could see that my character would serve a very useful function as a 'role model' for *Del*. I guess, without realising it, I'd entered a new phase of my life and I was delighted, though not entirely surprised, that as *OFAH* ran on to a second, third and eventually seventh series, *Boycie's* appearances became increasingly regular. In the early days he's a tricky, sneering, unsympathetic sort of a chap, but he mellows as he ages.

Reluctant Homecoming

On September 22nd *On the Razzle* opened its major run at The Lyttleton. It was a relentless cavalcade of high and low Stoppardian wordplay. While some of his verbal gymnastics might have benefited from a little restraint, this piece represents Stoppard just having fun: no philosophy, no intellectual undercurrent, not even any literary references. The audience is kept laughing through two hours of shenanigans, mistaken identities, malapropisms and romances.

The play required a lot of controlled energy, prompting Stoppard to say, 'One false move and we could have a farce on our hands.'

We had a great cast, with Felicity Kendal playing *Christopher*, one of the young rakes. Dinsdale Landen was *Zangler*, with Ray Brooks, and the wonderful Michael Kitchen as *Melchior*.

Michael was going through a patch of vagueness and confusion at the time over his relationship with Joanna Lumley. He loved her, he said, but he didn't know how to deal with it. This confusion manifested itself in a strange indecisiveness. He came in one day having swapped his lovely elegant old Mercedes for a tinny little new BMW.

'Why on earth did you do that?' I asked, astonished.

He shook his head in bewilderment. 'I don't know.'

One evening he asked me back to his flat, where he told me that I was the first person he'd asked into his flat for years, and we talked over a bottle or two. I'd told him I was not a good person to advise over personal relationships. I was an expert only in how *not* to handle women!

I liked him, though, and maybe the talking helped. We became good friends for the length of the run of our play.

Joanna came to see the show one night when Debbie was there. I introduced them and Debbie couldn't resist telling her about the last time Joanna and I had met.

'My husband did a scene with you in the *New Avengers*,' she said, 'and he remembers looking right up your skirt.'

It was one of those excruciating moments when I would have liked the ground to swallow me up.

Less excruciating had been my experience as the hindquarters of a horse. Thomas Henty (Tommy Cooper's son) was usually the beast's back end, but he was off sick and I was asked to step in. It was a little cramped, like the machine I had to trundle around beneath Brewster Mason as the *Ghost of Hamlet's Father* fifteen years before in Stratford, only this time, I was being straddled by Felicity, which made it much more bearable. She, of course, was charming and funny about it and, considerate as she is, didn't kick me about too much. Peter Wood was so delighted with my horse's arse, he left a note in my pigeonhole at The National's stage door. 'Dear John, thank you for your *demi-cheval.*'

Peter won that year's Olivier and Society West End Theatre awards for *On the Razzle* – well-deserved icing on the *gateau*, I thought.

If six months was a long wait between making my first *Only Fools* and its airing on TV, I had a twenty year wait for my next piece of television acting to appear. I was booked to play a blind French soldier to one of my own great comedy heroes, Frankie Howerd, in a series called *Then Churchill Said To Me...* in which Frankie played Churchill's batman, and, like *Lurcio* in *Up Pompeii*, addressed the audience directly in a conspiratorial way.... 'Ooh dear! The war's not going well, no it's not!'

To my great disappointment, Frankie was not in a happy frame of mind. He found it very difficult adhering to a script, because, as a stand-up, he was such an instinctive ad-libber, and as a result, his timing went to pieces.

He would say morosely between takes, 'I always wanted to be an actor, you know.' And as he spoke the hall-mark floppy jaw and famous disgruntled moue would come into play, because that was how he really spoke. And, poor man, he wasn't too healthy at that stage, but every time he said, 'Ooh, I don't feel well!' we all laughed, even when we realised he was being serious.

Sadly, because of the war-time content, some sensitive soul in the Government deemed it unsuitable to go out while we were at war with the Argentineans over the Falklands. For some reason, after that, it wasn't released until 1993, a year after Frankie had died.

Boycie Stakes a Claim

In March 1982, Marina Martin called me to come in for *Boycie's* second appearance in *Only Fools and Horses*. I was chuffed. The viewing figures for the first series hadn't been terrific (at a time when satellite TV didn't exist). The Christmas special on 28th December attracted 7.5 million and the BBC, whose upper echelons are not populated by lovers of working-class culture, had been very low-key in their approach to promotion. Nevertheless there seemed to be a good groundswell of support from the audience, which was by no means exclusively working class. I also had a feeling that if *Boycie* appeared for a second time, he would become a more important player.

The episode I was booked for, the third of Series Two, was called *A Losing Streak*, in which *Del Boy* and *Boycie* cross swords for the first time. In a classic display of bravado, *Del*, who'd been out gambling the night before and lost £150, was now very short of wonga. His way out is to challenge the richest man he knows to a game of poker, to be staged in the Trotter flat in Mandela House. *Boycie* and *Trigger* (Roger Lloyd-Pack) turn up for the session, and as the evening wears on, *Boycie* cleans *Del* out of everything – all his money, the Trotter van, Grandad's cash, jewellery and a pocketful of loose change. Until, of course, *Del* manages to turn the tables on *Boycie's* cheating by cheating himself, and get it all back.

Production started on May 30th, and I loved working with Ray and John, David and Nick again, and meeting up with Roger Lloyd-Pack; they had developed into a great team, especially now the show had a bit of a track record. There was a tricky moment, though, when some of the piles of cash we'd been using, issued with great bureaucratic brouhaha by the BBC bean counters, had disappeared. Nobody could imagine who might have nicked it; theoretically it could have been anyone on the set.

After much shuffling and increasingly shifty sideways glances as we all wondered who'd done it, the cash was discovered on top of the shade of a lamp that had been drawn down over the game, then lifted out of our eye-line – big relief all round.

The whole episode was filmed in studio, so we had a live

audience throughout; from their response, I had the impression they remembered *Boycie* and were glad to see him again. It was the first time I'd worked on the show with a live audience, and after their unrestrained reaction I left the set that day knowing, with a bit of luck and good scheduling, this show had legs, and there would be more gigs in it for me. The episode aired at the beginning of November and drew around 7.5 million viewers.

A secondary but important result of making that episode was my meeting Tim Combe in the BBC Club afterwards. Tim was an ex-BBC producer who had recently formed a new theatrical agency with Carey Ellison. By a neat coincidence, Marina Martin had just pruned me from her agency, so I was happy to join the new firm, and they seemed happy to have me.

Shortly after I'd filmed the episode, one of my most loyal directors, Douglas Camfield, cast me as *Corporal Dupré* in his eight part TV drama, *Beau Geste*. I'd worked with him on *Dr Who, Seeds of Doom* in '76, and several other BBC dramas. Douglas was a massively resourceful and confidence-inspiring director whom I greatly admired. He had a reputation for pulling off the most impossible scenes, on time and under budget.

The legionnaires' fort for this production had been placed in a vast sandpit at Binnegar Heath, near Wareham in Dorset – a popular location with TV companies making desert stories. The problem was that when it rained, the ground took ages to drain and, as a desert it looked, frankly, unconvincing. On one occasion, Douglas had booked a group of stunt horse riders to race across the 'desert' and storm the fortress. He had been allocated them for just half a day, and the forecast wasn't good. I found him round the back of a dune, physically on his knees in the sand, crossing himself vigorously, like an Argie player after scoring a goal, while genuinely pleading with God for good weather – which, I'm glad to report, he got.

By this time, although Debbie and I were still trying to make our marriage work, an air of desperation had crept into the process and we hadn't found any of the spontaneity between us which I would have loved. Maybe I hadn't reckoned with her very powerful urge to succeed and to become a star. I've observed over the years that being a big star is about two things – a massive desire for stardom, coupled with an exceptional talent. Debbie had the massive desire, all right, and she had talent, for sure, but it wasn't unusual enough; and her urge for stardom was badly skewing the rest of her life. She suffered colossal disappointments when she got the breaks, and then found they hadn't moved her on.

She had also become more insistent about sex at key moments in the month. She was anxious to have children and was beginning to fret about the lack of result. Of course, I had some inkling of the powerful feminine urge to bring forth life, and the way it can completely take over a woman's psyche as the clock ticks. At the same time, I knew from the embarrassing operations on my testicles in my youth that they may not have been performing as fully as they should – despite my face-saving posturing at the time. However, I thought I couldn't have been totally dysfunctional in view of what had happened when I was twenty-one and working in Cambridge when Carmen, with whom I'd dallied a few months before, pitched up and told I was in serious danger of becoming a father. I'd given her what seemed like a whopping sum of money at the time (which was what she said would resolve the situation). I only saw her again briefly, once, when she turned up in Kew and acted as if that had never happened.

When Debbie finally announced that she was pregnant, I had mixed feelings; I already had serious doubts about the long-term prospects of our marriage, but I was also very relieved for her sake. I could only look on with sympathy as I watched her collapse with disappointment when she came back from a visit to her gynaecologist. He had told her she must have had an ectopic pregnancy, and the baby had gone.

Debbie, always a fighter, wasn't going to give up easily, and insisted on signing up both of us for an exhaustive series of fertility tests. When a final set of results arrived and I opened the letter in the drawing room at Alexandra Road, I felt like I'd stepped on a rake. These conclusive results revealed unequivocally that my sperm count was pathetic; there was absolutely no chance I would ever have kids of my own, and Debbie's lack of babies was due to me, not her.

This was painful to me in a way I couldn't understand at first; but I guess the simple truth was that although I'd never had any serious complaints in the coupling department, and had not, up until then, been yearning for offspring, no man likes to think his seed will never bear fruit.

I realised then that the previous 'pregnancy' had been a phantom event, brought on, I guess, by the strength of Debbie's need for children; and there must have been another culprit for Carmen's pregnancy – if it had ever happened at all.

For my part, over the years since, I've learned to live with my inability to father a child, and married as I am now to the lovely Carol, with whom I've been for nearly twenty years, we haven't allowed lack of issue to become an issue.

I'm happy to say that Debbie and her next husband, David Janson, did go on to have two super daughters, one of whom, Ciara Janson, played *Nicole Owen* in *Hollyoaks*. But at the time, Debbie, was knocked flat by the news. Although she was still only 26, she was truly devastated, which only added to the pressure and revealed more cracks in our already shaky marriage and probably triggered its inevitable collapse. It wasn't long before I discovered that she'd found somebody else, although she still seemed reluctant to let go entirely of our relationship.

I felt terrible about it, and realised that, out of a wish not to hurt people, or maybe, more selfishly, a desire not to be disliked by others (the old trouble – see Beth), I'd gone into a marriage which I should never have considered. At the time I didn't know why I'd married her, and even from this distance, I still don't know. Nevertheless, I'm very fond of her and I still feel bad that I was less than honest with her.

Of course, I can see with hindsight that Debbie and I were miles apart in our priorities and ambitions, but she moved through life like a whirlwind and I guess for a while I'd got all caught up in it. As our marriage had tottered on, the big disappointment for me was that Debbie had become so preoccupied with her career that I found myself running around, putting out the fires she'd started. I didn't particularly blame her – after all, she was still only twenty-six and I guess she thought she had everything to play for. Sometimes, though, I felt as if I were fulfilling a role in her fantasies, while she allowed her attention to wander elsewhere. When living together became impossible, I knew one of us had to go; and as good chaps go, I went. Debbie stayed on in Alexandra Road.

So, in early 1983, I found myself living with my old boozing and gardening mate, Michael Slater, and his wife, Alison. They had, as it happened, a spare room in their flat in Earl's Court. As Debbie's dog had taken precedence in Alexandra Road, and the Prune had continued to live with my parents in Epsom, I thought of taking him with me to my new billet. But before I could, tragedy struck. He'd been out walking with my father and my mother's dog. Dad had crossed the road from the Downs, assuming my mad hairy dog was with him. But the Prune was lagging and when he did cross the road, he was hit by a speeding car. The poor old hound, who had been my good friend through some tricky times, was dead in an instant.

Although I hadn't spent so much time with the Prune in recent years, I missed him hugely and felt sadder about losing him than I have about quite a few fellow humans who have gone before me.

By a fluke or sleight of hand, Slater had managed to get himself headed-hunted as PR person for some spurious organisation. He was more full of bullshit than ever, but still good fun to be with. In any case, I was well occupied because I'd just landed a role in the second cast change in Dario Fo's hit play, *Can't Pay? Won't Pay!* at the Criterion. Into the new cast with me had come Patricia Quinn, Trevor Allan, Su Elliot and David Cardy.

Fo's play was a clever farce which had been running successfully in London for eighteen months, with Alfred Molina in my role, that of *Giovanni*, a Milanese Communist Party member outraged by his wife's militant food thieving; Fo himself had played the part in Italy. The plot centres on two Fiat workers and their friend, a policeman who persists in trying to explain the concept of law and order in what is a parable about state authoritarianism. I loved the play, the part, and the underground, secret place that the Criterion Theatre is.

Curiously, when Fo came to London to see the production he was asked if he enjoyed it. 'Yes,' he said, 'but I did not recognise the play.' I suppose in England we do this kind of political farce in a less surreal way than in Italy, where they would put it on in football stadiums, and Fo would use the opportunity to harangue his audience with his particular brand of left-wing politics.

On our first night Patricia Quinn's husband, (later Sir) Robert

Stephens, turned up full of beans – and booze – and gave me a great smacking kiss on the lips to let me know how much he'd enjoyed the show. Afterwards I went with them and Debbie (with whom, happily, I was still on friendly terms) to dinner at the *Caprice*. Debbie's mother, Mary came too, accompanied by an old client of hers, Lonnie Donegan. Lonnie had been a great role model (if such things existed then) for me when I'd been *Johnny & the Bandits* in my greasy youth. Thus I was much in awe of him, and was cringingly embarrassed when Robert Stephens, getting on for legless by then, started giving me notes on my performance: 'You could have been a lot quicker there, my dear' – and a lot more of that sort of thing.

Lonnie was appalled. 'Why did you let him do that?' he asked, as Robert staggered to his feet to make his exit with Patricia (forgetting to pay his half of the bill).

Although Debbie and I were living apart, we were both keen to let the split happen on amicable terms. Once, though, as I was driving past our old house, I felt a terrific pang when I spotted her walking out of the door with her dog. As she bounced off down the road, looking terrific as always with all her usual feisty energy, I recognized, at a distance, all that I'd seen in her that first time we'd met in the studios.

I thought of Harriet, too, whom I'd left in New York without ever bringing our strangely vigorous relationship to any kind of resolution. Why did I do this? I wondered. Why did I allow my relationships to drag on and overlap and never have a clean break? After I'd got back from the States, friends here had asked why I felt guilty about Harriet, when she'd refused point-blank to come to England, but I still felt it was my fault that I hadn't seen it through, one way or another.

I was acutely conscious that I hadn't really achieved closure, either, with the volatile, exasperating but lovely Sarah Venable. These unresolved relationships spun round my head, colliding with feelings of guilt over the handling my marriage to Debbie. I felt almost sick with confusion some of the time, and hated the thought that I seemed to be blundering through life, damaging every woman I bumped into.

In this unstable condition, I continued my run in *Can't Pay? Won't Pay!* at the Criterion, riding the ups and downs of the show as best I could. On the whole, it was doing really well and I was enjoying it, but I was extremely frustrated when, halfway though my contract, Peter Wood asked me to play *Fag*, valet to *Jack Absolute* in Sheridan's *The Rivals*. It was to go on at the Olivier Theatre at The National, starring Michael Hordern and Geraldine McEwan. It was an enjoyable part in the sort of production you might kill to be in. But I was unavailable, and I just couldn't do it. What a blow!

For a few days I was inconsolable, and my misery was compounded when Michael Kitchen (who'd also been in *On the Razzle*) came to see the Fo play. 'You done good,' he said to me after the show.

I told him about the offer I'd had from Peter Woods, which sounded fairly puny beside all the offers he'd had to turn down for various reasons. But he was sympathetic. 'Hang on in there,' he said. 'These things often work out.'

And, after a month or two of chafing at the bit, it turned out he was right – things did work out, with great jamminess, when Barry James, who had taken on the part of *Fag* decided, for reasons I never heard, to come out of the show at exactly the same time my stint in *Can't Pay? Won't Pay!* came to an end.

I went to see a couple of performances before I started rehearsals about a fortnight later. The day I arrived, I must have been in remission from the depression in which I'd been wallowing – mainly over Harriet, but over my parlous love life in general – because I almost froze in my tracks the moment I saw across the rehearsal room a stunning new potential object for my attention.

I was taking over as *Fag*, the valet, while *Lucy*, a maid was played by a slender, lovely raven-haired creature, Sabina Franklyn, daughter of the late Bill (*Sch... You Know Who*) Franklyn. I'd seen her only on TV when she'd played *Jane Bennett* in the BBC's 1980 *Pride and Prejudice*. I'd admired her then; in the flesh she was even more exciting.

With Michael Hordern, Patrick Ryecart and Geraldine McEwan as the wonderful *Mrs Malaprop*, this *Rivals* was a top-notch production, and now I was looking forward to it even more; especially, too, because it was being directed by the excellent Peter Wood.

Peter was a curious blend of the magnificent and the intolerable.

When he spoke about the period of the play, the history of comedy, or the role of the stage down the ages, it was as good as listening to a masterclass on Theatre. At the same time, he was a brilliantly inventive producer/director.

But there was also a harsher side to him.

If he was unhappy with the way an actor was performing, he would keep them back on-stage, pinning them there with his acerbic wit, while instructing the rest of the cast to remain in the auditorium to be an audience.

'I cannot *bear* it!' he would cry. 'I *won't* pay all this money to listen to a mouse with bronchitis – this is one of the greatest theatres in the world – we need a *lion*! a lion who'll come on with a roar that says, *Here I am!*'

His unfortunate victim would gaze back glumly, perhaps a little defiantly, protesting. 'But you said exactly the opposite yesterday!'

'Oh *please*!' Peter would groan. 'Don't expect me to be consistent.'

Only the show's stars – Hordern and McEwan – escaped his brutal ragging.

I knew my turn would come, sooner or later.

'Oh dear...' he sighed with deep gloom. 'I keep employing you because I *thought* you were a good actor.' He was shouting now, as if I'd mortally offended him. 'You certainly need a *director*, don't you?'

Without the usual gap of half an hour's hindsight, I had an answer for him at once. 'Yes, I dare say,' I replied. 'When am I going to get one?'

The rest of the cast in the auditorium burst into gales of laughter.

Peter, to his credit, produced a wry grin. 'Touché,' he conceded.

From then on, I had the key to dealing with him; if you stood up to him, and responded instantly, he would respect you for it.

But displays of such cruelty were quite common. During my time at *On the Razzle* and *The Rivals* I saw at least three people in tears, and several very hot faces.

David Rintoul, a fine actor and a very likeable man, took over the role of *Falkland* in *The Rivals* – one of the hardest roles in Restoration Comedy – and he was struggling. Most actors have strategies for dealing with the nakedness and vulnerability they feel when they know they haven't quite got to the character. David's was to use big, expansive gestures while delivering his lines.

Peter Wood stopped him in mid-flow. 'David, can you tell me why you're playing your character like an Armenian carpet seller?'

It was malicious and cruel, but it was apt, and terribly funny.

I was down in the stalls, and roundly booed our director.

David was mortified. After that, he tried to drop the gestures that suggested he was indicating the size of his carpets. His arms hung self-consciously by his sides. But his instinct to use his hands wasn't entirely eliminated and survived in much smaller gestures.

Peter Wood's voice boomed from the auditorium, 'Oh, I see: *Falkland* isn't a carpet seller any more, he's a blasted penguin!'

David, determined not to be crushed, blurted out a fruity Scottish expletive, and went on to develop a superb *Falkland*.

Michael Hordern and Geraldine McEwan were exemplary leaders of the company, happily chatting to all the company, and with great charm.

For all his vicious haughtiness, Peter Wood was undeniably inspirational – though maddening, too, in equal parts. Nevertheless, *On the Razzle* and *The Rivals* at the National remain two of my career highlights to this day.

The other bright side to *The Rivals* was Sabina. Soon after we'd met she told me she was involved only in the tag end of a relationship; and she certainly didn't appear to be averse to spending time with me, despite her father's warning...

'Watch it,' he'd told her. 'He's got a reputation as a bit of a womaniser.'

Frankly, he could talk!

Besides, I never felt that I really fitted the definition of a 'womaniser', according to the Oxford Dictionary: *a man who enters into numerous casual sexual relationships with women.*

Looking back, I think I would call myself a serial romantic, a man who loves the idea of falling in love, and gets into trouble by not letting go properly and by allowing relationships to overlap. At least, though, in one sense, Bill was right – I certainly wasn't a man's man, in as much as I always preferred the company of women to that of a gang of beer-swilling, dart-chucking, chauvinistic males, ever since my brief early career as an estate agent, when I'd tried to hang out with the young bloods at the Marquis of Granby in Epsom. They would stand around guffawing about their exploits with women in battered MGs, raising pints and not much else, whereas I actually enjoyed *being* with women.

On the other hand, because I was, and always have been in the broadest sense, interested in women, I always like to give them a thorough scrutiny, which is often construed as flirting.

As it happened, her father's warning did nothing to deter Sabina. After we'd toured the play to Plymouth and Bristol, she announced to her previous boyfriend, actor/director Michael Cameron, that she had met me. After snarling a little and referring to me – she reported – as 'John Callous', he moved out of her flat in Carmichael Court, Barnes.

That summer, I heard that my old friend and former housemate, Eric Lander, had kept himself together enough to land a star role in a West End production of *The Business of Murder*. I went to see him at the Mayfair Theatre, where he was giving a terrific performance. It was nine years since we had shared the cottage in Kew, and I marvelled at the man's inherent talent and his ability to bring it back into play despite the excesses to which he had undoubtedly exposed himself.

I was still living with Michael Slater in Earl's Court at the time, but my relationship with Sabina had developed. Thus I now found myself under pressure both from Debbie, who was having second thoughts and wanted me to come back, and from Sabina who wanted us to get married.

Not for the first time, I felt trapped – mostly by my own lack of decision. On one absurd occasion, I was round at my old house, talking to Debbie, when we heard that bang-crunch-tinkle sound of a woman parking nearby, and found that Sabina had driven round the corner, to do some kind of drive-by recce, and, in an act of reverse serendipity, had unintentionally hit my car.

Despite this, though, I was spending a lot of time with Sabina. We shared the same sense of humour with a wonderful and witty spontaneity which I'd missed with Debbie. She was also a woman who liked to give orders and expected to be obeyed (like many of the women who have figured in my life – for it has often been my lot to be with ladies who make decisions when I can't be bothered).

Sabina's own career was progressing well with a long-running part in *Keep it in the Family* for Thames Television and, provided I did as she said, she was easy to get along with. But after the Debbie debacle, for which I mostly blamed myself, I was anxious not to get committed too deeply, too soon.

In the very last throes of our marriage, I went with Debbie's mother, Mary Arnold to see Debbie play opposite Omar Sharif in the biggest stage role she ever had – before or since – in *The Sleeping Prince* at the Chichester Festival Theatre in the summer of 1983. She'd more or less revived her *Hollywood Babylon* Marilyn Monroe performance for the part, and it just wasn't working. Although Sharif was a charming companion on a couple of pub crawls we enjoyed in Chichester, I knew he wasn't really happy with Debbie's performance. Amazingly, and presumably because of Sharif's pulling power, the production did go on to the Haymarket in the West End for a few weeks that autumn.

When I went to see it there, Sharif – the *Sheriff of Omar*, as I knew him – was in a foul mood with Debbie, who'd committed some unacceptable act of chutzpah. I didn't discover quite what it was, but she told me that as the curtain came down, Sharif hissed at her, 'I will destroy you!' This didn't sound promising.

He didn't destroy her, as it turned out, since she went on for years appearing in British TV soaps, even surviving thirty-seven episodes as *April Branning* in *East Enders* in the mid 1990s.

At the end of September, my new agent Tim Combe was in touch to tell me I had two more dates for *Only Fools and Horses*.

The first was for what was the sixth episode of Series 3 – called *Wanted* – in which *Rodney* goes to the aid of an old woman who has fallen down in the street. She immediately starts shrieking 'Rape!' and *Rodders* rushes home to *Del*. *Del* knows she's a batty old thing who's let out of her institution at weekends and regularly makes accusations of this sort. For a laugh, he winds up *Rodney* by telling him that the police are searching for the 'Peckham Pouncer', and *Rodney* goes into hiding.

It was a characteristically lively episode and the team were really bouncing off each other by now. When it was aired on the 15th December it drew over eleven million viewers, and the show by then was recognised by BBC as a real rising star, and – important to the corporation's image – set firmly in the field of popular, non-elitist entertainment.

A week later we made *May the Force be with You*. Curiously, this episode was aired the week before *Wanted* and drew just under 11 million. It was especially interesting to insiders because it included the first appearance in the show by Jim Broadbent, as *DI Roy Slater*. (Had I somehow subliminally suggested the name of my old friend and dodgy bounder, Michael Slater, to the writer?)

This *Slater* had been at school with *Del Boy* and *Boycie*, and was well known to them. He had bumped into *Rodney* in the pub while on the trail of a batch of nicked microwave ovens. He doesn't let on to *Rodney* that he's a copper, and *Rodney*, knowing no better, asks him up to the flat in Nelson Mandela House.

Del's jaw nearly falls off when *Rodney* ushers *Slater* in, but before *Del* can get rid of him, *Slater* spots one of the missing microwaves and threatens to stitch up *Rodney* on a phony drugs charge if *Del* doesn't let on who he bought them from. *Del* ends up becoming a grass, to save his brother's bacon.

Given that Jim Broadbent had been an earlier choice for *Del Boy*, it was interesting to see them working together and speculate what might have been. It worked well – well enough for Jim to come back and do two later episodes between jobs in his increasingly busy movie schedule.

Boycie didn't appear in the next episode, *Who's a Pretty Boy, Then?* when two new characters entered the cast, Paul Barber as *Denzil* and Kenneth MacDonald as *Mike*, the new landlord of the *Nag's Head*. They both became long-running, key characters, and great friends, right up until Ken's untimely death in 2000.

Wanted had been my fourth appearance as *Boycie*, and I'd recognised by now that John Sullivan liked to set up satellites to revolve around the main characters, allowing him to bring them in from time to time as it suited him. Very often, though, he would get so carried away with a character or an idea he would end up simply writing too much, and some great vignettes we'd recorded ended up on the floor of the edit suite. But he had established by now that *Boycie's* function was to provide a source of envy and aspiration to *Del Boy*; and that however much *Del* may have despised *Boycie* for his superciliousness, he had to admire him too, and *Boycie's* ongoing role in the show was safe, if the show itself was to be ongoing. And here the physical differences between myself and David Jason came into play. *Boycie's* a tall, vaguely posh-looking geezer, whereas *Del* looks a bit unpolished and not quite right – like the dodgy wares he sells.

Only Fools and Actors

One evening early in 1984, towards the end of my run in *The Rivals* at The Olivier, I had an unexpected visitor to my dressing room after the show, in the form of Cathy, the enthusiastic American literary agent I'd met in New York three or four years before. She had told me then that she might be able to do something with my South African play, but I'd heard nothing from her about it and, frankly, had given up hope.

Now she'd brought with her the pleasing proposition that if I came over to NY and worked on *Cut the Grass* a little more, she would introduce me to a guy who would put it on in an off-Broadway showcase theatre.

For me, right then, still somewhat caught between guilt feelings over my divorce from Debbie, and Sabina wanting to make plans for our future, Cathy's suggestion couldn't have been better timed. It offered a perfect escape route for me – an excuse to do nothing about the hopelessly confused position I was caught in, between finally leaving Debbie without doing too much damage, and avoiding any commitment to Sabina which I might regret. I even welcomed the possible chance to bring some kind of resolution to my relationship with Harriet, which seemed to have been left dangling, despite the *Dear John* letter she'd sent.

Cathy seemed pleased when I said I would come to New York, and offered to put me up in her apartment until I got some accommodation fixed up. With no immediate prospect of fat earnings – at least until the play found its way on to Broadway – I wasn't about to book into The Algonquin.

I arrived at Cathy's flat in Christopher Street, Greenwich Village, thoroughly knackered and dazed after the flight and the usual hassle of getting in from JFK Airport on the Subway. I was even more confused when she told me bluntly that there was only one bedroom, which I would have to share with her. And there was only one bed.

Through sheer naiveté, it simply hadn't occurred to me that this was what she had in mind. I couldn't recall at any stage in our agent/client relationship her signalling a desire for corporeal congress. I made this clear as tactfully as is possible with a single-minded New York career lady and moved out the next day. Fortunately I still had a few contacts to pick up from my last sojourn in '79-'80, and I was excited about settling down in my new persona as a Greenwich Village scribbler. I quickly hooked up with a number of the people I'd got to know before, but, almost immediately, my life became complicated when Sarah Venable showed up, wanting us to get together again.

Although I'd gone to New York to do the play, I was also hoping to see Harriet, to clear up the tangle of our unfinished affair – which had been important to me at a key time in my life. I called her old number; she wasn't there; she was in LA, and sounded angry that I hadn't let her know earlier that I was coming to New York. I was disappointed, but turned my attention back to rewriting the play, which Cathy thought I had to do if I was determined to get *Cut the Grass* on in the States while I had a real chance.

Despite some initial hassle with US Equity over my appearance in it, the play was produced and shown at a small but well-connected showcase theatre on 42nd Street. Located with one or two other similar small theatres in what looked to me like an old warehouse building, it was run by a contact of Cathy's. For the female part, we had to cast an American actress who obviously had nothing like the fluidity with the accent that Moira Downie had been able to bring to the roles. As the Americans who came to see it were completely unfamiliar with the South African version of spoken English, the accent wasn't too critical anyway, and the show attracted a good number of viewers and producers for its week-long run. I was delighted that the piece appeared to have worked in New York as well as in Europe while the political circumstances in South Africa had become volatile, and word was seeping back that the apartheid regime was showing signs of unravelling.

However, it was to be another six years before Nelson Mandela was released from the *Victor Verster Prison* in Paarl. A group of New York African-Americans involved in drama came along, and like the British-Africans who came to see the show in Croydon, they were surprisingly engaged by it, and amused by the notion of a woolly English liberal trying to take on the regime like this.

One of the producers who came, Joe Cacaci, wanted to take the show up to a small theatre in New Rochelle, which he'd dedicated to showcasing and developing plays, away from critical pressure, with a view to bringing them back to an off-Broadway theatre. He spent months wrangling over *Cut the Grass* with US Equity, stressing its social value and informative qualities, and insisting that it was my story and I could tell it better than anyone else. But the American actors union were in the midst of an eyeball-to-eyeball stand-off over some paltry differences between the UK and US *per diem* expenses payment systems.

I could have done with a few *per diems* (living expenses paid to actors while they're working in a play or movie) while I was living as a dimeless Greenwich Village writer. When British actress Paula Wilcox got in touch to say she was in New York, and we should meet up, I hardly had enough wonga to buy her a beer.

In the meantime, I'd been out a little with Sarah. She was working in a TV series where she had to dress up as a species of jolly little bear – ears, fur and paws and whatnot – in *Romper Room,* a very popular kids' programme. She said how sorry she was that it had gone wrong for us last time in New York. She'd left her husband by then, but she and I had drifted further apart than I realised, and it was more an exercise in nostalgia than an expression of rekindled passion. I was hanging out with several of the American actor friends from the British American Repertory Company, including Harriet's brother, Davis Hall. A few weeks after my phone conversation with her in LA, Davis rang me and told me that she had turned up in New York. I rang her and we met, but she was rather prickly right from the start. I guessed Davis had told her about Sarah Venable coming round a bit early on. I explained that it had just happened, and wasn't part of my reason for returning to the *Grande Pomme.* But she was doubtful, and saw competition where it didn't exist. She still fascinated me; she looked tremendous and I still knew why I'd felt so strongly about her the last time I'd been in the States. But she gave me a really hard time about not keeping in touch. There was an argument, which climaxed, unexpectedly, with her saying she might be coming to London, and she would call me when she got there; I never heard another word from her.

After Joe Cacaci had battled on with the union, and Cathy had flogged the play round to any likely takers for another month or so (both without success), there seemed nothing much else that I could do, although Joe promised to keep on trying. I'd survived, sort of, by doing a few illicit voice-overs, and eventually ran seriously short of money. However, at least the play had had one fresh airing.

Back in England, little had changed. I met up with Debbie and she agreed it would be sensible for us to bring our marriage to an end formally with a divorce. We sold the house, and once again I found myself homeless. Once again, a woman came to the rescue. Kind Sabina suggested that I move into her place in Carmichael Court, a two-storey flat not far from the Thames and a short walk from the *Bull's Head* in Barnes.

After I'd been back for a while, Joe Cacaci phoned from the States to tell me that despite pushing it for six months, he'd finally given up trying to persuade American Equity to let me do the male part in my own play. 'I told 'em they were doing an American actress out of a great part, but that didn't cut any ice.'

I was deflated; I'd been sort of hanging on to the idea that I would be going back to do it; and there was very little happening for me in London. No episodes of *Only Fools and Horses* were made that year, and no fresh episodes aired. However, in June, a technicians' strike at the BBC had put the kybosh on a lot of new drama production, and the Corporation had decided to repeat selected episodes from the first three series of *OFAH*.

Episode One, *Big Brother*, went out at a good time – 9.30 pm, on June 13th. This episode and the others that were repeated all achieved far better viewing figures that they had first time round. This had the effect of bouncing the BBC comedy drama department into commissioning a fourth series, to run from early in the following year.

I was booked for three episodes to be aired in early spring, 1985.

I'd agreed to spend Christmas with Sabina, so when I found I had to drive out of London to Dorking just before the holiday, I took the opportunity to call in on my parents in Epsom and leave them some presents.

My father opened the door looking alarmingly scruffy. At the sight of his only son, not a scintilla of joy flashed across his sixty-six-year-old face.

'What the bloody hell are you doing here?' he asked, not making any effort to open the door wider.

'I came to drop off a few presents I've got for you and Mum.'

'She's not here,' he answered triumphantly, and I even thought for a moment he was simply going to close the door.

'That's OK,' I said quickly. 'I'll bring them in.'

He relented and held the door to admit me. He turned and wandered unceremoniously back to the kitchen where a mess of newspapers was spread across the table.

He reluctantly offered me a coffee, and I sat down opposite him. I was alarmed by how much he had deteriorated. Ever since he'd retired three years before, he'd let his appearance slip. He often didn't shave, he wore increasingly scruffy old clothes, and his manner had become notably surlier.

I did my best to build a conversation. I told him how I was booked for three more episodes of *Only Fools*.

'That rubbish!' he snorted.

Absurdly, I felt like crying. Only once in my career had he ever commended me for anything – *Dirty Linen*, in 1978 – and he'd subsequently backtracked on that a little. I was very depressed by his absolute refusal to admit any validity in what I was doing now.

I decided for once to retaliate. I had never told him before that I'd once seen him in London, by chance, when he hadn't seen me.

'Can you tell me something, Dad?' I kept my voice steady as I faced him. 'A few years ago, when you were still working, I happened to be driving up from a place on Millbank when I spotted you in one of those little streets just behind. It was definitely you, and I was about to stop and call out when you went up the steps of one of those smart Georgian terrace houses and disappeared inside.'

I'd often wanted to ask him about this strange, unexpected incident. His destination looked like a private house, but there he was, in full civil service attire, with briefcase. I thought he might offer some perfectly plausible explanation, like he was attending a working lunch with the Minister – he was, after all, one of the secretaries at the department.

But he didn't. He looked up and glared at me for a few moments without speaking. I could almost see his mind turning over as he decided how to answer what he'd obviously taken as an accusation.

'I don't know what you're talking about,' he said, eventually. 'That wasn't me. That's the trouble with you people, you live in a fantasy world. And you always were full of it.' He stalked from the room.

I never discovered the truth. Perhaps he was a kind of John le Carré character – *the Spy who Came in from the Kitchen*.

More likely, it was a generational thing.

He didn't consider it proper to talk about personal things – not even the fact that his sister, Enid (who still lives in Sheffield) gave birth to an autistic child and was left to bring her up on her own. Enid in, the end, dedicated most of her life to caring for Cathy and has made a great contribution to the work done by the Autistic Society.

I always liked Enid – she's very loyal and still has a good dose of the family sense of humour. 'You can tell 'em at the BBC your Auntie Enid won't pay the Licence Fee if they don't give you another series,' she once told me with a determined twinkle in her eye.

But my father never discussed her circumstances with me.

Life in Sabina's flat in Barnes was always full-on. I was busy, she was busier. She had the female lead in *Full House,* a new sitcom on Thames TV, with the first six episodes going out in January and February 1985. She was very sociable and generous with her time, a lot of which seemed to be spent advising girlfriends on how to deal with recalcitrant men. I was a little alarmed that she was considered such an expert. But with Sabina, life generally was light-hearted and a lot of the time hysterical. She had a punchy sense of humour and took delight in ribbing her friends – in the gentlest possible way. People were in and out of her flat, and I had become less of a pub habitué, compared with my sessions in the Greyhound and the St Margaret's Hotel. The time when I'd enjoyed hurling back five or six pints at a sitting (or a standing) was passing, but I would go along and listen to Humph Lyttleton when he was playing at the Bull's Head and meet up with old chums in the Coach & Horses in the High Street – still a favourite thespian haunt.

Although *Only Fools* had been growing all the time, I'd been in just four episodes of the first three series, and the recognition factor that came into play over the next five years hadn't appeared by then. The truth is that, of course, there's a big buzz in having played a character known to so many people, but it does have its downside.

When I rejoined the *Only Fools* team in early 1985, the greatest change was the absence of Lennard Pearce who had played *Grandad*. He had died very suddenly on the 15ᵗʰ December, after Ray and John had already started making the first episode of Series 4, *Happy Returns* (in which *Boycie* doesn't appear). *Grandad* was originally written into the plot, and Lennard had even made one scene for it before he died. The footage had to be scrapped and *Grandad* written out.

Lennard had appeared in all bar one of the twenty-four episodes made so far, and there was a great deal of affection for him among the viewers – who absolutely recognised the character – and, of course, among the team. He was a third grandad to John Sullivan's own kids, and one the least offensive men you could meet.

I didn't know Lennard well; *Grandad's* appearances were confined largely to him shuffling round the flat in his slippers. I'd worked with him directly on only one episode, *A Losing Streak*, when *Boycie* makes one of his rare visits to the *Trotter* flat to play poker. But I'd had a good chat with him in the Green Room then and found him a truly charming old boy. He was easy-going and very relaxed about the fact that he had found his only real success, so late in his career. The South London growl he adopted for the part was immensely warming, although, in reality, it wasn't quite so rough. 'I've been so lucky this has happened now. I've been a naughty boy, you see, and I'm living on borrowed time,' he told me mysteriously.

I arrived back at the BBC in January to make *Strained Relations*, which was going to be an important episode, based around the wake for *Grandad*, whose demise, obviously, had been triggered by Lennard's death. I was looking forward to seeing all the team again, and it was great to be involved in a show that had become hugely popular by then. The joy of being back for the first time in over a year was somewhat – though not hugely – marred by a headline that had appeared on January 5ᵗʰ in a Sunday tabloid, under the banner headline:

'BOYCIE WAS A THREE-TIMING ROMEO LOVE RAT'

Whichever way you look at a headline like that, it's hard to extract anything positive from it, and I certainly didn't. Amazingly, although I'd been expecting a merciless barracking, my colleagues on the show were quite *sotto voce* about it.

One of them – probably David – was unimpressed. 'Only three? I should've thought you could have done better than that!'

At least I didn't find myself forced into giving fatuous explanations, or justifying myself. It was only afterwards that I discovered the story had been planted by Debbie's mother, Mary Arnold, who had simply rung the paper and supplied some photographs.

They'd put up a shot of me with my arms around two blondes, who were friends of Debbie's, at a party we had given at our house. The unavoidable implication was that Debbie had been a victim of my callous philandering, and that I was a complete bastard.

Mary had always said that I'd treated Debbie badly, although she was never able to be specific about it. She had certainly been peeved when we'd got divorced, and although Debbie had forgiven me, her mother had not. Debbie never issued a denial of what had been said, but she did apologise to me, and told me it was nothing to do with her.

Looking for my way out of the labyrinthine Television Centre after a day's shoot, I stopped off at the bar, where I bumped into my first wife, Carol Robertson. Since I'd last seen her, Carol had taken her strong managerial skills from stage management to television production and the year before, she'd produced an eight part series, *Driving Ambition*, for the BBC. She commiserated over the Love Rat story, we had a great chat over a drink, remembering our youthful courtship in Llandudno's Happy Valley, and she even offered me a job, which suggested, at least, that she didn't still feel angry with me for running out on our marriage nearly twenty years before.

Strained Relations was originally aired on February 28th. It was a special episode. On the one hand, it said 'Goodbye' to Lennard Pearce and *Grandad;* on the other, it ushered in Buster Merryfield as *Uncle Albert*, who went on to feature in another thirty-seven episodes.

Buster came by the part in a bizarre way. After Len died, there had been a great deal of heart-searching about when, how, or even whether or not he should be replaced. Clearly it wasn't possible just to insert another actor to play the same part, so John Sullivan had to come up with some plausible device to bring a different, but similar aged sort of character into the flat at Nelson Mandela Mansions.

Buster wasn't sent up for the part by an agent, in the normal way; he'd simply written in to the producers, more as a fan, to say how sorry he was that Lennard had died. He was an actor, but only in a small and frankly sporadic way. For most of his career he'd worked in a bank, first as a clerk, and then as a manager, only allowing his love of acting take over once he'd retired from that life. He'd also, in his younger days, been a seaman and a keen amateur boxer. He had met Lennard on a job, and kept in touch with him. Although he hadn't a lot of professional acting experience, he asked if, by any chance, they were thinking of replacing *Grandad*, could he be considered?

When John and Ray first saw a picture of Buster, he looked almost too different – like an old seadog with his weathered face and massive, snowy whiskers. Not risk averse, John and Ray auditioned him, and it was only when they saw him in the flesh, with his jaunty air and twinkling eye that they could see he might work. John made much of *Uncle Albert's* old naval yarns and his tendency to bore everyone with them. On top of that, they discovered that Buster could play good singalong pub piano, and that gave him added potential down at the *Nag's Head*, now set to feature more in the show. They responded to these particular qualities, despite his lack of experience, and took him on.

Grandad's death had come as shock to *Del* and *Rodney*, and the regulars at the *Nag's Head*. After they have all gathered around the graveside, with North London cousins who have brought along *Grandad's* brother, *Uncle Albert*, the whole party retires to the flat for a riotous wake. *Rodney*, more overcome with grief than the others, gets to know *Uncle Albert* who, being an old seaman, tries to cheer him up with naval yarns.

When *Del* and *Rodney* think all the guests have gone, *Albert* emerges from the bathroom. The cousins have gone, and *Albert* has to stay the night. *Del* drives across London next morning to return *Albert* to the cousins, but he finds they've moved their mobile home, and no one knows where. *Del* guesses it's a ploy to get rid of *Albert*, but he's not at all keen on letting him stay on in the flat. He sends him off to find lodgings at the Seamen's Mission, only for him to turn up an hour or two later to report that it's been pulled down and replaced with posh flats and a marina.

Del and *Rodney* have no choice now; they have to keep him. In this way, the three-cornered *Trotter* household is kept intact.

Sullivan's script is a great example of his adroitness in reacting to events and producing a great plot to fit.

I introduced myself to Buster, who, after commiserating over the headline in the *Sunday ShagRag*, told me frankly about his status as little more than an enthusiastic amateur. He was understandably cautious, though. He'd seen all the earlier episodes and loved them.

'Oh gawd!' he confided in me. 'I just hope I don't bugger it up.'

After the shoot we all agreed that John and Ray had been right, and *Albert* would be a worthy replacement for *Grandad* in the *Trotter* household. He became a very popular character – a cheeky lovable rogue with a catch phrase of his own.. 'Durin' the war...' always presaging some rambling yarn, which became part of the *Only Fools* lexicon. I really looked forward to the *Nag's Head* scenes where *Albert* played the pub 'joanna', usually with some dodgy-looking bird of a certain age egging him on.

A week or so after making *Strained* Relations, I was preparing for the next episode, which was also to herald the arrival of a significant new character.

Like *Arthur Daly's* infamous *'Er Indoors*, *Boycie's* wife had never appeared. She had been mentioned more than once, most tellingly in *A Losing Streak*.

Boycie, chatting with *Del* in the *Nag's Head*, refers to her *en passant*.

'I said to Marlene the other day – you remember Marlene...?'

'Yes,' *Del* says with a sideways nod of the head. '*All* the boys remember Marlene.'

Boycie reacts a second later, with a quick double take and a frown at *Del* – a timeless, and telling moment.

It was clear that *Boycie* was set to become a key player in *Only Fools*, while the show itself, now attracting 14-15 million, was an unequivocal hit. Perhaps to avoid accusation's of aping the well-crafted *Minder*, John Sullivan decided that in view of *Boycie's* status, now was the time to introduce his wife to the public, in an episode called *Let Sleeping Dogs Lie*.

Ray and John with customary canniness had cast Sue Holderness for the part. I hadn't worked with her before, and hadn't even met her, but I knew her reputation for being an original and strong performer. Self-possessed and always a professional, she turned up for her first day's filming in character – brassy and petite, in a pretty good approximation of *Marlene's* 'style', busty top, short skirt, tons of make-up and rattling with bling.

Right from the start, we could see she was going to fit in with the rest of the cast. In her very first scene, her bottom was pinched by *Del Boy*, whom she had never met before. She took this in her stride, and later, she had to kiss *Duke,* the Great Dane puppy who was the star of the episode, as well as *Del Boy.* It was hard to say which she enjoyed most.

In any event, even for an experienced actress, it can be quite harrowing to be saucily intimate with total strangers, especially with a husband waiting for her at home.

Everyone agreed that our scene together had been a real success, and as we wrapped up the shoot, we all assumed that *Marlene* would make a follow-up appearance before very long.

With my track record, the last thing I needed was another wife. But I would never have guessed that twenty-five years later *Boycie* and *Marlene* would still be together.

Index

Index

Index